International Federation of Library Associations and Institutions
Fédération Internationale des Associations de Bibliothécaires et des Bibliothèques
Internationaler Verband der bibliothekarischen Vereine und Institutionen
Международная Федерация Библиотечных Ассоциаций и Учреждений
Federación Internacional de Asociaciones de Bibliotecarios y Bibliotecas

IFLA Publications 102

Libraries in the Information Society

Edited by
Tatiana V. Ershova and Yuri E. Hohlov

K · G · Saur München 2002

IFLA Publications
edited by Sjoerd Koopman

Recommended catalogue entry:

Libraries in the information society
/ [International Federation of Library Associations and Institutions].
Ed. by Tatiana V. Ershova and Yuri E. Hohlov.
- München : Saur, 2002, 172 p. 21 cm
(IFLA publications ; 102)
ISBN 3-598-21832-X

Die Deutsche Bibliothek - CIP-Einheitsaufnahme

Libraries in the information society
/ [International Federation of Library Associations and Institutions].
Ed. by Tatiana V. Ershova and Yuri E. Hohlov. - München : Saur, 2002
(IFLA publications ; 102)
ISBN 3-598-21832-X

∞

Printed on acid-free paper
The paper used in this publication meets the minimum requirements of American National Standard for Information Sciences – Permanence of Paper for Printed Library Materials, ANSI Z39.48.1984.

Printed / Bound by Strauss Offsetdruck, Mörlenbach

ISBN 3-598-21832-X
ISSN 0344-6891 (IFLA Publications)

CONTENTS

PREFACE

This book is an attempt to bring together works related to the changing role of the library as a social institution in the emerging Information Society, which were prepared by IFLA participants during 1998-2000.

The present collection offers articles written by library and information specialists in different parts of the globe – Africa (Namibia), both Americas (Canada, Mexico, USA), Asia (China, India, Korea), Australia, Europe (Russia, United Kingdom). Its thematic scope ranges from conceptual considerations on Knowledge Economy / Society to purely practical issues of library management and sustainability in a transforming socio-cultural environment. This approach allows to present both wide geographic and broad problematic scope, which hopefully will be of interest to many library workers and decision makers all over the world.

In this book libraries are looked at from different perspectives:

- Institutions, which mobilize information and knowledge for social and economic development;
- New windows of what electronic advances offer to people, including those with physical disabilities;
- Knowledge servers providing knowledge interface to people, consolidating information and networking global knowledge;
- Parts of information networks and new partnerships to be established to better serve the modern users' needs;
- Gateways for information, tools to bridge digital divide – both within countries and between countries;
- Treasure-houses of human knowledge, which participate in knowledge innovation, and become an important link in the knowledge innovation chain;
- Brokers that will help make local and indigenous content available on the global information infrastructure;
- Institutions, which can successfully deal with diversity – cultural, linguistic, and growing diversity of information resources.

These are many, but not all roles the libraries can play in the changing society to ensure that they are not superseded by other players. To ensure this, libraries have to evolve from institutions to conservate and to provide access to a patrimony towards an inalienable part of a distributed global knowledge warehouse, to become service oriented rather than collection building oriented, to analyze and use ICT and marketing techniques that can be harmoniously combined to make the library an institution heavily demanded by the Information Society. This is what all works presented in this collection deal with in their authors' hope to be of real use to the library community.

The Okinawa Charter on the Global Information Society adopted at the G8 summit in 2000 says: "Our vision of an information society is one that better enables people to fulfill their potential and realise their aspirations. To this end we must ensure that IT serves the mutually supportive goals of creating sustainable economic growth, enhancing the public welfare, and fostering social cohesion, and work to fully realise its potential to strengthen democracy, increase transparency and accountability in governance, promote human rights, enhance cultural diversity, and to foster international peace and stability". Library can be viewed at as an IT contributing to the achievement of above goals.

We all are sure that libraries have an irreplaceable and growing role to play in the emerging Information Society. They can support wealth creation by ensuring equal access to information and the opportunities afforded by knowledge. They can be important tools to fill the growing gap between the information rich and the information poor. They provide, through their widespread physical network, a cost-effective infrastructure for life-long learning. They can become a strong basis for innovation by rendering both most recent and historically valuable publications, which are relevant to those seeking new ways of development.

For us there is no doubt that investing in libraries means investing in the future.

The editors would like to express their sincere gratitude to all colleagues who have made this book possible: the authors for having shared their valuable ideas and experiences, IFLA Editorial Committee for having endorsed the publication, Dr. Claudia Lux personally for her moral and organizational support, and last but not least, the Saur Verlag for having responded to the proposal to bring this collection of articles to the attractive physical form immediately recognizable by all library professionals in the world.

Tatiana Ershova
Member of Standing Committee,
IFLA Section on Management and Marketing

Yuri Hohlov
Chairman of Standing Committee,
IFLA Section on Information Technology

TO BE OR NOT TO BE: PUBLIC LIBRARIES AND THE GLOBAL KNOWLEDGE REVOLUTION

Qihao Miao

Shanghai Library, Shanghai, China

Abstract

Beginning with an introduction to the global Knowledge Revolution and the related concepts, the paper argues that while National Information Infrastructure is somewhat technology-centered, the new concept of National Knowledge Infrastructure is biased to human, the current focus of the international community on knowledge assessment and National Knowledge Infrastructure provides an opportunity for the library community, especially public libraries, to recover and expand its role in the society. So far, however, most public libraries have not yet involved themselves fully in the Knowledge Revolution. To be proactive, public libraries should assume their role as knowledge server by interfacing knowledge with people, organizing knowledge, consolidating information and networking global knowledge.

The paper then follows up the points with case study in China, including an initiative started from a most impoverished province and a re-engineering effort of a leading public library in this country. Both are aiming at mobilizing information and knowledge for social and economic development through public library system. The experiences of China prove that public libraries can be critical players in the National Knowledge Infrastructure, and the current efforts can be substantially upgraded if making full use of available information infrastructure and cooperating with counterparts elsewhere and other knowledge institutions. To conclude, the paper appeals IFLA for taking the responsibility to alert and organize the librarians all over the world, in order to participate pro-actively in the global Knowledge Revolution

1. Introduction

In May 1997, a simple ceremony was held in the new building of Shanghai Library. The front compound, surrounded by Roman-styled pillars, was named "The Knowledge Plaza" during that event. It was an appropriate naming choice, given that libraries often sport the banner of knowledge as their logo. Knowledge, after all, is one of the core missions of the library.

Now, knowledge has been placed in the spotlight of the international arena. We are told that the developed world is entering an era called "The Knowledge Economy" (or Knowledge-based Economy), that a "Knowledge Revolution" is occurring which may have significant impact upon not only developed but also developing countries. Ironically, however, many libraries seem to be indifferent in this revolution. The key question for the library community today, therefore, is to be or not be participating in the global Knowledge Revolution on a pro-active basis.

To answer this question, the paper will provide analyses and evidence to show that the "Knowledge Revolution" can be another renaissance for the library community. The library can be an integral part of the information highway, allowing people to access the untold wealth of knowledge available electronically from diverse sources. At the same time, the library can serve as a humane and people-centered place of rest and relaxation. It is a local base, plugged into both the global knowledge economy and the micro-realm of its immediate surroundings. In effect, it becomes a bridge linking powerful computer networks with even the most impoverished end-user.

2. The Coming of the Knowledge Revolution

To understand what is the Knowledge Revolution and its relation with library and librarian, we should start from some basic concepts.

2.1 Information and Knowledge

While the two terms "information" and "knowledge" tent to be used interchangeably, slight but significant difference remains. Discussion about the conceptual distinctions among data, information, intelligence and knowledge has taken place for a long time. A well-known model is pyramid-like, in which data is on the bottom, then information, then knowledge, and finally wisdom or intelligence at the summit. This simplified model shows that knowledge is a part of information, but not all information can be called knowledge. The rapid technological progress in information processing and the better understanding of both concepts reveal a need to separate knowledge from information [1]. This need can be seen in the divorce of the further two categories of knowledge: codified and tacit [2, pp.12-14].

Codified knowledge is sometimes called explicit and focal knowledge [3]. It is normally embodied in media, and can be transformed, transmitted and taught. Tacit knowledge, on the other hand, may be in the mind of educated people, or in the form of skills and know-how needed to handle or improve codified knowledge. The last few years have witnessed the rapid advancement of science and technology in general and information technology in particular. People can process knowledge which is explicit, embodied and codified much easier and more cost-effectively than knowledge which is tacit. The access bottleneck has therefore been moved to that knowledge which is intangible, invisible and only in one's mind. The principles and regularities of this kind of knowledge flow are, to a large extent, unknown to us.

2.2 Knowledge-based Economy and Knowledge Revolution

The term Knowledge Economy can be traced back to early 1990s [4]. According to an OECD report issued in 1996, it is an economy directly based on the production, distribution and use of knowledge [2, p. 7]. On the way to the Knowledge-based Economy, a radical paradigm transformation is occurring in economic and social systems, This shift has been driven, in the past few decades, by technological innovation. Advances in high technology areas are changing the basis of economic growth. The easy and inexpensive availability of massive digitized data and information has been instrumental in creating new products and services. The Knowledge Revolution is the process of paradigm shift on the way to Knowledge Economy. As the term "revolution" implies, the process and its related labor pains will touch, globally, all aspects of human life. A milestone in the serial activities concerning the Knowledge Revolution is the '97 Global Knowledge Conference held in Canada June 22-25 last year, sponsored by the World Bank and the Canadian Government. Several government leaders and the Secretary General of the UN attended the conference.

2.3 National Knowledge Infrastructure

A National Knowledge System is defined as a "network of institutions in the public and private sectors whose activities and actions motivate, create, access, assimilate, diffuse, and use knowledge for productive activity and promotion of public welfare" [5, p.7]. A similar concept, namely, that of a National Knowledge Infrastructure, appeared in the

June 30 version of the outline of '98 World Development Report [6]. It is interesting to compare the key elements of the National Knowledge Infrastructure (NKI) with those of the National Information Infrastructure (NII), particularly their sequence (See Table 1). According to the provisional outline of the 1998 World Bank, knowledge networks are relationships of educated people and their organizations. There is an explicit difference between the two. In short, the NII is, to a large extent, a technological infrastructure, while NKI is a human infrastructure.

Table 1. Compartson of Key Element of NII and NKI

National Knowledge Infrastructure (NKI)	National Information Infrastructure (NII)
1. Educated people	1. A wide and ever-expanding range of equipment
2. Knowledge institutions	2. The information itself
3. Knowledge networks	3. Applications and softwarw
4. Telecom infrastructure	4. Standards and transmission codes
	5. The people: vendors, operators, and service providers

Source: NKI [6]; NII [7].

3. Public Library As a Part of Knowledge Infrastructure

3.1 Knowledge Revolution for Public Libraries: Curse or Blessing?

Especially in developing countries, public libraries seem to be less advanced in terms of computing capabilities than academic and company libraries. Public libraries have been less than enthusiastic about the advent of information age. Some librarians have felt that many traditional library jobs would be substituted by computers and network systems. In some pessimistic arguments, traditional librarianship as a profession has been sentenced to death. The only question left to determine is how soon that death will occur. Even optimistic commentators have viewed the role of the librarian in the information age as a passive intermediary who is a mere beneficiary of the achievements of other players. In both views, the librarian is not an active agent of knowledge creation and distribution in the ages ahead.

It may partly explain why there is no significant presence of public libraries in the knowledge-related activities by World Bank. A database search on the official website of the GK'97 conference revealed, for example, that only seven librarians attended; there were more than 2000 other participants. Among these seven were six from universities or learned societies, plus one library network specialist from National Library of Canada, which is the host country of the conference. There are more than one hundred working sessions covering a broad spectrum of the theme, but the word "library" was mentioned only once within a phrase "digital library", in any of 97 rapporteur reports available on web after the conclusion [8]. While information revolution and information economy imply an emphasis on technology, the Knowledge Revolution emphasizes more human aspects of information provision. Accordingly, this presents more an opportunity than a threat to public libraries, because, ultimately, libraries are people-centered institutions.

The following characteristics of public library should remain as advantages in information age:

- Public library is the primary terminals reaching the wide range knowledge consumers, so that it understands the "whole market";
- The experiences of cataloging, indexing and classification of literature are in fact a basis of knowledge organization in a boarder sense;
- The physical space of public libraries, thought by avant-garde commentators as out of date, may constitute the natural premises to gather people together;
- Public libraries are the very unique in spreading information and knowledge lifetime to those people beyond the reach of information infrastructure.

3.2 Library: Key Link of the National Knowledge Infrastructure

Library should be, by nature, an essential part of the knowledge infrastructure. In some sense, knowledge management is just another name of librarianship [9]. As outlined in a vision statement of the Library of Congress of the USA, "The Library is in the unique position to be both catalyst and participant in the intellectual process that transforms information into knowledge, and knowledge into wisdom" [10]. The UNESCO Public Library Manifesto also designates public library "the local gateway to knowledge" [11]. But sticking to the tradition is far from enough for library to keep up with the technology-triggered Knowledge Revolution. Some librarians, mostly those from academic or special libraries have been early adaptive to the new change. A few "Knowledge Center" or "Knowledge Hub" have been established, or re-engineered, within university libraries. These centers differs from ordinary library not just by name but also by function. Knowledge Centers are making full use of computing and communication technology and re-positioning themselves as learning facilities, for example, University of California at San Francisco established a knowledge center collaborated with its library [12], Mitchell C. Brown proposed a "Knowledge bases"-databases that contain knowledge in library [13]. A serials of publications on the new role of librarians also noticed the trends, some called for a national knowledge strategy [14], some exploring the function of librarian as knowledge engineer [15, 16].

Library has been conceived as a part of "soft infrastructure" for business activities [17], which is a somewhat supporting role. With the concept of National Knowledge Infrastructure, library's function for the economic and social development can only be enhanced. The library in developing country will not always a black hole to swallow public funding, but can also make much more explicit contribution to the economy, it can be same essential, if not more, in the information age as in the past history of human being.

3.3 Public Library: Towards a Knowledge Server

I would rather use server instead of hub to describe the function of library in the knowledge infrastructure. Hub is just a locus of communication, the word "server" would be more appropriate. As a server, the library converges social knowledge, adds value to it, produces new knowledge and diffuses it, as requested.

3.3.1 Interfacing knowledge with people

With the establishment of information infrastructure, the interface is needed more than ever between (i) machine and human being; (ii) codified and tacit knowledge; (iii) culture and economy; (iv) knowledge and its consumers; and (v) developed and developing world. Public library has been understood as public access point to information highway [18], but unlike other Internet Service Providers, which also provide access, public libraries can act as an off-line relay, by downloading and sending network-available information and knowledge to those out of the network reach, or by attracting people to the nearby libraries to access Internet. The library building can be a place for gathering educated people to communicate and create tacit knowledge, and interpret tacit knowledge into codified knowledge.

3.3.2 Organizing knowledge

The gray literature, digital materials and Internet resources are remolding the job of cataloging and indexing into a concept of knowledge organization. The new age may open a room for a higher level of knowledge organization, for instance, the building of "collection-on-web". While cataloging Internet has already been in agenda [19], the library collection on web may go further, it comprises network available information selected and re-organized by librarian, (who should be the best to do that!) in meeting the need of its own patrons: those who frequently visit the library server. The fact that the collection is in the local web sites may be much significant in developing countries, where the telecommunication infrastructure are always a bottleneck, the waiting time is often too long for users to endure. The web collection also permanently stores in library server the selected Internet resources, which are valuable to future users, and as we are aware, may be short-lived otherwise.

3.3.3 Consolidating information

The consolidation of information can be seen as a role of interface either. It is deemed as important for developing countries to make information more "usable". The concept is not new [20], but may be new for public libraries, our own experiences tell that if public library will play a more direct role in the local development, it can not just stop at the mere technical processing of literature, some further manipulation may be needed. In many cases, the users ask for an answer to specific questions beyond the reach of ordinary reference service. There is a long argument as how far the librarians should go to collect, compile and synthesize information to meet these specific needs, this is not only a problem of fee-or-free, but also on the border of library service. In the Knowledge-based Economy, the line of demarcation between library and other information services must be more ambiguous. On the other hand, network and the digitalization of information will reduce the cost of consolidation dramatically, a cost-sharing mechanism can be arranged more easily.

3.3.4 Networking global knowledge

Localism is both the strength and weakness of the public library. With the global networking of library community and other information servers, local library can go global. Knowledge networking is not just a problem of Internet, but of international collaboration of knowledge institutions. Some proposals on the international cooperation have been raised, for examples, on the cross-cultural cooperation on knowledge exchange [21], and for decision-makers in developing countries [22]. Based on the traditional relationship of inter-library loan, it is not difficult for library community to collaborate on knowledge networking.

Not only scientists and government decision-makers but man-in-the-street as well may need information elsewhere even abroad. There is a story in China about a farm girl who suffered a strange disease, she eventually cured with the help of a listserv in the Internet, through which tens of international doctors provided their knowledge and advice about the disease which was only documented in another country some years ago. Every time when I told the story in lectures and meetings, I was asked by the audience how to do that. In that case, the disease is so strange and serious that worth publicizing in news media, and the help came from information professionals of a medical research institution. Of course, most information seekers will not so lucky, the case and these questioners make me believe that local public library should and can be catalyst in this global knowledge networking.

4. Public Libraries in Knowledge Revolution: the Chinese Case

Although the term "Knowledge-based Economy" is gaining popularity among learned societies of China due to the publication of the Chinese version of the above-mentioned OECD report, the Chinese "knowledge industries" in general, and the library community in particular, may not be aware of all that is happening under the umbrella of the Knowledge Revolution in the rest of the world. But independently, a parallel development, driven by indigenous momentum, can also be found in China.

China is an economy with a dual structure. A few industrializing provinces and cities in the coastal areas are catching up quickly to the developed world, while for many other regions, poverty and illiteracy are still the urgent problem. Both, however, are facing the same dilemma concerning information and knowledge. The following story explains what the public library system in China has done and is going to do as an integral component of the knowledge infrastructure of this particular country; and how the cooperation of library community can help in this process.

4.1. Knowledge Project: Disseminating Information and Knowledge to the Unserved

The Knowledge Project in China was launched as an ordinary library promotion campaign, just like similar programs in other countries such as South Africa [23]. In 1994, it was first proposed by a provincial library of Guangxi Zhuang Nationality Autonomous Region (a Province de facto). The Province is one of the least-developed ones in China. Public libraries of the Province suffered from the serious shortage of funding. The backwardness of economic development is to blame, but long-term factors are also involved.

The project was thus proposed by the Provincial library and supported by the local governments in order to push knowledge flow through the library system. Specific measures included establishing a steering group; organizing book-reading and other related activities; pairing township library with a local company which would donate RMB5000 (about US $ 600) a year to the paired library; and soliciting contributions from local and overseas donators [24].

In three years of implementation, the Project achieved some results. More than RMB500,000 yuan and 1.5 million copies of books were donated to the public library system of the Province. Owing to the "pairing policy", 115 village and township libraries were established [25]. The Project was extended to the whole nation of China in early 1997. The steering committee for the National Project was formed by several State Ministries. The nationwide Knowledge Project is aiming at fostering national civilization and social progress by encouraging book-reading and knowledge dissemination through the public library system. The Guangxi Knowledge Project is totally a local initiative. The particular significance of the Project is to bring information and knowledge to those unserved otherwise. This is a huge challenge, and, in fact, can be looked upon as a positive step in accomplishing the coming Knowledge Revolution. But the project in Guangxi Province also reveals some critical problems yet to be solved.

First, the vicious cycle engendered by a lack of information is hard to break. Can the library alone change the poor performance of local enterprises in a few years? Some enterprises felt unsure if the pairing could be continued. Second, the Knowledge Project in the original form has a clear limitation in that there is difficulty in understanding and applying modern information and communication technology (ICT) to concrete situations. This ignorance of ICT results in not only slow progress, but also the absence of up-to-date information, which may be of great importance to the local economy, and which would make progress sustainable. Until recently the Knowledge Project had not paid enough attention to take the advantage of Internet. Now the provincial library, together with other ten city and county public libraries, built up the network linkage and tapped information highway via the CERNET (China Education and Research Network) node in University of Guangxi. Before discussing further the need for improvement, let us look at the other side of the coin.

4.2 Re-engineering Shanghai Library

The relative prosperity of Shanghai makes it a city that represents the second face of China. The 1997 GDP per capita of the city is over US $ 3000. A recent survey found that in China's three biggest cities, among which is Shanghai, 33 per cent of the population uses computers, either in the office or at home. One fourth of these users, or over 8% of the population, can get access to the Internet through some means [26]. At the end of 1996, Shanghai Library moved to its new premises, which cost approximately US$7,500,000. By traditional indicators, such as extent of book collection and floor space, the new Shanghai Library is the second largest public library in China, second only to the National Library in Beijing. In a comparatively advanced information environment, however, Shanghai Library is nevertheless facing different challenges. When more and more information is digitized and could be processed easily by machine and reach end users without libraries, when an advanced information infrastructure "Info-port" is under construction, when Internet Content Providers are replacing some of library functions, librarians must ask themselves the following question: what is our niche in the competitive "knowledge market". Top managers have identified that there is a pressing need for the library to become re-engineered and actuated as a "knowledge center" rather than a book museum equipped with computers [27]. Behind the magnificent building and its state-of-the-art LAN-based integrated management system, there is an in-depth re-thinking of how the library should position itself at the threshold of the new millennium. Accordingly, a series of innovations have been implemented, some of these innovations may be thought to be radical and unorthodox by traditional library theorists:

- Subsidiary research units have been established to catalyze research by both in-house and contract experts;
- Established the designated Training Center to teach knowledge handling for information professionals and users;
- Organizing comprehensive cultural and academic activities to facilitate brain storming;
- Alerting the society-at-large by reporting new developments elsewhere in the world;
- Advising and consulting for business, based on both library collection and Internet search
- Building up a mechanism to support law-making of People's Congress and policy-making of local government

The purpose of all these efforts is to make a more direct contribution to local economic and social progress. In addition, these efforts are intended to prove the value of the library to society, while keeping basic service free to patrons.

4.4 The Need for Cooperation of Library Community and other Knowledge Institutions

The Knowledge Project and the case of Shanghai Library are in the same country, but both libraries involved may not be aware of some important and relevant events and ideas in other side. Although Shanghai Library, as well as other libraries in the comparatively rich regions in China, donates books from time to time to the libraries in poorer region, more achievements can be made if these libraries are perceived as partnerships in the knowledge networking. Shanghai Library, for example, may be in the position to help public libraries in Guangxi in the exploitation of Internet resources, it is possible that at the expenses of transporting the donated books, recipient libraries can benefit much more.

On the other hand, the re-engineering of Shanghai Library should have obtained more momentum if we had known earlier the World Bank actions and the methodology of knowledge assessment. There is a great room for collaboration of libraries and other institutions worldwide. In most situations, not the library but the professional organizations and other knowledge institutions are the source of information and knowledge, just as in the story of that farm girl mentioned above, but library can help the end users to find and reach these sources, so that the collaboration of the whole knowledge institutions are so important.

5. Library and Knowledge Revolution: Conclusions

The Knowledge Revolution provides an opportunity for the library community, especially public libraries, to recover, and indeed expand, its key role in the national knowledge infrastructure:

1. In the last few years, with the ever-growing availability of technological tools that enable easy and inexpensive transmission, distribution and transformation of codified information, the third millennium of human existence will witness an era in which knowledge will become vital, and the tacit knowledge will be the bottleneck.
2. The focus of the international community on the Knowledge Revolution is both necessary and timely. It is critical that the library community understand the opportunity presented by the process of paradigm shift. They should be not onlookers but full stakeholders in this revolution.
3. The experiences of China are a case study to show that public libraries can be a critical player in the social knowledge chain. As the world moves toward the information age, libraries can make contributions to the economic and social development in both less-developed and comparatively rich areas. The Chinese case tells us that some of current efforts are lacking, and will continue to be insufficient without the full use of available telecommunications and network infrastructure. The lessons from China also reveal that cooperation with library community and other knowledge institutions may greatly upgrade the current efforts.
4. A global collaboration of libraries can make a tremendous contribution in enhancing and facilitating knowledge networking. Public libraries, with their

traditional relation to ordinary people at large, can have a unique role of channeling latest information and knowledge to those out of the other terminals. IFLA, as a representative body of the international library community, should undertake the responsibility to alert and organize the librarians all over the world, particularly those in the developing countries to participate pro-actively the global Knowledge Revolution.

References

1. Building the European Information Society for us all: The final report by EU High-level Expert Group. – An executive summary: April, 1997. – Mode of access: http://ispo.cec.be/hleg/Building.html: November 27, 1997.
2. The Knowledge-based Economy / OECD/GD (96) 102. – Paris, 1996. –46 p. – An executive summary. – Mode of access: http://www.oecd.org/dsti/: October 13, 1997.
3. Tacit Knowledge / Sveiby, K. E. – An executive summary. – Mode of access: http://www.sveiby.com.au/polanyi.html: December 29, 1997.
4. For examples: The Knowledge Economy: The Nature of Information in the 21st Century. Annual Review, December 1993. – Nashville/Queenstown: Institute for Information Studies, 1993-1994; Digital Economy: Promise and Peril in the Age of Networked Intelligence / Tapscott, D. – McGrraw-Hill, New York, 1995. – P.44-48.
5. Prospectus for National Knowledge Assessment / Committee on Knowledge Assessment, Office of International Affairs, National Research Council. – Washington, D.C.: National Academy Press, 1996. – Mode of access: http://www.worldbank.org/html/fpd/technet/prospect.htm: December 24, 1997.
6. Knowledge for Development / World Bank: Version of provisional summary, 30 June, 1997. – June. – Mode of access: http://www.worldbank.org/html/fpd/technet/wdr98/world.htm: Jan 5, 1998.
7. National Information Infrastructure: Agenda of Actions, U.S. Government Report. – September, 1993. – Mode of access: http://sunsite.unc.edu/nii/NII-Agenda-for-Action.html: Jan 10, 1998.
8. The official website of the Global Knowledge '97. – Mode of access: http://www.globalknowledge.org/.
9. Koenig, M.E.D. Intellectual Capital and Knowledge Management // IFLA Journal. – 1996. – Vol. 4, N 22. – P. 299-301.
10. The Library of Congress in the Year 2000: A Vision, Management and Planning Committee. – Washington, DC: The Library of Congress, 1988. – VIII p.
11. UNESCO Public Library Manifesto. – 1994.
12. http://www.fsu.edu/~fsus/general/depart.html
13. Knowledge Management: A Library Perspective / Brown, M. C. – Mode of access: http://www.lib.lsu.edu/sci/chem/SLA/presentation.html: December 29, 1997.
14. Etheridge, L. S. National knowledge strategies and the library of the future // FID News Bulletin. – 1994. – Vol. 7/8, N 44. – P. 142-145.

15. Lancaster, F. W. From custodian to knowledge engineer: the evolution of librarianship as a profession // Journal of Information, Communication, and Library Science. – Vol. 4, N 1. – P. 3-8.

16. Annual Review of Information Science and Technology: LIS professionals as knowledge engineers / Poulter, A. at al. – 1994. – Vol. 29, Chapter 9.

17. Library 2000: Investing in a Learning Nation: Report of the Library 2000 Review Committee. – Singapore: SNP Publishers Pte Ltd., 1994. – P. 91-93.

18. Libraries as public access point to the information highway: A Draft Position Paper, Canada's Coalition for Public Information / Shiu, J. – 1997. – Mode of access: http://www.uccb.ns.ca: October 31, 1997.

19. "Cataloging Internet" project in University of Toronto. – Mode of access: http://www.fis.utoronto.ca/library/cir/: December 26, 1997.

20. Saracevic, T. Processes and problems in information consolidation // Information Processing & Management. – 1986. – Vol. 1, N 22. – P. 45-60.

21. Miwa, M. International Cooperation of information Consultants: Towards the Effective Exchange of Electronic Information // International Forum on Information and Documentation. – 1997. – Vol. 1, N 22. – P. 29-36.

22. New Methods for International Collaboration in Science, Technology, and Innovative Policy: the IDRC-IFIAS Knowledge Brokering Initiative: Draft, 1997. – Mode of access: http://www.worldbank.org/html/fpd/technet/gk-methd.htm: 27 December, 1997.

23. Serving the Unserved in the Year 2000 / Gerike, E.M. // 63rd IFLA General Conference.

24. Mai, Qunzhong. The Knowledge Project: an important action for the impoverished areas to develop library undertakings // The Journal of the Library Science in China. – 1996. – Vol. 22, N 105. – P. 13, 21-24. – In Chinese language.

25. Li, Xiaobing. Survival and development of village and township libraries // Library World. – 1997. – N 3. – P. 39-41, 45. – In Chinese language.

26. Wen, Hui Bao. – 1997. – July 18. – P. 10. – In Chinese language.

27. Miao, Qihao. Automation, Digitalization and the beyond: Re-engineering Shanghai Library // Proceedings of the International Symposium on Academic Libraries in the 21st Century. – Shanghai Jiao Tong: University Press, 1996. – P. 32-39.

DRIVING LIBRARIES TOWARD A SUSTAINABLE FUTURE

Dawn Maddern

Caloundra City Council, Caloundra, Australia

Abstract

Libraries face new challenges in term of accountability and funding process. They are also challenged by the new windows of opportunity electronic advances have offered them.

In searching for ways to deal with these changes they must look to the community for confirmation of the validity of any new roles, and must be to shift focus as the community requires.

They must acknowledge the right of funding bodies to expect full justification of financial support and they must present arguments that have sound economic and social rationale.

They must also consciously seek out new partnerships across sectors-partnerships which will enrich their communities, impress the funders, and ensure their long term survival...

My discussion today centres on library services as a whole. The personal computer and its connectivity has empowered space challenged library services, such as mobiles, beyond all expectation. The restrictions created by the size of the service, or the location of the service, are effectively negated by the communications line. Access to information via the web has changed the small or mobile librarys' ability to deliver forever. This is particularly true in Australia, where connectivity has arrived at a time when major management changes are taking place at all government levels. Today I will talk about Local Government, or the local Council, through which public libraries in Queensland operate. Council sets the service level and provides over 80% of the funding. The remainder comes in the form of a grant from the state government.

Australia, like many other countries, has embraced new economic theory as the linchpin for future sustainability. National Competition Policy has played a major role in altering the organisational structure and practices of many local government authorities. Workplace reform aimed at increasing productivity levels, strategic planning, and the implementation of accounting models better suited to a competitive environment have changed the face of public libraries operating under the banner of local government forever.

Greater emphasis on customer driven planning and operational activities signifies greater accountability for the products we produce back to the community. Detailed surveys targeting specific outcomes will provide the rationale for service change. Libraries need to be aware that this is a two edged sword: regardless of best practice or trendy direction, the only assurance for continued survival will be successfully fitting the library key products to the local community. Best fit to your community as reflected in community feed back to all levels of government.

These critical changes will have long term repercussions for service delivery in public libraries. There is no doubt that technological change has transformed the library forever. As part of the wider organisational structure of Council, libraries will be increasingly required to be accountable through performance measurement, closer alignment to structured policy, and transparency: both to the elected members and to the community, about what we hope to achieve through the vast and expensive networks set up in the name of advancing information exposure.

In this paper I make no distinctions in the type or quality of service the public can expect from a large library, or through the smallest mobile library.

Technology has progresses libraries beyond the argument of the viability of, or indeed, the necessity of a PC on the desk or in front of a user. Even the oldest, most undistinguished mobile library can be wired simply and cheaply to provide access to the global information network. In Australia, connectivity is the major cost variable.

A greater co-ordinated effort is needed to ensure that remote and isolated communities are not disadvantaged by lack of infrastructure to ensure cheap consistent and speedy communication pathways. In Queensland, major discussions are currently taking place between government and service providers to address the obvious inequity in the provision of internet services to our coastal strip for less than $2 hour while many outback towns pay $12.00 for the same privilege.

Addressing the training issues surrounding new technologies will continue to be a major issue for efficient service provision. The best equipment, the best will, and the best facility will not deliver if staff are not adequately trained. Training does not stop once staff understand search and bookmarking processes - training must be seen in its broader context, and must address the future of libraries as publishers, libraries as interpreters, libraries as intermediaries.

The organisational and cultural changes necessary to ensure that training is on the financial agenda, and is accepted as a key financial investment, are significant. To further support expansion of training opportunities away from navigation, and towards manipulation or creation, a major shift in the priority training receives in budgets, and in the development of a case for new financial initiatives, is necessary.

The profession expends a lot of energy discussing the ***global*** information change. But what of the ***local*** information change? Here is a whole new opportunity for the local public library - with the emphasis on the **local**! Information kiosks are springing up in service stations and shopping centres, offering interactive opportunities to the individual in a variety of financial return formats.

What of the local community information database? The value of information is not debased just because it is local and should therefore be easy to obtain. But is it? Often it is easier to find the telephone number of the nearest foreign embassy than it is to find out the number and name of the current president of the local tapestry club. Libraries are very well placed to develop key local information systems which can then be made available to a wider audience. The library of the future will rely heavily on structured community feedback through a range of surveys which will heavily influence further funding opportunities. The importance of getting it right at the local level cannot be emphasised enough. Technology should not just be seen as a **global** contribution to the quality of life of communities. The local information economy has immediate, long-term and sustainable implications to the perceived community value of the library. Libraries also have the opportunity to act as brokers in the development of local web pages specialising for a particular market: tourism, beach conditions and surfing reports, local cultural event web pages.

A further opportunity on the home front is Council information. The internally developed Council Intranet offers a wealth of information which can have a positive influence on the quality of life of residents. There are major efficiency gains to be had in local government as stronger partnerships between traditionally quite separate departments are developed. Branch libraries and the mobile are often the only evidence of Council presence in the outer suburbs and rural areas. Could the library, through the Council intranet, provide access to other Council services? Libraries have a high profile in the community. Individuals use library services to their own advantage and retain a positive image of the transaction. Other Council departments, on the other hand, often only connect with the public in a negative situation - a complaint, a dog in the pound. Libraries are securely entrenched in community goodwill: here is an opportunity for the rest of Council to benefit from some reflected glory- and it won't hurt the library's next budget bid, either!

Can the public library extend this further? In Queensland there are 121 local government authorities with 322 public library facilities and 19 mobile libraries, dotted about the state. All local authorities have at least one library with access to the Internet, most have all. By extension, all of these public libraries have access to each other. There is a plethora of federal and state government agencies who want access to the grass roots community. Often the type of access required is limited to distribution and reception of specialised information. Libraries are perfectly placed to become the brokers of that information exchange.

In Queensland, a trail is presently being conducted with the state's admissions body to a university (QTAC). Prospective students come to the library to make an admission application via the Internet. Details are downloaded and feedback to that student comes back to the library, where the student can continue to adjust information, and ultimately have a tertiary place confirmed. The library staff facilitate this process. The trail has enormous implications to prospective students living in remote communities, to the accuracy of detail keyed in, and to the timeframes for acceptance. Such facilitation of education and information creates new opportunities and relationships for libraries in all communities, especially the small and isolated, and has enormous potential Australia wide.

In Victoria, where services from banking institutions have been shrinking in rural townships, mobile libraries are trailing the delivery of electronic banking facilities.

The opportunities are endless. Libraries, if they are to take advantage of their unique spread and connectivity, will need to develop new marketing skills and to redesign their objectives to include electronic brokerage as a legitimate and non threatening use of the public library.

Libraries have no divine right to spend from the public purse. Technology has created a host of opportunities for libraries to improve their service delivery

- better database management and more efficient control of resources
- cheap, comfortable and supported access to the internet
- instant E mail connectivity
- access to local information in a hypertext environment

However, in our new world of stricter accountability and transparency, the subsidised library infrastructure must take steps to ensure that the community really do find the library indispensable. In the first instance that the right to access information is necessary and desirable. In the second instance that libraries are a cheaper, more efficient and more democratic dispersal of information services than a privatised alternative- which would not be accountable to the public in the same manner as are libraries, and may ultimately lead to monopolistic control of information.

Public Libraries are challenged by the new window of opportunity electronic advances have offered them.

- They must look to the community for confirmation of the validity of any new roles, and must be prepared to shift focus as the community requires.
- They must acknowledge the right of funding bodies to expect full justification of financial support and they must present arguments that have sound economic and social rationale.
- They must consciously seek out new partnerships across all sectors- partnerships which will enrich their communities, impress the funders.

Libraries must do all of these things, and do them well, to ensure that they have a place, a mandate, a right to exist all through the 21st century!

LIBRARIES AND NATIONAL INFORMATION POLICIES AND/OR NATIONAL *IT* STRATEGIES - A SURVEY

Hellen Niegaard

BTJ Denmark Ltd, Copenhagen, Denmark

December the 10th 1948 almost 50 years ago United Nations adopted one of it's most visionary documents of impact to all human beings in countries all over the world: the Universal Declaration of Human Rights [1]. Celebrating the declaration this year has proved its continuing importance and relevance - and the ever-existing demand to live up to its intentions. In the fields of libraries article 19 of the document states " Everyone has the right of freedom of opinion and expressions: this right includes freedom to hold opinions without interference and to *seek, receive and impart information and ideas through any media and regardless of frontiers"*. In her paper [2] at the Contributed Paper Sessions of last year's IFLA conference in Copenhagen Marian Koren, NBLC in the Hague illuminated how the concept of right to information has developed from being at first primarily understood as a mass media issue and journalist's rights to freely move around the world in order to seek and gather information to a more broad concept, which stresses freedom of information as freedom of expression towards today's third sense of understanding, putting the weight on the receivers of information. Underlining that it is considered most important *that individuals have access to information*. In this view, people have a right to know, a right to uncensored news and information. A perspective that has gained influence scientifically according to Ms Koren and that is being used now world wide including within institutions of United Nations. A concept also reflecting the intentions of the most important international document of Public Libraries: UNESCO's Public Library Manifesto [3]. The manifesto was first published in 1949 and lately revised in 1994. The document states the role of public libraries as *local* gateways to information, to knowledge and culture and it underlines that the services of the libraries are provided on a basis of equality of access for all human beings. It also stresses that collections and services of the libraries have to include all types of appropriate media and modern information technologies as well as traditional materials, and it underlines that they should not be subject to any form of ideological, political or religious censorship, nor commercial pressures. A concept which taking the development of the information society into consideration put libraries in a central position when working for fulfilment of article 19.

Furthering Access to Information through Public Libraries

The information society generates and consumes enormous amounts of information and at the same time information technological progress has made it easier to process, store and communicate information and knowledge in new ways. Alone the ever-accelerating Internet generates innumerable quantities of information supported by a still ongoing decrease in telecommunication costs as well as in hardware prices. However the large amounts of information available also creates a number of different problems, because it is difficult to assess exactly what information is available and how specific groups of citizens may get at it. What does it take to meet that development? For libraries as well as for their originators and "sponsors". The development calls for new actions from all types of libraries including the public libraries and the way they store and make available their collections. However also for new actions of more fundamental character from the authorities financing libraries and the way these authorities take advantage of libraries' services and include them in national planning, when dealing with the needs of the information society and aiming at furthering access to information for all citizens. In the light of this situation creation of a national information policies and IT-strategies are needed more than ever everywhere. As the revised edition of UNESCO's manifesto emphasises "The public library is the responsibility of local and national authorities. It must be supported by specific legislation and financed by national and local governments. It has to be an essential component of any long-term strategy for culture, information provision, literacy and education". A couple of years ago IFLA's Section of Public Libraries therefore decided to find out whether IFLA's member states actually have established or are developing national information policies and - or national information technology strategies. And if positive, whether they include libraries.

National Information Policy / IT Strategies - a Survey

In 1996 / 97 a survey was carried out. A questionnaire consisting of 25 questions was sent out to all national library associations or national libraries – in two rounds. Of IFLA's *then* one hundred and almost forty member states, only about 30% did answer so far. However survey results indicate a rather clear trend. This trend is introduced below and will be followed by an introduction to two countries' different ways of tackling needs of the information society in regard to promoting access to information through libraries. The Section will later this year inform Professional Board of the survey results in a report. It will be two sided and intends on one hand to reflect how member states aim at providing access to information via tools such as national information policies (NIP) and national IT-strategies (NITS) and will on the other hand also put forward suggestions for any relevant IFLA actions in the field.

Though the responses more or less represent all parts of the world and include both developed and developing countries the Section decided at its Spring Meeting earlier this year in Cleveland to make an extra effort in order to have more answers and thereby make the survey more representative. Therefore questionnaires have been sent out once more this summer to countries, that did not respond before. Furthermore countries that did answer, but stated they had not yet or were about to have any form of NIP/NITS will be contacted again ahead of the report. In case responses from this last round differ fundamentally from the results introduced here, an article will be published in IFLA Journal or at the Internet together with the final report to Professional Board, which the Section will do for PB's December meeting this year. It will thus not be appropriate to go into details of all responses at this moment however in stead concentrate on the main lines of the survey, as it has given a rather clear picture of the importance of the issue.

Survey - Results and Indications

Formal conclusions so far are; about 100 nations did not reply. Maybe because the questionnaire was too difficult. Or maybe because it was wrongly targeted - or maybe because some of the countries did not have any national information policies or national IT strategies at that time and therefore did not report; though the questionnaire included possibilities to do so.

As to the issue, the conclusions are; it is definitely an issue. IT is forcing the agenda everywhere. Where policies and strategies are developed – it seems less difficult to develop and establish such policies and strategies than to follow up sufficiently. In the majority of the countries having NIP/NITS, these appear to comprise a range of activities of various relevant institutions including new ways of co-operation between them as well as development aspects of IT as such. But a few countries state that their policies and/or strategies only comprise library matters.

To the question whether they have or have not either national information policies or national IT-strategies 11% says no, while 89% represent four different groups, dealing with either NIP or NITS or both. Thus 24% claim to be under way to develop NIP/NITS or is discussing the issue and the need for such policies and strategies. Before giving the report to Professional Board this group will be contacted once more as probably some of the countries might now have established NIP or NITS.

Of the 65% positive answers 32,5% are in fact countries having both a formal (sort of) National Information Policy and National IT strategies; the group includes countries from Africa, Asia, Australia and Europe. In all these countries libraries and their services are mentioned in general, while 19% of them specifically talk about public libraries and several of them include other types of libraries as well.

Another 32,5% report to have either NIP (11%) or some sort of NITS (21,5%), and of these countries only 8% do not refer to libraries at all. In fact some 57% of the positive answers include libraries and library services as an important instrument when planning the way a nation should meet and act in regard to the demands of the information society. A very clear and both for libraries and for authorities or governments interesting response, a result that has settled with the widely spread impression that libraries and library services often are forgotten when governments and authorities deal with issues of fundamental importance to the development of their societies. It is thus a response that calls for new actions from IFLA in order to further access to the information, knowledge and culture via library collections and services all over the world. One step of action should be a formal invitation to UNESCO, UN's organisation for education, science, culture and information and media, to revise UNESCO's guidelines on National Information Policy: Scope, Formulation and Implementation [4]. Being developed thirteen years ago, the guidelines do not cope with current developments within the fields of communication and information technology nor the latest IT tools, their possibilities and problematic aspects. A revision is very much needed and might perhaps be done as a common project between UNESCO and IFLA in the near future and should in that case be based on a formal contract.

The Role of Libraries

In almost all the countries NIP and/or NITS was adopted recently (1993-1997. Implementation and evaluation (following-up) of NIP/NTIS are almost everywhere the responsibility of national (or federal) government alone, however in a couple of countries also of local authorities. Most countries have appointed a particular body or committee to be responsible for co-ordination. Where libraries play the central role of the NIP/NITS, often the national library or a similar institution is responsible. The role of the libraries includes of course all traditional library tasks - comprising both traditional collections and IT-services but this is not all.

In different words several countries see the future role of libraries as public access points to knowledge and information, "gateways to information", as a bridge between information strong and information weak citizens, as information centre toward a national IT development and as partners in processes of standardisation etc. Target groups are generally "the public in general, educational and scientific institutions, as well as national business". NIP/NITS is put into practice in a number of ways - varying from legislation and other state initiatives to national programmes and projects. A part from a few exceptions funding derives everywhere from public budgets; state and/or local level, mostly state. To the question "What progress have been made due to NIP/NITS?" allocating of funds is together with co-ordination the most common replies. When asked about the importance of libraries being a part of NIP/NITS, answers are very positive in general, though some do underline that one thing is adopting NIP/NITS another is to make the intentions come through. In the following the situation of two of the answering countries will be briefly introduced: Finland's and Malaysia's; both are among the countries to having a combination of NIP and NITS.

A Couple of Examples

The unpredictable rapid development of information technology has created an information society where all kind of information is available to principally everyone. In this situation a number of countries have established or further developed national information policies and IT-strategies, among those are Finland and Malaysia.

In Finland (5 mio inhabitants), a government position paper [5] in 1995 outlined an information society strategy stipulating that each administrative branch prepare detailed action plans to implement a strategy with the aim of providing every citizen the opportunity to acquire the new skills (of the information society) needed and to obtain access to information. The Ministry of Education focuses it's activities on education, research and culture, providing institutions concerned with modern information networks, and guaranteeing schools at all levels the opportunity to use these networks and the services offered by them. Libraries were also included in this development, since they are considered crucial in providing these services to everybody. The paper was followed by a national strategy [6] covering the period until 1999. The goal of these strategies is to guarantee all citizens equal opportunities in the new information environment. These strategies show how levels of education and research can be raised with the help of information technology. They simultaneously suggest how national competitiveness can be improved and employment opportunities increased, how people's access to and use of information can be promoted and how basic skills in using modern technology can be learned by everybody. They also encourage citizens to faze new challenges arising in an ever-changing society. The key elements here are high-quality education, training, research and culture, with opportunities for lifelong learning available to everyone. By international standards, the information society in Finland has already achieved a high level of developments in terms of social, communication and information technology measures. The technical infrastructure as a whole in Finland is also rather sophisticated, and in certain fields Finland must (autumn 1997) be considered among the world's most interesting countries in regard to such development. Some central goals have already been mentioned another is to build education and research networks into an open global network. The ultimate goal, the Finnish Information Highway, is a consortium of local, regional and national networks as a part of an open global information network. When it comes to libraries (archives and museums) a number of initiatives have been taken. Professionals in the information services have for instance been given extensive in-house training since it became obvious that the new information technology is going to change the nature of their work fundamentally. University libraries, which are public, form the backbone of scientific libraries and a centrally purchased library system has been integrated and constitutes the basis of research libraries services in the country. Access to information is one of the fundamental rights of all citizens, and the Finnish public library system (municipal libraries) forms the basis of initiatives in order to fulfil this right. An overall aim is to prevent citizens from becoming alienated in the information society by offering them adequate services and access to Internet etc at the public library. In 1998 extra funds to be used specifically in public libraries are 10 mln FIM, while the total 1998 funds for the information strategy is around 265 mln FIM.

Through the National Information Technology Council the Malaysian (19 mio inhabitants) Government has introduced a number of IT policies and projects in order to transform Malaysia into a digital nation. In the Governments Vision 2020 [7] a long term development is scheduled. In 2020, the overall goals are that "All Malaysians will have access to information and learning through a national infostructure for personal, organisational and national advancement" and that "Information and knowledge applications will provide the basis to further enhance quality of life". The major thrust is of Vision 2020 is to develop an information-rich society, which nurtures science and technology culture and changes the education system with emphasis on IT teaching and learning. The library IT development is stated in the "National Policy on Library and Information Services" [8] and designs a three-tier library development plan for library services based on three levels: national, state and rural level. At the moment in Malaysia there are approximately 8.500 libraries of different type and size. They are the National Library, 13 university libraries, 300 special libraries, 14 state libraries, 189 municipalities, district, rural and mobile libraries and about 8000 school libraries. The State libraries are responsible for the development of the state wide library network that extends to districts, towns and villages, and initiatives in the IT area are numerous. One is the development of nation-wide public libraries will bring information services to local communities in the cities, to the villages and to remote areas. The JARINGARD ILMU (knowledge network) is linking state libraries with the Internet. Internet access is soon supposed to be widely available in the public libraries at local and village levels. Thus introducing information technologies to rural communities is expected to mainstream development and thereby making a quantum leap into a new technological era in Malaysia. A development connected to the recent decision of the Malaysian Government to set up 500 Desa Wawasan (Visionary Villages) to promote the use of IT also in the villages. Libraries will be an integrated part of these villages.

To conclude - IT is definitely forcing the agenda world wide in general, but in particular in the library sector. All nations need to deal with the information society. The explosive development in formation technology has forced and will force governments all over the world as well as many international organisations to start public debate on the information society, its possibilities and problems and the way it is structured in each country in order to contribute both to nations and to individuals positive development. It calls for innovative thinking to find ways and means of preventing social isolation among the information weak in all countries, first of all through improved educational efforts however also through establishment of open national information networks which will enable more people to take advantage of the benefits of the information society. Neither in human nor societal terms can any country afford not to deal with these matters and must sooner or later develop and support new communication structures, it is therefore highly relevant for them to set up and adopt national information policies and/or IT-strategies, and not least to see that such tools include all appropriate means such as the services of the libraries.

IFLA's Standing Committee for Public Libraries appointed mid 1995 a special ad-hoc group, to work with the NIP/NITS issue. Members: Francoise Danset, France, Peter

Klinec, Slovakia, Philip Gill, UK and Hellen Niegaard, Denmark. When FD and PK left the committee in 1997, Nic Diament, France and Ilona Glashoff, Germany joined the working group.

References

1. Universal Declaration of Human Rights: United Nations adopted 10 December 1948.
2. The right to information as a condition for human development / Koren, M. // IFLA conference in Copenhagen, 1997.
3. UNESCO Public Library Manifesto, 1994.
4. Guidelines on National Information Policy: Scope, Formulation and Implementation: General Information Programme and UNISIST (PGI-85/WS/14). – Paris, 1985.
5. National Strategy on Education, Training and Research / The Ministry of Education. – Finland, 1995.
6. Towards a Culture-Oriented Information Society / The Ministry of Education. – Finland 1996. – Mode of access: http:// www.minedu.fi/eopm/strategi/2.html.
7. The National Information Technology Council of Malaysia: National IT Agenda. – p.1-16.
8. Jaafar S.B., Negara P. Developing national information and knowledge infrastructure // Regional Conference on Public Libraries: Planning future needs. – Malaysia., 1997.

PROBLEMS CREATING A NEW IDENTITY IN EAST GERMAN LIBRARIES

Claudia Lux

Zentral- und Landesbibliothek Berlin, Berlin, Germany

The night of November 8-9, 1989 – the Wall falls in Berlin.

Noon on November 9, 1989: In the eastern part of the city, in the Berlin City Library, a library normally filled with hundreds of users, total emptiness. Not a reader in sight.

A few kilometres away, behind the Wall into the western part of the city, crowds inundate the America Memorial Library, lines waiting patiently to enter in front of the entrance. A reader from East Berlin returns a book on November 9 which he had borrowed in August 1961 and could not return because the Berlin Wall had been erected over night closing off his part of the city from West Berlin.

The situation on the first day after the Wall fell made clear what the following months would confirm: novels of western authors, glossy and political weekly magazines, books on cars, West German law and marketing strategies are in demand and are only available in book stores or libraries in the western part of the city.

This situation did not change substantially for the following years, for while libraries in East Germany had great stores of literature, which were suddenly not in demand, and they had no money to buy new books

Libraries in East Germany were suddenly confronted with fundamental changes:

- external changes resulting from the political and cultural environment
- internal changes resulting from technical developments and change of status.

Today, in 1998, nine years since the fall of the Berlin Wall, the first visible results and new developments can be seen in East German libraries.

A. External Changes Resulting from the Political and Cultural Environment

1. Adaptation to Decentralized Political Structures

With the political unification of Germany on October 3, 1990, the East German regional precincts became dissolved and five new federal states were created: Mecklenburg-Vorpommern, Saxony-Anhalt, Saxony, Thuringia and Brandenburg. East Berlin with West Berlin became a single federal state. This introduced a new federal structure into East Germany:

A central Ministry of Culture no longer existed, instead the federal states and communes were responsible for education and culture and consequently make decisions on financing. The East German Library Law of 1968 is no longer valid. Library financing stopped being a compulsory duty and became a voluntary service of companies, communes and the federal states. For many libraries and librarians the change of financing became a threat to existence.

2. Takeover of West German Organizational Structures

On all political levels the new organizational structure was adopted to that found in West Germany. Each West German federal state with its cities and communes became a partner for a new federal state in East Germany and its communes. From 1990 to 1996 several thousand West German civil servants were sent to the new states in order to provide structural assistance and to help introduce West German structures and organigrams there.

Almost half of all libraries in East Germany fall victim to this reorganization, they were closed not only by companies, but also by communes and cities, library personnel were dismissed, the book holdings were literally disposed of.

Unification was very expensive – the East German economy, from which tax revenues were supposed to come, were in a crisis. More and more businesses were liquidated and dismissed their employees. The communes hardly had any money and therefore reduced their support where they had the authority to make decisions, and that was almost only in the area of culture. Some libraries could retain their employees only for a year in temporary positions. A radical dismantling of staff occurred and more and more became unemployed.

For those libraries which remained, the organigrams of the West German partner-cities were taken over, job descriptions for all employees were rewritten and reassessed, but because of the lack of money expenses were cut. For political reasons, leadership positions were advertised anew. Staff changes in light of new media or new technology were hardly considered. There was no time to really develop new organizational and management structures. Thereby the responsibilities for libraries became just as disperse, as they were developed over decades in West Germany and they remained traditional.

Many former heads of East German libraries are removed from office and not allowed to work. In this way, their knowledge of the organization was removed, too. The positions are advertised anew and the leadership positions initially are almost always filled with young and old directors from West Germany

Only a few library employees in East Germany strove immediately following the fall of communism to assume leadership responsibilities. This was especially true of those who before as members of the state party or the business union leadership were used to making decisions and organizing. Those leaders are confronted with judgments and prejudices from others and also from their own library.

Others waited to be asked and begged. However they demanded that they would take no responsibility or make any decision. To the contrary: many East German colleagues consciously accepted no responsibility, because they knew the internal structures too well, better than the new leaders from the west. Much is difficult, because old leaders and party members were still in the house, because old animosities have not been forgotten and yet, the major consensus must be on the new : money, new technology and legal regulations.

In addition to innovations and changes in their private lives, librarians had also accept them in their jobs. At times their own positions stood to disposition - at many libraries they had to apply again for their current position, a position that they had held perhaps for 10 to 20 years. They were - in some instances several times - checked - both on membership in the former GDR state security as well as evaluated on the work they had done.

In the new order, qualification papers are more important than job experience, which one had practiced successfully for years. Everything is checked exactly, but on the basis of western public service wage agreements. To them it appears to be unfair that those who already in the old state system had the best training, because they were conform to the state system, now receives the best chances in the new system, too.

Those who also had been refused training opportunities also had no possibility to improve themselves in the new system – an exception being if they took part in a re-training - however without the preference of being granted time off from work to take part and without the security of knowing that they would also receive a corresponding position upon successfully completing the studies.

The responsible administrative level for the new management of the library frequently came from West Germany and first had to learn the particular social and communications patterns of the New German States. Federal decentralization in the cultural area promoted very different developments in the libraries. Their success depended on some few factors:

- the position of the library in the West German partner federal state/ West German partner city
- self-initiative and negotiation skills of the new, respectively also old, leadership with often new partners at the administrative level
- knowledge, training and reeducation in the new competition-oriented surroundings
- high cost-awareness and the ability to obtain additional money sources

Two to three years after the fall of communism, the internal structure in most libraries was firmly in place and their position was laid out within the political surroundings.

3. Professional Instruction and State Guidelines are Abolished

At such a time, in which above all western structures were introduced in East, political and professional instructions from above were missing. They have crumbled away and have not been replaced, because they do not exist in the West to the same extent as they had been present in the East.

The guidelines and regulations of East German ministries are no longer valid. In West Germany there are professional recommendations for which implementation is voluntary. This means that things can be attained only through the self-initiative and commitment of the individual library. Information about West German recommendations is almost only available from the German Library Institute, which at this time has an extremely important consultation function. This is also reinforced with former co-workers of the East German library consultation institute. Recommendations and consultations are completely voluntary for the libraries.

New ordinances are only issued by the state government or the city and they are concerned with legal connections, regulations for library usage, ordinances on fines or circulation regulations.

4. New Argument with Local Politics

Politics in the libraries is no longer regulated by guidelines laid down by the State, but now through policies for allocation funding, by budgetary rules and staff regulations. Since state guidelines no longer exist, locally elected officials freely make decisions about the public libraries in their city and, likewise, professors preside over the development and budgets of their university libraries. A completely new type of lobbying is therefore necessary for libraries in order to secure their future politically. Recognition for „silent“ but continued performance or for achievement of self-proscribed goals is no longer on the agenda. The library is judged by the fulfillment of divergent expectancies form outside dependents.

5. Economic Policies Dominate Cultural Policies

If libraries are voluntary financed by the commune from tax revenues, then the pressure of justification and argument increases that they are important for economic development, that they provide a substantial contribution for the community. Although this contributes to a reinforced motivation to provide information with better access to databases which is now possible following the fall of the old system, the necessary knowledge of English is still lacking and the patrons - especially small and average-sized businesses (for example, in Magdeburg or Cottbus) - have no money to pay for these services. Libraries have a good position if they are located in a town where a new university is established such as Frankfurt/ Oder, which as a European university with connections to the eastern neighbors has a special importance and receives support on a European level.

Also those public libraries win in the political environment, which aggressively present themselves as positive location factors for social problems or for bringing life to the center of the town, such as happened in Rostock or Dresden. However, this has become increasingly more difficult, since libraries must be less active as an educational and cultural factor and become increasingly active as an economic factor (for example, as a frequency provider for businesses and stores of a district). This means that totally new demands are placed on the image of the East German librarian.

6. Adaptation to a Changed Cultural Environment

To the changed responsibility also comes a changed cultural policy, which first of all wants to get rid of as much as is possible from the GDR period. This tendency is visible in all cultural areas and also extended to the book holdings of East German libraries. In comparison to the federal republic, East Germany had a low title spectrum in publications and low book prices. This meant that a large part of the East German annual book production could easily be made available with multiple copies in the libraries.

Into the west the title spectrum is large and book prices high. In the east-libraries at least 40% of the holdings are replaced as they are no longer current. The readers drive to nearby West German or West Berlin libraries. With the currency union from June 1990 until 1993, funding was made available from a special program of the federal government for "rebuilding holdings in the East". Gifts of duplicate copies from West German libraries were made, because also older western literature was in demand. Only a few libraries, such as the Ernst-Abbe-Library in Jena, reciprocally exchanged their own duplicate titles with West Germany. One remained largely passive and accepted gifts and decided what was no longer wanted. A radical holdings revision took place in the city libraries - but it only lasted until 1998 when the holdings had been replenished. As a matter of fact, these holdings were often better than those in West German libraries, where budget cuts did not permit replacing the holdings to the same extent and many holdings from the 70's were retained. The university libraries also got money, primarily so they could purchase new textbooks for the students.

At a time when their own future was uncertain, librarians had to orient themselves to a completely different publishing and bookseller structure, as well as make selections from a flood of offers. West German publishers and booksellers enjoyed a flourishing business. For the special program was also understood as economic assistance for the book trade.

The transition period was exploited by businesses at the expense of libraries. Thus libraries of administrative agencies experienced difficulties obtaining the necessary literature even though the budget had been given money by the communities for the necessary literature. Employees in these administrative libraries generally did not have professional library training. Some publishers capitalized on this. They sold the new administrative heads car, dog and sport magazines for their own personal interests, made subscriptions for television magazines or compiled very quickly and poorly, expensive loose-leaf collections for legal problems. For one or two years anything could be sold in East Germany. Hardly anyone knew what the budget for professional work, for legal literature and for official gazettes would be. The German Council of Municipalities and the German Library Institute began intensive training for administrative librarians. They were again to get access to „their" budget, manage the organization and control of subscriptions and acquire knowledge about the serious book and magazine market.

7. Reeducation, Reeducation, Reeducation

There was no end to the travels of western consultants and the demand for training in basic activities - the structure of the book trade and publishers, methods of procurement, discounts, legal problems of library work, correct budget management, new library materials from labels to book binding, library furniture, dealing with representatives of publishers and companies, etc. The daily requests were infinite. At the same time, readers began to make demands and raise questions – especially for new magazines and books, for legal assistance for the daily life – from the choice of school to filling out income tax forms, health insurance, etc. In the public libraries those new novels were purchased which had been featured in bookstores, television and media advertisements – former authors from the east were forgotten. Non-fiction and professional literature was completely reoriented.

Advanced computerization of East German production suddenly became completely obsolete, previous programming knowledge was no longer in demand. Small, fast computers, different programs, databases, printers were on the market – what should one buy, what not, where does one get training for it? All these problems occurred simultaneously and intensively, and as never before, money was always the central issue, also for the urgently necessary reeducation.

8. Western Influence and Counter Tendencies

Virtually all the changes were strongly western dominated. In the area of consumer goods it changed so quickly that counter movements, such as fairs and special markets for products from the East were organized. In the library environments the partners changed. Bookstores were sold, privatized and staff changed. Publishers folded, different new ones emerged. Big West German publishers flooded the East German market with advertisements and products. The customer in the libraries increasingly demanded those works, which they had been made aware of through the advertising. However, a counter movement also demanded a rethinking of old GDR values, where libraries in their importance for the culture had been more important. But also the West German libraries strongly saw their disadvantages as a result of the unification - the economic reductions to support unification resulting in the fact that they could not buy any new books and had to reduce staff. In the East and in the West there were many who wished that the Berlin Wall would return.

A difficult situation arises when nostalgia and progress strongly collide. It is a time of real changes, where regrets surface at the realization of how many old structures and connections have been changed in both parts of the country. And hope that much can be saved in the new age is widespread.

In addition to the western orientation of the contents, leadership from the west was installed in the big East German libraries. In smaller libraries this also happened, but by no means so often. The candidates from the west had worked with the new computers, they knew the new library materials of the suppliers and in particular they knew the western book trade and publisher policies. Most important, however, was that they were acquainted with the legal regulations and the prescribed budget management – even if that was – in reality – not so different from that in East Germany.

There were few differences in the internal organizational structures of libraries, which were still organized according to acquisitions, cataloging and circulation.

Until 1998 attempts were still made to apply an East German payment, which however, only was effective for a few of the important leadership positions. Only in library committees was value placed on representation of East German libraries, assurance of East German participation was achieved, different dues were paid - until East German librarians increasingly rejected this special treatment and demanded real equality with West German colleagues.

9. Change as Change from Outside

The new society in East Germany changed with increasingly speed in the first years following the fall of the Wall. Problems and decisions, new possibilities and interests had priority in the daily lives. Those things which for years had been impossible were now caught up on: education, a driver's license, travel, buying a house, etc. Inheritances and property claims assumed importance in the private sphere. Jobs and earning money were wishes in addition to the uncertain library perspectives. Much private time was now needed for organizing problems which now had to be regulated privately: rising rents, taxes, health insurance, choice of doctor, Their child's place in the kindergarten, etc. Only after people had grown accustomed to all this could they bring their individual identification to the profession and to work, and thus bring organization of the library more into the focal point.

Change came from outside and was rarely instigated from within. Thus, the library was changed as a result of external influences. Where should a new identification come from? It was more difficult if the changes were instigated from within. Even library leadership from the west signified „foreign change" and thereby caused problems of identification with what was new. Only those changes which helped individuals make decisions were able to mould „leader" spirits which had been cramped by 40 years of dictatorship – to form a new identification.

B. Internal Changes Resulting from Technical Development

10. New Responsibility for Decision-Making in East German Libraries

After political structures were stabilized and leadership levels were clarified, could processes of internal change develop. However, the new possibilities of decision-making in libraries were not simple. Decisions about new books and periodicals, about new furnishings were easy to make - but decisions in the new western environment were more difficult. Regulations on how purchases were made, what had to be observed so that all competitors in the free market were justly treated and an economic selection made, all these things had to be taken into consideration.

Many new situations create a network of new decision-making authority, which was dependent on rules one had to know. There was a fear of making decisions which, because of ignorance, could be wrong and which could be quickly discovered and criticized by the responsible authorities. At the local level in public libraries this played a greater role, since they were more directly regulated by their administrations than the university libraries. The decision-making competencies which they had exercised during the transition period following the fall of communism, when much had still not been newly regulated, was now taken away from them.

Just as the decision-making responsibility of the library director had first to be adjusted to a new framework focused externally, so also the internal decision-making process had be moulded anew. Old and new leadership structures existed side by side with different levels of willingness to make decisions. Some structures in the libraries facilitated any decision-making responsibility; conversely, many staff members didn't want to be responsible for any decision and thus didn't „buy-in" to changes which had to be made.

11. New Perception of Self-Competencies in East German Libraries

In the meantime, eight years have passed since the fall of communism. New rules have been established, even though they still were not accepted everywhere. East German librarians were increasingly realizing that their own professional training was at least as good as that of their western colleagues, only that they did not have as much experience, for example with data processing. On the one hand, they could still draw on their own experiences; simultaneously, however, technical change processes had to be implemented and thereby basic structures of the library had to be changed and these changes accepted.

The attitude that all of one's previous activities had to be rejected and everything western had to be blindly accepted - in book selection, in cost-awareness, in furnishings and in technology, - had been overcome. Conditions were now reassessed and one recognized more strongly one's own abilities to create good organizational forms and influence meaningful changes. It was clear that East-West changes were no longer the determining factors, but that general technological development demanded new challenges, which had to be met. There was, however, also a group which even today emphasizes that nothing basically need be changed. It had been noted that about 20% of East German employees were actively engaged in making changes and 20% were strongly retentive. The remaining 60% acquiesced, usually when the change has occurred.

And thus a situation had arisen which in itself was no longer distinguishable from that found in West German libraries which were likewise exposed to new changes brought about by technological innovations. There one also found both groups, those seeking change and those seeking to preserve old structures, as well as those acquiescing when change finally pushed its way through resistance to change!

12. The Transformation Process in the Creation of a New Identity in East German Libraries

With these contradictory internal positions – wanting to entirely change oneself or waiting until one is forced to change – it is difficult for libraries to find the way to a new identity. Today it is no longer the transformation of the East German society into the West German society, what is clear is that the changes involve the whole society, and both East and West must face this transformation process. The chances for East German libraries are currently, however, much greater, since they have already accepted many changes and are still undergoing processes of change – even though the desire to finally settle down is also great.

Creating a new identity in East German libraries is only possible if even more changes and innovations are introduced, – in spite of the tremendous upheaval which has already taken place. This means that familiar procedures must be relearned and changes must be accepted. It also means that innovations are introduced positively for the library patron, who has to adapt himself to the changes and innovations in the library. Again re-education plays a crucial role. This can only be implemented when those professional and technical skills which are necessary for the changes has been learned. Unfortunately, only in the initial years after the fall of the Wall was there money to train for „adapting to the west"; now what is required is that technological innovations be mastered. Modernization with staff and technology means that the transformation processes continue, even though library staff have just gone through a period of change. Simultaneously, there are a variety of negative influences from an environment with high unemployment, increasing poverty and with financial difficulties for libraries, so that these steps of transformation sometimes appear hopeless.

Nevertheless, taking the willingness to change in East German libraries as a basis, re-education is required in order to master the new media and the new processes. Training must be intense, so that one does not so easily revert to the familiar ways. Changes in organizational procedures are frequently viewed as being merely an „electronification of old procedures" and training must convey deeper basic restructuring necessities which are also intronsically tied to the new responsibilities.

a. Identity Through Success and Recognition

Even if libraries during the GDR period didn't receive any special material support, they were, however, imbedded in a cultural system which was responsible for them and assure their continued existence. Today, the existence of the library must be secured during a period of financial difficulties, since the new political structure is frequently focused on problems other than libraries and the material base for libraries is being withdrawn – evident cuts both in staffing reduction as well as in decreasing acquisitions budgets.

A counter-trend was recently re-emerging in eastern Germany recalling again the allegedly good „old times" when the library was part of the solid government system. It goes without saying that since the fall of the GDR-system, the density of the library network has been rapidly reduced. Very many small reading rooms and small libraries, but also many mobile libraries and larger branch libraries closed in the „reading country" GDR. It was a point of discussion whether the service had become better or worse as it was made more economical. What remained was the service for the patrons, what changed was how the new services would be offered.

The new trend for success and recognition looks at the cost benefit for each library. Here one must take a stand in order to survive. Survive is only possible if everything is changed completely – new books, new media, new technology, new furnishings, because patron expectancies have increased. Libraries only receive recognition if performance improves - and in particular with less staff. Only those who comprehend and experience this trend will survive. Thus, the situation for all East German libraries may be more difficult, but it is also more exciting than before. And it is clear that especially middle-sized city libraries, such as those in Rostock, Berlin-Mitte or Jena, are able to gain a new identity by capitalizing on recognition obtained with extended opening hours, Internet access and other new media in their collections.

b. Identity Through New Creativity

In order to have a successful library today, colleagues in East German libraries have a special talent: their old creativity. Creativity was widespread in East Germany: one created something wherever there was a deficiency and made things possible for the patrons. This creativity required much time, but now time is no longer available. Services must be delivered quicker and better, and whoever needs as much time as he needed before will not be able to meet the demands. Masses of information and new books must be coped with – there is no longer any time to look for mistakes, to check, to discuss. High quality must be delivered immediately. But creativity is needed today in order to supply better services for readers and patrons. This creativity, which was restricted by rules and adaptation, could be reawakened if motivation for new goals could be invoked in East German libraries.

c. Identity Through Conscious Globalization

Prior to the fall of the Berlin Wall, globalization was not possible in the East, one oriented oneself to his own library and his own country. Incidentally, this tended to be the case in West Germany, as well. The upheaval in East Germany occurred however, at a time in which globalization was under intense development. This was accompanied by a new pressure for modernization and language competency that East German librarians were forced to confront. Today, globalization means that one must understand English in order to translate information, ideas and processes from the international area to help patrons in one's own library. It also means one must translate his own information and make it accessible globally. Some libraries in East Germany have begun to intensively give English courses and Internet training. In this way, the journey to a new identity has begun.

d. Identity Through New Organizational Structures

The first things which are visible in transformation process are new services. This was the only way in which a new identity can be developed in East German libraries. When they have caught up, they must be better than West German libraries, in their holdings, in technology, in employee training. If they are able to maintain their commitment to change and not be satisfied with what they have attained halfway to their goals, there will be an interesting future. The global information society places these demands on them. These new organizational structures exist - in Rostock, in Dresden, in Berlin, in Halle, in Frankfurt/Oder, in Potsdam etc. Others are satisfied that they have created improved external conditions and thus continuing education of staff has stagnated.

But success has proven those right who continue and become involved in the process of further changes, this process can be summarized as follows:

- formal changes take place in East German libraries - book holdings, furnishings, buildings
- formal changes only create a new identity if recognition and success are present
- new strategies are based on a strong orientation toward the patron, cooperation with sponsors, convincing politicians and public opinion, and achieving the goals of the digital library.

- competency of continuous learning, change and improvement is required and has begun
- competency in new technologies, foreign languages (especially English) and teamwork is imperative. In particular, competency in the service are required
- in order to secure this on a long-term basis, new management methods must be introduced, those in leadership positions have the task of promoting goal-oriented discussions and moderating between the different interests.
- this means that the staff must be actively involved in the processes and execute changes.
- for this, new organizational structures, such as teams and task-force-working groups, must be created in order to alleviate the fears of making one's own decisions.
- the criteria for success are customer satisfaction, high use statistics and acceptance in both the social and political environment.

The way to the future of East German libraries is a giant leap, not leisurely development, and requires continued efforts.

THE GROWING GAP BETWEEN THE INFORMATION RICH AND THE INFORMATION POOR, BOTH WITHIN COUNTRIES AND BETWEEN COUNTRIES - A COMPOSITE POLICY PAPER

Edited by Alfred Kagan

University of Illinois, Urbana/Champaign, USA

Introduction

The IFLA Social Responsibilities Discussion Group was officially established in December 1997 to address the role of libraries in society. It is currently affiliated with the IFLA Education and Training Section. The group is initially concentrating on the following themes:

- Equality of access to library collections and facilities,
- The growing gap between library rich and poor both within and between countries,
- The "right to know."

This policy paper was developed from the six discussion papers prepared for the 1998 IFLA meeting in Amsterdam and the comments received at our first open meeting. Much of the following text is taken directly from the papers (see http://www.ifla.org/VII/dg/srdg/index.htm#8). The themes of the discussion papers were: rural library development (Kalpana Dasgupta, India), literacy in libraries (Josephine Andersen, South Africa), fees for library services (Kristine Abelsnes, Norway), human resource development (Dennis Ocholla, South Africa), the electronic information gap (Alfred Kagan, US), and North-South library cooperation (Ismail Abdullahi, US). Each theme will be addressed in turn, including concrete proposals for action.

The information rich and poor are often defined in two separate and distinct ways: The North vs. the South (rich vs. poor countries) and the gap between the elite and the disadvantaged within countries. Our project seeks to unite these ideas. To a greater or larger extent all countries have information gaps. The United States and South Africa are examples of two countries that have extremely skewed distribution of wealth, resulting in excellent information services for some and poor or non-existent services for others. Although the United States is rich, its distribution of wealth and information is becoming more unequal. On the other hand, the great majority of South Africans are poor, but there are now efforts to equalize the standard of living that was constructed under apartheid. We believe that libraries, library associations, and those who work in libraries have a social responsibility to address these issues in whatever context they find themselves and in all countries. We hope that the IFLA Professional Board will endorse the following recommendations and provide administrative and monetary support for implementation.

Dennis Ocholla defines the information poor in five ways: 1. The economically disadvantaged populations of the developing countries (The South); 2. Rural people who are often geographically isolated by lack of communication and transportation systems; 3. Those disadvantaged by cultural and social poverty, especially the illiterate, the elderly, women, and children; 4. Minorities who are discriminated against by race, creed and religion; and 5. The physically disabled. The following remarks are focused on addressing the needs of these population groups.

Rural Library Development (Dasgupta)

The most extreme information gaps are between illiterate and neo-literate people in rural villages and rich urban populations. Kalpana Dasgupta reminds us that information is a prerequisite for all development activities. The goals must be to see that the right information reaches the right clientele in the most comprehensible format at the right time. For example in India, rural libraries have helped educate people in local history, village traditions, methods of cultivation, public health, and the message of the freedom movement against British colonialism. The diversity of the rural population must be analyzed in order to plan appropriate library services. Interpersonal forms of communication such as information exchange in marketplaces, water sources, and places of worship must be discovered.

It is necessary to find out how rural communities use information as an aid to the adoption of important innovations and new practices that are crucial with the development process. Before establishing libraries the following information should be developed: village environment (geography, livelihood, education, etc.), peoples' needs (physical, intellectual and psychological), availability of resources, infrastructure facilities, and attitudes of the people. It is important to pay special attention to women, students, young adults, children, and neo-literates. Rural libraries can act as information and community centers to improve living conditions and the quality of life. Local authorities must be empowered to create such institutions.

Recommendations. IFLA should develop a research program on rural library development in coordination with national library agencies. The focus should be on empowerment of local authorities to process appropriate information in comprehensible formats for diverse rural populations.

Literacy in Libraries (Andersen)

Another way to look at the growing information gap is to explore the extremes between illiterate and highly educated people. Josephine Andersen explains that illiteracy often results in unemployment and unemployability. She notes that 36% of the citizen's of her country, South Africa, are illiterate. The problem is historical, and she quotes former Prime Minister Verwoerd (1958-1966) who said "There is no place for the Bantu in the European community above the levels of certain forms of labour." In fact, the acquisition of literacy and education has often been seen as a threat to those in power. This was just as true in the United States during slavery days as in apartheid South Africa.

Illiterate people often do not have access to an environment conducive for learning. Public libraries are ideal learning places and can provide the right surroundings and conditions conductive for human development, even in rural areas without electricity. Libraries must be involved in their communities, and literacy is a library responsibility. Public libraries must promote lifelong learning but often are not equipped to do so and lack librarians with appropriate skills. Literacy programs can be based on Paulo Freire's revolutionary Language Experience Method. Freire advocates problem solving and dialogue between teachers and new learners to encourage critical thinking and creativity. This method contrasts with the "banking method" where teachers "deposit" information in the learners.

Recommendations. IFLA should urge library and information schools to promote adult basic education skills as a component of their curriculums. IFLA should promote literacy training as a basic library service.

Fees for Library Services (Abelsnes)

Kristine Abelsnes quotes the Unesco Public Library Manifesto: "The public library shall in principle be free of charge." The public library must be supported by specific legislation and financed by national and local governments. Libraries are an essential component of any long-term strategy for culture, information provision, literacy and education. Library service is a common good, and free access to information is the backbone of a free and democratic society. Publicly funded libraries are most of all political instruments; they are not businesses.

However, there is a conflict between ideals and economic realities. The dilemma is that library fees can exclude some users, but not charging fees may exclude some special services that in turn may create revenue for basic services. We strive for equal access but even small fees discriminate between users, decreasing library use especially among children and young people. We see a trend in rich countries to protect so-called basic services and charge for supplemental services. However there is no consensus as to what services are basic and what services are special. What is expensive today may be cheap tomorrow, and what seems extra today may be considered basic in the near future. Furthermore once a library charges for one thing, it is easier to decide to charge for something else. Some argue that fee based services generate revenue to subsidize basic services. However experience has often proven the reverse. When supplemental services do not fully recover costs, they result in the poor subsidizing the rich.

Information is not free, but libraries can make it freely available to the community. Information is more than a commodity; wide access to information can empower citizens and therefore be a method of wealth distribution. Commercial information providers have a social responsibility to their communities and public libraries. If we abandon free-of-charge public libraries, we can expect political support for our libraries to erode and even fade away. This could lead to libraries being eventually integrated into the market. This would effectively end any hope of equality of access and cede information access entirely to the commercial sector.

Recommendations. IFLA should take a strong position against fees for basic services broadly construed. IFLA should be an advocate for public libraries in their negotiations with commercial information providers, and promote a price structure based on ability to pay.

Human Resource Development (Ocholla)

Dennis Ocholla discusses library and information education in Africa and the Third World generally. He compares LIS education to the political realm, quoting Ali Mazrui's insight that Africa has borrowed the wrong things from the West: the profit motive without entrepreneurial spirit and the acquisitive appetites of capitalism without creative risk-taking. Similarly, LIS departments are thrilled with modern information systems but apathetic to their development and maintenance. Instead of lavishly spending money on Western goods and services, it is necessary to address the plight of the information poor.

LIS departments are generally found in universities, and university graduates often dread working with the poor, the illiterate, and in rural areas. These graduates are alienated from the majority of the population who see universities as ivory towers. We must provide students with the knowledge that inculcates a service culture. Libraries can help empower the information poor in tackling their challenges and responsibilities. Graduates must understand their role in transforming the information poor into information consumers, especially because the information poor are often fragile users who are easily discouraged by elitist information providers.

Such a reorientation begins with the selection of dedicated LIS students. Once enrolled, fieldwork is an excellent device for sensitizing students to work ethics and providing a sense of belonging and responsibility. Academic performance is necessary but not sufficient for advising students on various specializations. Such decisions must also take service attitude into consideration. Continuing education and informal education is a life-long process. LIS departments can reach out to their alumni and provide workshops and seminars. Keeping up these contacts can provide feedback for continuous revitalization and improvement of LIS programs. Library and information schools can be catalysts in promoting information access and use by disadvantaged communities through their products, programs and activities.

Recommendations. IFLA should encourage library and information science schools to adopt a socially responsible orientation, including the promotion of a strong service ethic towards all population groups.

The Electronic Information Gap (Kagan)

The Dakar Declaration on the Internet and the African Media (1997) called for creating a culture of online communications and ensuring African content on the Internet. Kagan cites the Declaration as just one example that people and institutions everywhere want electronic access to information and are working towards their goals. As opposed to every country's elites, most of the world's people must contend with all the barriers associated with poverty. Regarding electronic access, Zulu noted the following barriers: lack of adequate electricity; lack of good computer environments (dust, humidity, and heat); poorly developed telecommunications infrastructures; few qualified people to maintain equipment; large illiterate or semi-literate populations, lack of foreign exchange, language barriers, lack of national information policies, and lack of ability to upgrade obsolete equipment. Let us be mildly optimistic that solar energy, microwave and satellite technologies may prove useful in addressing these enormous problems.

Herbert Schiller has described the phenomenal growth of corporate power in the rich countries including the deregulation of economic activities, privatization of functions once public, and commercialization of activities once social. To receive assistance, poor countries must contend with the World Bank's structural adjustment programs that mandate privatization, currency devaluation, removal of trade restrictions, cuts in subsidies, and severe reduction of services such as health and education. And such aid comes with Eurocentric cultural strings attached. Corporate media has the power to choose what ideas to present and regulate what people think and believe.

As opposed to a "public good," transnational corporations view electronic information as a commodity. Microsoft dominates personal computing and tries to control Internet content and commerce through the arrangement of selected icons on its desktop. Many have praised the Internet's diversity and profound democratic effect, but commercialization runs in a counter direction. There are also questions of language and local content. English is the dominant Internet language, and although most countries now have at least minimum presence of the web, the great majority of content is still provided from Europe and North America. Furthermore, minorities within rich countries are also marginalized. For example, a recent study of United States students found that 73% of white students had their own computers as opposed to 32% of black students. Libraries have a social responsibility to try to equalize access to electronic information. We will need to become much more politically active within our professional associations and our societies to promote universal access to information.

Recommendations. IFLA should promote the development of local content electronic resources. IFLA should promote policies and develop programs that equalize access to the Internet.

North-South Library Cooperation (Abdullahi)

Ismail Abdullahi begins from the premise that national development necessitates the cooperation of all sectors of a national economy and the integration of economic, social and cultural advances. Development therefore requires increased access to information. The countries of the North have recognized this and use information extensively. The rapid growth of information technology is further increasing the already large gap between the information rich and poor. There is a lack of sufficient cooperation and resource sharing between North and South and a lack of development infrastructure in the South. The goals should be to remove all barriers of library resource sharing and provide equal access by any individual from any geographical location to the sum total of the world's knowledge.

We have recently seen a high degree of interest and activity in library development and cooperation in developing countries. But Salman has recognized the following problems: lack of essential infrastructures for national information systems, shortages of skilled people, underutilized information services, unsatisfactory access to locally produced information, access to a very limited quantity of foreign and international information literature, and lack of application of new technologies. Furthermore, government monopolies have often stifled the flow of information due to unwise telecommunications policies and lack of resources. Policymakers in Africa and elsewhere often do not perceive the importance of information for national development. Librarians must work to change these attitudes to information and technology transfer.

Recommendations. IFLA should promote greater resource sharing between the North and South, including Southern links to the information superhighway. IFLA should research the education and training needs of Southern countries in order to plan the development of appropriate information infrastructures. IFLA should urge appropriate government agencies to develop policies conducive to the development of information infrastructures.

The Profession, Library Associations, and IFLA Structure

The first open meeting of the Social Responsibilities Discussion Group was held on August 16, 1998 in Amsterdam. There were a number of comments addressing IFLA's structure and the need to mainstream the issues of social responsibility. One speaker asserted that IFLA's Regional Sections are marginalized within Division 8, and noted that there was a proposal coming for changing the structure. It was noted that the Regional Section on Latin America and the Caribbean was holding a panel on the information gap in

Amsterdam. This speaker noted that there is probably more support than we know about within IFLA. Another participant noted that such issues are pervasive in librarianship, and that many of us are librarians precisely to address such concerns. Another speaker lamented that information gap issues are hardly talked about in one of the rich country associations, the American Library Association. There was consensus that the Discussion Group should try to mainstream social responsibility issues within IFLA.

Recommendations. IFLA should reevaluate its structure in order to better address information gap issues. IFLA should compile a report on how various library associations are addressing these issues.

References

Rural Library Development

1. Dasgupta, K. Libraries: Responding to Societal and Community Needs: Paper Presented at the Seminar «Libraries: changing information concepts and Sources» / The American Centre Library. – Calcutta, 1993.
2. Kumar, P. S. G. Freedom of Information: Presidential Address Delivered at SL-All // India Library Conference, Goa University, Goa, January 5-8, 1995.
3. Role of Public Libraries as Communication Centres for Socio-Economic Development: Paper Presented for the Seminar «Two Decades of the Foundation, of the Raja Rammohun Roy Library Foundation». – Calcutta, 1993.
4. Vashishth, C. P. Libraries as Rural Community Resource Centres. – Delhi: B. R. Publishing, 1995.

Literacy in Libraries

5. Christie, P., Butler, D. The Right to Learn: the Struggle for Education in South Africa. – Braamfontein: Ravan Press and Johannesburg: Sached Trust, 1985.
6. Infolit. Annual Report. – August, 1996.
7. Koch, E. Limiting Those Liquid Assets. Leading Edge. – 1996. – N 6.
8. Learn and Teach. – 1994. – September.
9. Lunsford, A. A., The Right to Literacy. – New York: The Modern Language Association of America, 1990.
10. Schamber, L. The Role of Libraries in Literacy Education. – Syracuse, NY: ERIC Digest, 1990.
11. Underwood, P. CALICO News. – 1997. – December. – P. 2, 4.

Fees for Library Services

12. ALA Goal 2000. – Chicago: American Library Association, 1994.
13. Bakken, F. The Possible Role for Libraries in the Digital Future: Paper Presented at the EBLIDA Conference and Workshop, New Developments in Electronic Copyright, Copenhagen, 12-13 February, 1998. – Mode of access: http://www.kaapeli.fi/~eblida/copenhagen/bakken.htm.

14. Latimer, K. Free To Fee: the Current Account from an Academic Library: Paper Presented at the 62nd IFLA General Conference, Beijing, 25-31 August, 1996.

15. Unesco Public Library Manifesto. – Paris: Unesco, 1972.

Human Resource Development

16. Mazrui, A. A. Cultural Forces in the World Politics. – London: James Curry, 1990.

17. Mersham, G. M., Rensburg, R. S., Skinner, J. C. Public Relations, Development and Social Investment: A Southern African Perspective. – Pretoria: J.L. van Schaik Academic, 1995.

18. Sturges, P., Neill, R. The Quiet Struggle: Libraries and Information for Africa. – London, Mansell, 1990.

19. Warner, A. S. Making Money: Fees for Library Services. – New York: Neal-Schuman, 1989.

The Electronic Information Gap

20. Dakar Declaration on the Internet and the African Media: Issued by the seminar on Internet, an Opportunity for Media and Democracy in Africa?, Dakar 7-10 July, 1997. – Dakar: Panos Institute, the Pan African News Agency, 1997. – Mode of access: panos@sonatel.senet.net.

21. Arruda, C., da Conceição, M. Libraries, New Technologies and Human Resources: the Challenge to the 21st Century. 1997 IFLA Paper, Copenhagen, 073-CONTR-3-E.

22. Chun, D. Exclusive Agreements with PC Manufacturers and Microsoft Regarding Operating System Software // Info-Policy-Notes: News from Consumer Project on Technology. – 3 June 1998. – Mode of access: http://www.essential.org/listproc/info-policy-notes/.

23. Hoffman D. L., Novak T. P. Bridging the Racial Divide on the Internet // Science 280. – 1998. – 17 April. – P. 390-391.

24. Hansell, S. News-Ad Issues Arise in New Media. // New York Times. – 1997. – 8 December. – P. 10.

25. Haywood, T. Info-Rich - Info-Poor: Access and Exchange in the Global Information Society. – London: Bowker Saur, 1995.

26. Mchombu, K. J. On the Librarianship of Poverty. // Libri. – 1982. – Vol. 3, N 32. – P. 241-250.

27. Ott, D. Power to the People: the Role of Electronic Media in Promoting Democracy in Africa. // First Monday: Electronic file. – Mode of access: http://www.firstmonday.dk/issues/issues3_4/ott/index.html.

28. Patrikios, H. A., Levey, A. L. Survival Strategies in African University Libraries: New Technologies in the Service of Information. – Washington, DC: American Association for the Advancement of Science, Sub-Saharan Africa Program, 1994.

28. Schiller, H. I. Information Inequality: the Deepening Social Crisis in America. – New York, London: Routledge, 1996.

29. Shapiro, A. L. New Voices in Cyberspace. // The Nation. – 1998. – Vol. 266, N 21. – P. 36-37.

30. Srikantaiah, K., Xiaoying D. Internet and Its Impact on Developing Countries: Examples from China and India. – 1997 IFLA Paper, Copenhagen, 087-CONTR-6-E.

31. Zulu, S. F. C. Africa's Survival Plan for Meeting the Challenges of Information Technology in the 1990s and Beyond. // Libri. – 1994. – Vol. 44, N 1. – P. 77-94.

North-South Library Cooperation

32. Aman, M. Transfer of Information Technology to Developing Countries with particular Emphases on Africa: Paper Presented at the 2nd National Conference of African American Librarians, Milwaukee, Wisconsin, 1995.

33. Asali, K. Some Ideas on Cooperation between National Libraries in Asia and Oceania. // International Library Review. – 1980. – Vol. 12, N 1. – P. 13.

34. Begg, N. Development of Resource Sharing in Pakistan. // International Library Review. – 1980. – Vol. 12. – P. 299.

35. Bouazza, A. Resource Sharing among Libraries in Developing Countries: The Gulf between Hope and Reality // International Library Review. – 1986. – N 18. – P. 373-387.

36. Bowden, R. The Opportunities for, and Problems of, Regional Co-operation in Library Services in Developing Countries / Resource Sharing of Libraries in Developing Countries: Proceedings of the 1977 IFLA/Unesco Pre-Conference Seminar for Librarians from Developing Countries, Antwerp University,30 August – 4 September 1977. – Munich, New York: K. G. Saur, 1979.

37. Fernandes, T. Global Interface Design. – Boston: AP Professional, 1995.

38. Giplin, R. Equilibrium and Decline. / American Foreign Policy: Theoretical Issues. – Glenview, Illinois: Harper-Collins, 1989. – 124.

39. Joshi, K., Sauter V. L. The Opportunities and Constraints Affecting an Informatics Policy: The India Experience // Information and Management. – 1991. – Vol. 20. – P. 313.

40. Kent, A. Network Anatomy and Network Objectives / Library Resource Sharing: Proceedings of the 1976 Conference on Resource Sharing in Libraries. – New York: Marcel Dekker, 1977.

41. Mall, P. Should the Third World Have Information Technology? // IFLA Journal. – 1983. – N 9. – P. 296-308.

42. Parker, T. F. Resource Sharing from Inside and Out: Reflections on the Organizational Nature of Library Networks. // Library Resources and Technical Services. – 1975. – Vol. 19, N 4. – P. 352-53.

43. Salman, L. The Information Needs of the Developing Countries: Analytical Case-Studies // Unesco Journal of Information Science, Librarianship, and Archives Administration. – 1981. – Vol. 3. – October-December. – P. 241-246.

44. Zulu, S. F. C. Africa's Survival for Meeting the Challenges of Information Technology in the 1990s and Beyond // Libri. – 1994. – Vol. 44. – N 1. – P. 77-94.

KNOWLEDGE MANAGEMENT RESEARCH AND END USER WORK ENVIRONMENTS 2010

Wilda B. Newman

The Johns Hopkins University, Applied Physics Laboratory, Laurel, MD, USA

Abstract

Research in Knowledge Management and collaboration with the Johns Hopkins University, Digital Knowledge Center will allow focus on the future work environment of the University as a whole. The sharing of resources, perspectives, ideas, concepts, and work environments will create a synergy for developing profiles of end users and their Knowledge Management environments. It will look at the published information environment, as well as the overall "information" environment of end users. The research will review how end users currently access and use information and develop future scenarios of end user profiles and how these are structured, from a Knowledge Management perspective.

The definition of Knowledge Management as defined by the Gartner Group states that: "Knowledge Management promotes an integrated approach to identifying, capturing, retrieving, sharing, and evaluating an enterprises information assets. These information assets may include databases, documents, policies, procedures, as well as the uncaptured tacit expertise and experience stored in individual's heads" (www.gartner.com). It also includes content management, best illustrated in the "traditional or industrial age library," as well as process flows in automated environments. Knowledge Management is a very broad umbrella and includes by necessity many people of diverse educational and experiential backgrounds. Many of these people are outside the field of Computer Science and are playing an important role in defining and developing the overall understanding of Knowledge Management.

The Milton S. Eisenhower Library at Johns Hopkins University (JHU) has established an R&D arm that includes the Digital Knowledge Center (DKC) to assist with the transition of the information environment into the new millennium. The transition of this environment includes information that is both published and unpublished, as well as information that is internal and external to the organization.

The DKC has two major activities: (1) Evaluation of technology and determining where it is going and the limitations of that technology, and (2) Building collaborative relationships with other areas of the University in general. The DKC focuses are electronic pedagogy, electronic scholarship publishing, and emerging technology. The work proposed will take advantage of these focal points and promote a collaborative approach between the JHU Applied Physics Laboratory and the University as a whole in Knowledge Management.

The use of technology is prevalent throughout our facilities; however, we have yet to leverage that technology in ways that the organization begins to reap more fully the benefits that technology can assist in data, information, and knowledge delivery. This may mean internally produced content or externally produced content and include not only text and graphics but also muti-media, such as streaming video, digitized audio and real time content creation. Knowledge Management also includes procedures and processes that are related and embedded in the functional operations supportive of the infrastructure in the work that occurs as part of all divisions and levels of the University. For example, how will the executive, scientist, researcher, faculty or engineer conduct his or her business, make decisions and manage? How will the administrative, business, or secretarial employees interact in the new environments? And, how will the Program Manager differ in how he or she manages the program environment? In other words, we need to think not just about what we do now, but rather what we do and how we would like to do it in the future. This will require new concepts, tools, and strategies. Basic to this are the building blocks that include knowledge processes, organizational culture, knowledge support, and information technology infrastructure, as noted by Richard N. Fletcher, Principal, Energy Futures Research Associates, Dallas, Texas.

"The future Eisenhower Library will carry forward the digital and network revolutions in the creation, distribution and use of scholarly information but will also integrate a more market-based, customized and entrepreneurial approach to the packaging and delivery of information. The MSEL will become a center for research and development in the application of technology; an aggregator and publisher, and not just a consumer of scholarly information; a campus hub for working with faculty on the integration of technology and electronic resources into teaching and research; a national center for lifelong learning opportunities for information professionals; and a provider of information services to broader academic, research and business communities.

"This vision for the Eisenhower Library predicts a significant moderation in the cost increases for knowledge acquisition as the traditional model of scholarly communication is replaced, a redefinition of the MSEL as a virtual resource not limited by time and space and so dependent on buildings for the housing and use of information, and a positioning of the Library as a successful competitor in the information market, and for corporate, foundation and federal investment."

Knowledge Management has many definitions, but is generally acknowledged to be the next "age" or revolution, in businesses and organizations and is seen as a discipline. The concept behind Knowledge Management is applying an environment of management to the most valuable asset of an organization, its knowledge. The research proposed will pursue Knowledge Management as previously defined, that is, as an integrated approach to information assets. These may include databases, documents, policies, procedures, tacit expertise and experience, as well as content management. Collaboration with the Eisenhower Library's Digital Knowledge Center will allow focus on the future work environments of the University as a whole. Further, sharing resources, perspectives, ideas, concepts, and work environments will create a synergy for developing profiles of end users and their Knowledge Management environments. To accomplish this research the following tasks are identified.

TASKS

- Task – 1 Research the field of Knowledge Management and arrive at a recommended definition for JHU/APL and the University as a whole.
- Task – 2 Interview end users relative to how they work now and how they would like or need to work in the future, with the support of automation, in order to develop end user profiles, current and future.
- Task – 3 Develop VISION 2010 scenarios for end users with the DKC, including the Executive Manager, the Faculty, the Program Manager, the Scientist, the Researcher, the Student, the Administrative Support, and others as perceived.
- Task – 4 Based on the research and work with the Eisenhower Library and the DKC recommend an approach/es for APL and the University for Knowledge Management 2010, including system development and application access.

- Task – 5 This task will be used to assess the research project on Knowledge Management for the Laboratory and the University overall.

An Advisory Group will be formed that includes staff from the University, as well as the APL, including the Director for Research and Exploratory Development. The Advisory Group will be given regular status reports on the work as it progresses and will be asked for feedback on the process.

The JHU/APL is committed to the field of Knowledge Management with the work of the Research and Technical Development Center and the establishment of an Information Operations Program Development Office, and is one of the Laboratory's strategic plan areas for increased focus in new business development

The DKC at the Eisenhower Library offers a significant opportunity for additional research and collaboration in Knowledge Management, with likely benefits of feeding the efforts of the Laboratory directly, as well as supporting the strategic initiative of APL in its goal to further benefit the government and commercial sectors, while directly supporting the University as a whole. This field is a broad discipline with multiple layers in both depth and breadth, and will require people from many different perspectives for an organization like the Johns Hopkins University to meet the challenge of this next information era.

References

1. Harvard Business Review on Knowledge Management. – Harvard Business School Press, 1998. – P. 221.

2. Davis, S., Meyer, C. BLUR: The Speed of Change in the Connected Economy. – Addison Wesley, 1998. – P. 265.

3. Naisbitt, J, Aburdene, P. Megatrends 2000: Ten New Directions for the 1990s. – William Morrow and Co., Inc., 1990. – P. 384.

4. Electronic Book'98 Workshop: Turning a New Page in Knowledge Management. – 1998. – 8-9 October. – NIST.

5. Gartner Group Symposium: The Future of IT / Itxpo97. – 1997. – October.

6. Coen, R. Hoogenboom M.C., Gemini C. Web-Enabled Applications Programmed on the Net: How to become a Web-Enabled Enterprise. – McGraw Hill, 1997. – P. 574.

7. Hackman, J. R., Oldham, G. R. Work Redesign. – Addison-Wesley Pub. Co., 1980. – P. 330.

THE ROLES OF KNOWLEDGE PROFESSIONALS FOR KNOWLEDGE MANAGEMENT

Seonghee Kim

Faculty of Library and Information Science, Dongduk Women's University, Korea

Abstract

Knowledge and Knowledge Management have emerged as a current 'hot issue' for many organizations. This paper starts by exploring the definition of knowledge and knowledge management. It then considers the partnership for knowledge management, and especially how librarians as knowledge professionals, users, and technology experts can contribute to effective knowledge management. It is concluded that knowledge professionals will have to move from the background to the center of the organizational stage, to jointly hold the reins of knowledge management.

Introduction

In this information and knowledge age, knowledge is the most important factor in the long term success of both an individual and organization. In fact, knowledge may soon be the only source of competitive advantage for an organization. These knowledge assets reside in many different places such as: database, knowledge bases, filing cabinets and peoples's heads and are distributed right across the organization. All too often one part of an organization repeats work of another part simply because it is impossible to keep track of, and make use of knowledge in other parts. Libraries as major functions of an organization need to know what the organization's corporate knowledge assets are and how to manage and make use of these assets to get maximum return. This paper explores the phenomenon of Knowledge Management (KM) from the viewpoint of a management academic with a professional background as a librarian. Then, the paper proposes new roles of librarians for maximizing the value of knowledge in an intelligent organization.

Knowledge and Knowledge Management

The organization's success depends critically on a successful knowledge management. Knowledge assets are the knowledge that an organization owns or needs to own to achieve its goals. Knowledge equals information, extracted, filtered or formatted in some way.

Knowledge can be divided into two types. They are tacit knowledge and explicit knowledge. Tacit knowledge consists of the hands-on skills, best practices, special know-how, heuristic, intuitions, and so on. Tacit knowledge is personal knowledge that is hard to formalize or articulate (Polanyi 1973). The transfer of tacit knowledge is by tradition and shared experience, through for example, apprenticeship or job training. Tacit knowledge in an organization ensures task effectiveness – that the right things are being done so that the work unit could attain its objectives. It also provides for a kind of creative robustness – intuition and heuristic can often tackle tough problems that would otherwise be difficult to solve. Whereas tacit knowledge is implicit, explicit knowledge is rule-based knowledge that is used to match actions to situations by invoking appropriate rules. Explicit knowledge guides action by answering three questions: what kind of situation is this? What kind of person am I or What kind of organization is this? and finally, What does a person or an organization do in a situation such as this? (March 1994). Explicit knowledge is used in the design of routines, standard operation procedures, and the structure of data records. Explicit knowledge enables the organization to enjoy a certain level of operational efficiency and control. It also promotes equable, consistent organizational responses. Those forms of knowledge can be found in any organization. The organization however, is skilled at continuously expanding, renewing, and refreshing its knowledge in all categories. The organization promotes the learning of tacit knowledge to increase the skill and creative capacity of its employees and takes advantage of explicit knowledge to maximize efficiency. In effect, the organization has acquired a third class of knowledge – meta-knowledge – that it uses to create and integrate all its intellectual resources in order to achieve high levels of performance.

The organization adopts a holistic approach to knowledge management that successfully combines tacit and explicit knowledge at all levels of the organization. Tacit knowledge is cultivated in an organizational culture that motivates through shared vision and common purpose. Personal knowledge is leveraged with explicit knowledge for the design and development of innovative products, services and processes Strategic vision and operational expertise are fused in creative action.

Where an organization's performance is heavily reliant on knowledge work then knowledge management is pivotal. Knowledge work emphasizes the use of professional intellect in activities which use individual and external knowledge.

Knowledge Management is a discipline that promotes an integrated approach to identifying, managing and sharing all of an organization's knowledge assets including unarticulated expertise and experience resident in individual workers. In other words, knowledge management is taking advantage of what you know. Knowledge Management involves the identification and analysis of available and required knowledge, and the subsequent planning and control of actions to develop knowledge assets so as to fulfill organizational objectives. Knowledge Management is not about managing or organizing books or journals, searching the inherent for clients or arranging for the circulation of materials. However, each of these activities can in some way be part of the knowledge management spectrum and processes. Knowledge Management is about enhancing the use of organizational knowledge through sound practices of knowledge management and organizational learning. Thus, Knowledge Management is a combination of information Management, Communications, and Human Resources.

The purpose of Knowledge Management is to deliver value to organization. The basic goal of knowledge management is to harness the knowledge resources and knowledge capabilities of the organization in order to enable the organization to learn and adapt to its changing environment (Auster and Choo, 1995). Therefore, Knowledge Management practices aim to draw out the tacit knowledge people have, what they carry around with them, what they observe and learn from experience, rather than what is usually explicitly stated. Managing knowledge goes much further than capturing data and manipulating it to obtain information. Davenport (1993) explains that knowledge management process is about acquisition, creation, packaging, and application or reuse of knowledge. Some examples of each of these types of knowledge management process are:

- Knowledge Acquisition: finding existing knowledge, understanding requirements, searching among multiple sources.
- Knowledge Creation: research activities, creative processes in advertising, writing books or articles, making movies, and so on.
- Packaging: publishing, editing, design work

- Applying or using existing knowledge: auditing, medical diagnosis;
- Reuse of knowledge for new purpose: leveraging knowledge in product development processes, software development.

The Partnerships for Knowledge Management

I have described the concept of knowledge and knowledge management. Knowledge–based systems forge new partnerships that bring together the organization's capabilities to create and use knowledge, organize knowledge, and build infrastructures that enable the effective management of knowledge.

Three groups of experts who need to work together as teams of knowledge partners are at the heart of the knowledge center. They are users, knowledge professionals including librarians, and technology experts.

Users are the individuals in the organization who are personally involved in the act of creating and using knowledge. Users, including the professionals, technologists, managers, and many others possess and apply the tacit knowledge and explicit knowledge. The knowledge and expertise they have is specialized and focused on the organization's domain of activity. Through their coordinated effort the organization as a whole performs its role and attains its goals. Through their knowledge creation and use, the organization learns, makes discoveries, creates innovations, and undergoes adaptation.

Knowledge professionals are the individuals in the knowledge center who have the skills, training and know-how to organize knowledge into systems and structures that facilitate the productive use of knowledge resources. They include librarians, records managers, archivists, and other information specialists. Their tasks include the representation of the various kinds of organizational knowledge; developing methods and systems of structuring and accessing knowledge; knowledge distribution and delivery; amplifying the usefulness and value of knowledge; knowledge storage and retrieval; and so on. Their general focus is to enhance the accessibility and quality of knowledge so that the organization will have an enlightened view of itself and its environment. The knowledge professionals design and develop knowledge products and services that promote learning and awareness; they preserve the organization's memory to provide the continuity and context for action and interpretation.

The knowledge technology (KT) experts are the individuals in the organization who have the specialized expertise to fashion the knowledge infrastructure of the organization. The knowledge technology experts include the system analysts, system designers, software engineers, programmers, data administrators, network managers, and other specialists who develop knowledge based systems and networks. Their general focus is to establish and maintain an knowledge infrastructure that models the flow and transaction of knowledge, and accelerates the processing of data and communication of messages. The knowledge technology experts build applications, databases, networks that allow the organization to do its work with accuracy, reliability, and speed.

In the intelligent organization, the knowledge of the three groups of users, knowledge managers, and KT experts congeal into a superstructure for organizational learning and growth. In order to work together in teams of users, knowledge professionals, and knowledge technology experts, each group will need to re-orientate its traditional mindset. Users will need to separate the management of knowledge from the management of knowledge technology. Knowledge technology in most cases has been heavily managed, whereas the management of knowledge processes – identifying needs, acquiring knowledge, organizing and storing knowledge, developing knowledge services, distributing knowledge, and using knowledge – has been largely neglected. Users need to understand that the goals and principles of knowledge management are quite different from the objectives and methods of knowledge technology management. Users could participate fully in these knowledge processes, not just as end-consumers of knowledge services, but as active agents in every activity of the knowledge management cycle, especially in clarifying knowledge needs, collecting knowledge, sharing knowledge, and transforming raw data into useable knowledge. Users should share the responsibility of identifying and communicating their knowledge needs, and not abdicate this work completely to the knowledge professionals (librarians) or knowledge technology experts. The most valuable knowledge sources in the organization are the people themselves, and they should participate actively in an organizationwide knowledge collection and knowledge sharing network. KT experts are the most prominent group in today's technology-dominated environment. The management of knowledge technology has remained in the media's spotlight for many years. KT experts have become proficient at fashioning knowledge-based systems that dramatically increase operational efficiency and task productivity. At the same time, the same systems are equally well known for the their inability to provide more holistic information about processes, subject areas, or even documents. Computer-based information systems concentrate on formal, structured, internal data, leaving out the informal, unstructured, external information that most decision makers require. KT experts need to move the user to the center of their focus – develop a behavior-based, process-oriented understanding of the knowledge user in terms of their needs and knowledge use dispositions. People in organizations are not content with structured transactional data, they also want knowledge technology to simplify the use of the informal, unstructured information that forms the bulk of the organization's knowledge resources. They also want external data: knowledge to help them understand how the external environment is changing, what other organizations are doing, and how the organization is doing. In other words, users want a web of formal and informal data, internal and external data that are meaningful to them for cultivating insight and developing choices.

The intelligent organization understands that the discovery and use of knowledge can best be achieved through strategic knowledge partnerships that combine the skills and expertise of its users, librarians as knowledge professionals, and KT experts. This collective synergy is necessary to weave an knowledge tapestry that draws together structured and unstructured, internal and external, as well as historical, current, and future-oriented knowledge; to create the tools and methods to access knowledge and select the best available knowledge sources; to design knowledge architectures based on a rich understanding of users' knowledge and communication requirements; and to integrate the organization's knowledge processes into a springboard for organizational learning and development. Through strategic knowledge partnerships, the intelligent organization can significantly enhance each of the knowledge processes that make up the knowledge management cycle.

The Roles of Knowledge Professionals for Knowledge Management

Knowledge Management has emerged as a key concern of organizations. Librarians have long been regarded as part of the support staff of the organization, working quietly in the background, often uninvolved in any of the critical functions of the organization. Information professionals have to recast their roles as an knowledge professional. In other words, librarians need to work as knowledge worker. Knowledge work is characterized by variety and exception rather than routine and is performed by professional or technical workers with a high level of skill and expertise. So those who exercise their intellects in any of these types of activities are knowledge workers. If librarian's work can be or is totally routinized, then they are an administrative worker (for example, gatekeeper), not a knowledge worker. That means that librarian's roles should be not limited to being the custodians or gatekeepers of information. Knowledge professionals will have to move from the background to the center of the organizational stage, to jointly hold the reins of knowledge management with users and the technology experts, to help steer and shape the knowledge policies, structures, processes, and systems that will nurture organizational learning. Knowledge professionals should be able to extract, filter and disseminate vital external knowledge. They also will design and develop workgroup application suites that are effectively platforms for knowledge management. Finally, they will work side by side with users in collecting and analyzing strategic intelligence; and to act as trainers and consultants who transfer knowledge gathering and research skills throughout the organization.

Conclusion

This study described the notion of knowledge and knowledge management and investigated the roles of librarians as knowledge professionals for obtaining an organization goals. The knowledge professional position will continue to evolve as the knowledge infrastructure develops. The precise role of the knowledge professional will depend on the organization structure and knowledge needs. The emphasis in roles of knowledge professional will likely change according to the needs of the user community and the level of technological sophistication.

References

1. Abram, S. (1997) Knowledge Management: Is this the Answer? – Mode of acces: http://www.informart.ca/sla/km/abram.
2. Auster, E., Chun W. C. (1995) Managing Information for the Competitive Edge. – NewYork: Neal Schuman, 1995.
3. Birks, G. (1995)Value-added Information Services: The Art of Being Synchronous with Your Corporation // Bulletin of the American Society for Information Science. – 1995. – Vol. 21, N.2. – P. 23-25.
4. Broadbeht, M. (1996) The Phenomenon of Knowledge Management: What Does it Mean to the Information Profession? – 1996. – Mode of access: http://informationoutlook.com/may/broadben.html.
5. Choo, C. W. (1995) Information Management for the Intelligent Organization: Roles and Implications for the information professions. – 1995. – Mode of access http://hoo.fis.utoronto.ca/fis/respub.
6. Choo, C. W. (1991) Towards an Information Model of Organizations. // The Canadian Journal of Information Science. – 1991. – Vol. 16, N 3. – P. 32-62.
7. Choo, C. W., Auster E. (1993) Scanning the Business Environment: Acquisition and Use of Information by Managers. / Annual Review of Information Science and

Technology. – Martha E. Williams. Medford, NJ: Learned Information, Inc., For the American Society for Information Science. – 1993.

8. Davenport, Thomas H. (1993) Process Innovation: Reengineering Work Through Information Technology. Boston, MA: Harvard Business School Press.
9. Davenport, T. H. Prusak L. (1993) Blow Up The Corporate Library // International Journal of Information Management. – 1993. – Vol. 13, N 6. – P. 405-412.
10. Fidel, R. (1994) User-Centered Indexing // Journal of the American Society for Information Science. – 1994. – Vol. 45, N 8. – P. 572-576.
11. March, J. (1994) G. A Primer on Decision Making: How Decisions Happen. New York, NY: Free Press, 1994.
12. Morgan, G. (1986) Images of Organization. – Newbury Park, CA: Sage Publications, 1986.
13. Murray, Ph. C. (1995) Information, Knowledge, and document management technology. – 1995. – Mode of access: http://www.ktic.com/topic6/.
14. Nonaka, I. (1991) The Knowledge-Creating Company. // Harvard Business Review. – 1991. – Vol. 69, N 6. – P. 96-104.
15. Polanyi, M. (1966) The Tacit Dimension. – London, UK: Routledge & Kegan Paul, 1966.
16. Polanyi, M. (1973) Personal Knowledge. – London, UK: Routledge & Kegan Paul, 1973.

GLOBAL INFORMATION INFRASTRUCTURE AND THE QUESTION OF AFRICAN CONTENT

Justin Chisenga

Department of Information and Communication Studies, University of Namibia, Windhoek, Namibia

Abstract

The paper looks at the question of African information and cultural content on the global information infrastructure (GII) and indicates how the continent can make a meaningful contribution to the development of African local content on GII. It presents a general picture regarding the development and access to the Internet on the continent and indicates that the basic infrastructure for Africa to contribute to the development of global information exists on the continent. It further examines the various ways and methods through which information with a strong African cultural content can be made available on the global information infrastructure. Major problems and constraints hindering the development and use of the Internet on the continent are highlighted, and activities that are required to be implemented in order to ensure that a meaningful contribution to the global information content is done in Africa are discussed. The paper concludes by indicating that unless conscious steps are taken to contribute to global information, millions of people on the African continent will never access information with their own content and, even in the electronic age, will forever remain consumers of electronic information and cultural products produced outside the continent.

We have the opportunity to add our unique touch to the new Net culture (Khaldoon Tabaza, *Star*, Jordan; January 16, 1997)*

Global Information Infrastructure

The world is slowly witnessing the development of the global information infrastructure (GII), a seamless web of communication networks, computers, databases and consumer electronics that will put vast amounts of information at user's finger tips (United States. Information Infrastructure Task Force 1994). Through the global information infrastructure, users around the world will be able to access libraries, databases, educational institutions, hospitals, government departments, and private organisations located anywhere in the world. The Internet, a global network of computers and networks is being seen as the front runner to GII, and is providing an opportunity and infrastructure for publishing and distributing all types of information in various formats in the shortest possible time and at the lowest cost. With millions of people around the world accessing the Internet and still a large number trying to do so, providing information content on the Internet has become a major business, economic, cultural and even political activity. Both large and small business institutions are marketing their products through the Internet. Cultural institutions such as music and film industries, national libraries, archives and museums are also establishing their presence on the Net. Political parties and governments around the world are also using the Internet to communicate their policies, programmes and ideologies.

The Question of Content

In spite of the wide spread of the Internet infrastructure and its use, it is generally felt that there is a dominance of the English language and the content that targets the needs of users in the United States and United Kingdom. As a result of this dominance a number of governments around the world are calling upon their citizens to produced local content in their languages and publish on the Internet, thus making a contribution to the development of local content on the global information infrastructure.

Calls, although not so loud, for publishing local content on the Internet are also being heard on the African continent. The number of African Internet Web sites is growing and almost all countries have local or internationally hosted Web servers (Jensen 1998). Although this is the case, the degree of comprehensiveness of the local content on these Web servers vary greatly. Generally, there are very few well established local content developers on the continent. In addition, most governments have no deliberate or conscious policies to enhance the African content on the Internet. Recently, the United Nations Economic Commission for Africa (UNECA) indicated that surveys have shown that Africa generates only 0.4% of global content, and if South Africa's contribution is excluded, the figure is a mere 0.02% (UNECA 1999. This sad situation should be a matter of major concern to the people of Africa, and especially information professionals on the continent.

Africa – Access to Global Information

Establishment of full Internet access on the continent has moved at a very fast rate since 1995. Mike Jensen (1998) painted the following situation regarding Internet development in Africa as at the end of 1998:

- only three countries (Eritrea, Somalia and Libya) had no local Internet access;
- there were almost 400 Internet Service Providers (ISPs) on the continent of which around 100 were located in the Republic South Africa;
- the total number of computers connected to the Internet, excluding South Africa, was almost 10000, as opposed to around 290 in 1995;
- although generally Internet access is concentrated in capital cities, the number of countries setting up Points of Presence (POPs) in some other major towns is growing. Angola, Benin, Botswana, Egypt, Ghana, Kenya, Morocco, Namibia, Tanzania, Tunisia, Zambia and Zimbabwe had established POPs outside the capital cities, while South Africa had about 70 POP locations around the country;
- use of 128kps links had become increasingly common and some countries had established 256kps;
- around 1,000,000 Internet users, of which about 850,000 - 900,000 are located in South Africa;
- French speaking countries had a far higher profile on the Web and greater institutional connectivity than Anglophone and Lusophone countries, due to the assistance provided by institutions such as the Canadian and French governments which are concerned with the dominance of English on the Internet.

Who has Access to the Internet?

In general, academic and research institutions appear to be in the forefront in establishing and using the Internet. Universities in many countries are providing Internet access to their faculties and research staff members while some have even started providing facilities to students. The industrial and commercial sectors are also using the Internet and setting up Web sites. Electronic banking and commerce through the Internet is also slowly becoming a reality on the continent with banking institutions in South Africa leading the way. Governments, although some of them initially appeared to have been opposed to the free flow of information on the Internet, have also started establishing their presence on the Web. A large number of international and non-governmental organisations operating in Africa have Internet access. Internet access from homes is also slowly taking shape.

Taking the above situation into account, although the number of people accessing the Internet is generally low compared to the total population of the continent, it can be said that the basic infrastructure and environment to contribute to global information and culture exist on the Africa continent.

Contributing to Global Information

The Internet presents a rare opportunity to the people and institutions in Africa to contribute to the development of the content of the global information infrastructure. The benefits of contributing to global information are many and include the following which were identified by the United Nations Economic Commission for Africa - UNECA (1996, 40). It will:

- make African people producers of indigenous information and knowledge and not simply passive consumers of imported information;
- [enable Africa] export information and knowledge and to participate pro-actively in the development of the global information infrastructure;
- provide African researchers and scientists with access to information on Africa generated from within the continent;
- enable African researchers and scientists to collaborate on equal footing with their peers around the world irrespective of distance;
- promote African cultural heritage, including the modern cultural sector of its rich and growing film and music industries

Contributing to the information and cultural content of the global information can be done in many ways, and the following are some of the ways through which this could be achieved. Some of these activities or projects are already being implemented consciously or unconsciously, although generally on a very small and sometimes uncoordinated scale:

- Local information content on Web sites
- Creating Subject Based Information Gateways
- Creating electronic databases
- Digitalisation of documents and artefacts
- Indigenous language orientation

Local Information Content on Web Sites

Access to the Internet on the content is slowly being followed with the setting up of Web sites and this is being done by academic and research institutions, libraries, museums, archives, national governments, financial institutions, international organisations, non-governmental organisations (NGOs), large and small business institutions, news agencies and media organisations, and even individuals. The best strategy for contributing to global information is for all these institutions and individuals to make a deliberate decision and provide a large amount of information with local content on their Web sites.

Libraries, Museums and Archives

Libraries, archives and museums are basically information and cultural institutions. They acquire, process, store and disseminate information in various formats. Some of the information being processed is unique in content and of very high cultural value, and in some cases, very limited in distribution. For example, most university and research libraries in Africa have for years collected copies of research reports, papers thesis and dissertations produced by students and members of staff. Most copies of these documents can only be found in these institutions. Archives in Africa have over the years collected unique current and historical records, while museums have in their collections rare art-facts and many other objects of great cultural value. If these collections could be made available in electronic format and accessed over the global information infrastructure, it will go a long way in contributing to the development and growth of Africa's information and cultural content on the Internet.

Unfortunately, most Web sites of these institutions do not contain much in terms of original local information, except for the brochure type of information (Chisenga 1998). In contrast, there is quite a lot of links to full-text information resources produced and stored on Web servers located in other countries outside Africa. It very easy for people from Africa to access information materials from the Library of Congress and other major libraries around the world than materials in a local university or national library, through the Web sites of libraries, archives and museums based in Africa.

Non-Governmental Organisations

Both local and international non-governmental organisations operating in Africa produce quite a lot of information materials with a large local content for public consumption. These organisations conduct research and work on projects whose end result is basically information. In addition, most of these NGOs have the capacity to establish Internet connection and set up local Web servers on which they could publish their information products.

Universities and Research Institutions

Africa has a large number of universities and specialised research institutions like the Institute for Southern Africa Studies (ISAS) of the National University of Lesotho; Institute of Ethiopian Studies (Ethiopia), Kenya Medical Research Institute, Institut Fondamental d'Afrique Cheikh Anta Diop (Senegal), Human Science Research Council (South Africa), Tanzania Commission for Science and Technology, National Council for Scientific Research (Zambia), Nigerian Institute of Social and Economic Research and many more. Members of staff of these institutions conduct research and participate in many projects within their communities, countries or regions, and therefore these institutions have the capacity to produce and publish information with a large African content on the Internet.

African universities and many other research oriented institutions should encourage their academic and research staff to publish their works on the Internet. In addition, they should also publish on their local Web server much of what they are currently producing i.e. annual reports, technical papers, consultancies reports, feasibility study reports, research reports from their specialised research units.

African Governments

African governments have already started setting up Internet Web sites and they should also take into consideration the question of providing adequate local content on their sites. Not only should they provide information targeting potential foreign investors, but also provided information for the consumption of the few Internet users in their countries. The U.S White House Web Site is a source of huge amount of information. Audio and video files, speeches and briefings by the Presidents, policy papers, etc. There is nothing preventing African governments from providing the same level of information services on their Web sites.

News and Media Agencies

Most news agencies in developing countries were established to counter the work of the major international news agencies and media such as the Agence France Presse (AFP), Reuters, Associated Press (AP) and United Press International (UPI), with the aim of trying to balance the flow of news and the seemingly negative reporting by the international media. National television and radio networks are established to serve the local populations. These institutions have put in place the infrastructure to collect news and information from around the country and disseminate such information to both local and international audiences. Using the Internet infrastructure, they can reach millions of people around the world and thus afford the people around the world a rare opportunity to access a wide variety of original and first hand news stories from the African continent.

Therefore, efforts being made by the South Africa Broadcasting Corporation (SABC), the Media Institute of Southern Africa (MISA), Pan African News Agency (PANA), Africa Online and a host of local newspaper publishers to distribute their news stories through the Internet must be commended. These institutions have set up Web sites on which news stories coming from Africa can be found. Online newspapers from Africa are providing an opportunity to a large number of Africans living abroad and other people interested in news from Africa to be up-to-date with events on the continent.

Individuals

Web sites being created by individuals in Africa are also slowly coming up. These sites could also be used as a means of providing information with local content. For example, Africa artists could exhibit some of their works over the Internet; great African musicians like Luck Dube (South Africa), Yousour N'dour (Senegal), Salif Keita (Mali), Baba Maal (Senegal), Khalid (Algeria), Astere Aweke (Ethiopia), Kofi Olomide (Democratic Republic of Congo), Angelique Kidjo (Benin), Papa Wemba (Democratic Republic of Congo), and many more could provide access to their Web sites where their fans could get information about their music, lyrics, and even sample audio files of their music; lecturers and researchers could provide their works on their home pages; and even Sangomas or traditional healers could also market some of their products on the Web sites.

Subject-Based Information Gateways

Subject-based information gateways (SBIGs) or virtual libraries, have emerged as one form of organising Internet information resources and ensuring that researchers, teaching staff and other serious Internet users have access to information which has gone through some form of quality control. Information gateways have been set up in a number of disciplines and the following are just, but a few of the gateways available on the Internet:

Social Sciences Information Gateway (SOSIG)

http://www.sosig.ac.uk

Engineering Electronic Library (EELS)

http://www.lub.lu.se/eel/

Dutch Electronic Subject Services (DutchEES)

http://www.kb.nl/dutchess/

INFOMINE World Wide Web virtual library

http://infomine.ucr.edu/

Edinburgh Engineering Virtual Library (EELV)

http://www.eevl.ac.uk

Information professionals in Africa should consider setting up subject-based information gateways of information resources produced on the continent. These could be in subject areas such as human rights, rural development, governance and democracy, agriculture and the environment, education, etc. Contributions to these gateways could be done by information professionals on the continent located in different countries. Establishing African based and managed information gateways could be one way of marketing the information produced on the continent to the rest of the world.

Electronic Bibliographic Databases

Most libraries and documentation centres in Africa have established local electronic databases. Many of them are using UNESCO's CDS/ISIS software and most of the databases created are bibliographic records of materials termed as 'special collections'. These are materials that relate to the their countries' or parent institutions' available in the collection. If these databases are made accessible and searchable over the Internet, it will go along way in identifying and knowing what information materials are available on the continent and where they are located.

For most CDS/ISIS users who have access to the Internet, a number of Web-based Interface programs for accessing CDS/ISIS based databases are have been developed and made available from the ISIS Users Forum Web sites at: http://www.bib.wau.nl/isis/. These can be down loaded from the site and implemented on the local machines. Unfortunately, Africa with quite a large number of CDS/ISIS users, only the National Archives of Namibia has its CDS/ISIS based databases accessible over the Internet at http://witbooi.natarch.mec.gov.na. Efforts to train information professions in publishing CDS/ISIS databases on the Web are slowly emerging and in June 1999 UNECA organised training workshop in Addis Ababa, Ethiopia, for a number of information professionals from around Africa at which skills in publishing CDS/ISIS databases on the Web were taught. It is hoped that participants at the UNECA workshop will soon be publishing their databases on the Web.

Digitalisation of Documents, Artefacts, etc.

Digitalisation of existing documents, manuscripts, artefacts, and making them accessible over the information superhighway is one major way of contribution to the cultural content of global information. Throughout the world, major digitalisation projects are being implemented. National libraries, museums and archives, with the support of national governments and sometimes private institutions, are spending millions of dollars on creating digital archives. Digitalisation of unique national libraries, museum and archival collections and materials will make these institutions become accessible to all parts of the world.

Unfortunately, efforts towards digitalisation of information materials on the continent are either non-existent or very negligent. Lack of funds, appropriate equipment and skills could be the major hindering factors to digitalisation of documents on the continent.

Indigenous Language Orientation

Africa is a continent of thousands of indigenous languages. While all foreign languages such as English, Portuguese and French, spoken on the continent, have institutions and governments fighting to ensure that they are well represented on the Internet, there seem to be no effort in advancing African indigenous languages on the Internet. Arguably, in terms of cost effectiveness, it may not be feasible to create Internet contents in all of the African languages. However, established African languages like Kiswahili (spoken in the East Africa) and Amharic (Ethiopia), spoken by millions of people, should have a presence on the information superhighway. Governments that have indigenous national languages (i.e. Sesotho in Lesotho, Setwana in Botswana) should also ensure that materials being produced in those languages also find way on the Internet. This is the only way African Internet users will find materials in their languages in cyberspace.

Problems and Constraints

While discussing the methods and strategies through which Africa can contribute to global information, it is important to take note and acknowledge the various problems and constraints to electronic information sharing and networking still facing the continent. Above all, Africa's capacity to contribute to global information will largely depend on how well these problems are solved. Jensen (1997, 13-15, 41) discussed in detail the following constraints:

- low level of computerisation in most countries
- scarcity of computers
- lack of proper guidelines on the use of computer facilities
- limited training and lack of skilled manpower
- lack of mechanisms to improve collaboration in areas of electronic networking
- vandalism of network infrastructure (i.e. copper telephone lines)
- high import duties on computer and communication equipment
- high price of Internet services in some countries
- lack of Internet bandwidth

It should be noted that the degree of the severity of the above problems differ from country to country. However, if the continent is to contribute effectively to global information, the above problems have to be attended to and a number of strategies and initiatives have to be adopted by both governments and information professionals. The political will of African leaders to establish a viable global information infrastructure on the continent is required and is already taking shape with the adoption of the African Information Society Initiative (AISI) document in May 1996 (UNECA 1996).

What Should be Done?

An enabling environment must be established across the continent, and the implementation of the following is considered to be very vital:

- African Information Society Initiative
- National Web servers
- Training of library and information professionals
- Training of technical experts
- Conscious government policies and efforts to contribute to global information
- Effective copyright laws and regulations

Africa Information Society Initiative

African governments and leaders have recognised the role information and communication technologies (ICT), if properly harnessed, can play in the development of the continent. They have also realised the various opportunities presented by ICTs in overcoming the priority challenges which hinder the continent's development in the following areas: job creation, health, education and research, culture, trade and commerce, tourism, food security, gender and development, man-made crises and natural disasters. As a result of this realisation and conviction, in 1996 they adopted the African Information Society Initiative (AISI) document prepared by the United Nations Economic Commission for Africa (UNECA) in which they agreed to establish an African Information Society. Among the recommendations made, the Initiative calls upon national governments to implement the following three which are very relevant to the subject of this paper (UNECA 1996):

- develop and use software and data that addresses the variety of languages used in African countries and oral traditions;
- encourage the development of value added information services including electronic publishing and networking facilities;
- support initiatives which build local content.

Implementation of the recommendations of the AISI document is the surest way through which the continent can contribute to global information.

Training of Library and Information Professionals

Library and information professionals on the continent are in a well placed position to make a strong contribution to the development of the global information infrastructure, by ensuring that much of what already exist in print format finds it way on the information superhighway. However, there seem to be a general lack of adequate skills that would enable them work in electronic information environments. Skills in the following subject areas are required:

- web page design, hypertext markup language (HTML) and the emerging extensible markup language (XML)
- use of electronic networks
- use of metadata
- evaluation of Web-based information sources
- setting up and maintaining subject-based information gateways
- management of electronic documents and collections

- digitalisation of documents

Skills in the above areas are very important if information professionals in Africa are to make a major contribution to global information.

Training of Technical Experts

There are very few technical experts to install and maintain electronic networks and computer equipment on the continent, and generally they are overloaded with work and cannot meet the needs and demands of Internet users. Therefore, dependency on foreign experts from outside the continent is still high and this is in spite of the many years of political independence most African countries have enjoyed. A deliberate policy should be adopted to ensure that establishment of electronic networks goes hand in hand with the training of people to manage and maintain the networks.

The Internet Society (ISOC) is contributing a lot to Africa in the development of technical expertise. Since 1993, ISOC has been organising training workshops for participants from developing countries at which a large number of individuals from Africa have attended. Training has been in host-based internetworking technology, backbone internetworking technology, network navigation services and national network management. Some of the exiting Internet Web servers and Web sites on the continent have been set up by people who have gone through ISOC's workshops. However, local initiatives are required from within Africa to train the required manpower.

Deliberate Government Policies

Governments and information professionals on the continent should adopt deliberate policies aimed at creating local content. Just as there are national libraries, archives and museums, African governments should also encourage and support the setting up of national Web servers at which local information could be published. They should provide support and funds for the digitalization of some of the materials in national libraries, archives and museums.

Copyright Laws and Regulations

The question of intellectual property in the digital information environment should also be addressed on the continent. Electronic publishing and production of various works of art and culture can only be very successful if content producers are assured that their works, even in cyberspace, will be protected by appropriate and effective copyright laws. Unfortunately, the situation regarding protection of intellectual property on the continent is not that good. The major reason is that in some countries, copyright laws are old and out of date and do not protect works produced in electronic formats. In other countries, laws protect only materials produced by certain sectors of the industry i.e. music or published books; and in others, the laws are almost non-existent. It should also be noted that some countries on the continent have not endorsed the many international copyright and intellectual property conventions.

In order to encourage the production of electronic information on the continent, African governments should enact and enforce appropriate copyright laws. Information professionals must take an active part in the establishment of effective copyright laws and also ensure that the new laws are not too restrictive.

Conclusion

The global information infrastructure is a global phenomenon with no borders. There are no restrictions on how much should be contributed to its growth in terms of the information content. Therefore, the onus is upon both African political leaders and information professionals to make a valuable contribution to the growth of the global information infrastructure. Political leaders should create a conducive environment by providing the required information communication technology infrastructure, while information professionals should use their information processing and management skills to ensure that information with a large African content is made available on the global information infrastructure.

For years, Africa has been a major market and consumer of information and cultural products from developed countries. Unless, deliberate steps are taken to contribute to global information, the continent's millions of inhabitants will never access their own content, and will forever, even in the electronic age, remain consumers of electronic information and cultural products produced from outside the continent. Fortunate enough, it is not too late. Africa still has the opportunity to add its unique touch to the new Net culture.

References

1. Connection community content: the challenge of the information superhighway - final report of the Information Superhighway Advisory Council / Canada. Information Superhighway Advisory Council (1995). – Ottawa, Ont.: Information Superhighway Advisory Council, 1995.
2. Chisenga, J. (1998) A Study of university libraries' home pages in Sub-Saharan Africa // *Libri*. – 1998. – Vol. 48, N 1. – March. – P.49-57.
3. Jensen, M. (1998) Africa Internet status. – 1998. – December. – Mode of access: http://www3.sn.apc.org/africa/astat.htm.
4. Jensen, M. (1997) Policy constraints to electronic information sharing in developing countries // OnTheInternet. – 1997. – November/December. – P.13-15, 41.
5. Notabaskken, D., Akhtar S. (1994) Does the highway go South? A report of the International Institute of Communications Pre-Conference on Southern countries interests. – Tampere, Finland, 1994. – September. – P. 3-4.
6. Smith, K. (1998) The Changing face of society // OnTheInternet. – 1998. – November/December. – P. 14-17.
7. Rao, M. (1998) Development almanac: the Internet in emerging nations // OnTheInternet. – 1998. – November/December. – P. 24-32.
8. UNECA. African content development: creation and dissemination: Paper presented at the First Meeting of the Committee on Development Information (CODI), Addis Ababa, Ethiopia, 28 June - 2nd July, 1999. – 1999.
9. UNECA. (1996) African Information Society Initiative (AISI): an action framework to build Africa's information and communication infrastructure. – Addis Ababa: UNECA, 1996.

10. Putting the information infrastructure to work (1994): a report of the Information Infrastructure Task Force's Committee on Applications and Technology / United States. Information Infrastructure Task Force. – 1994. – Mode of access: http://iifcat.nist.gov:94.

11. Vandecasteele, P. (1996) Networking on duty tracks // Computers in Africa. – 1996. – November. – P. 39-40.

* Quoted by Rao, M. 1998. Development almanac: the Internet in emerging nations // OnTheInternet. – 1998. – November/December. – P. 29.

SOUTH ASIA IN THE GLOBAL ELECTRONIC VILLAGE: ISSUES AND IMPLICATIONS

Jagtar Singh

Department of Library & Information Science, Punjabi University, Patiala, India

The Internet and its Impact

The Internet is an amazing development of our times based on the convergence of the computer and the communication technologies. The traditional constraints of space and time are no more there and the whole world is almost becoming a global electronic village. The developments in computer and communication technologies have made a significant impact on libraries and scholarly communication. Now it is possible to communicate from a networked workstation with anyone across the globe as well as have real time access to digital documents. Hypermedia and multimedia are other significant developments of our times. International collaboration is now possible in teaching, learning, publishing, and resource sharing via various networks. The Internet-based resources and services, such as e-mail, ftp, http, bulletin boards, mailing lists, scholarly discussion lists, computer conferences, electronic journals, digital databases, various browsers and search engines have a strong potential to provide massive access to one and all. In fact, the interactivity and interoperability of many of these networks and services must be integrated into our professional education and practice for value addition at every level.

Paradigm Shift and Globalization

There is a shift away from stand alone libraries to library and information networks. More and more people are talking of 'hybrid library'. 'Balance' between the print-based publications and digital documents has become a buzzword. There is a paradigm shift from ownership to access; just-in-case to just-in-time ; print-based publications to digital documents; stand alone libraries to networked systems; intermediary model to end-user model, command-based systems to menu-based systems; linear to non-linear mode of access; hierarchical to non-hierarchical systems; one-way dissemination of information to interactive communication; bundling of scholarly journal to its unbundling; stability to instability; physical format to formless data; top-down to bottom-up systems. Information has become fluid and transcendental. It is now separated from the containers in the process of digitization. Otherwise also, information has become fourth need and strategic input for the emerging information society. There is a paradigm shift in education also. Now-a-days, there is a trend towards individual exploration, apprenticeship, team learning, diverse and fast changing curricula. Above all now teacher is required to serve as a councilor and facilitator. This shift calls for the use of networked PCs, information access, skill development simulations, collaborative tools, email, networks, and a variety of publishing and access tools. As such, it is high time that we take cognizance of these changes and make our professional education and practice responsive to the needs of the emerging information society.

Existing Gap and Inequality

There are wide variations between and within the developed and the developing countries. Though the position of the elite institutions in the developing countries is relatively better, yet there is a perceptible inequality of access to the networked resources and services between and within the developed and developing countries on the one hand, and the elite and the ordinary institutions on the other hand. The developed countries and institutions are better positioned to reap the benefits of enabling technologies. But in spite of these technological developments, the existing gap between the developed countries and institutions and the less developed countries and institutions is increasing day by day, whereas the enabling technologies have a strong potential for bridging the existing gap between them.

Not to talk of India alone, the picture is not rosy in other South Asian countries also. In fact, we cannot call this world a global electronic village till the less developed countries and institutions are provided with networked workstations and training facilities. Nepal, Bhutan, Bangladesh, and the Maldives are four countries in South Asia where the position of library and information networking is far from satisfactory. India, Pakistan, and Sri Lanka are relatively in a better position. It would be appropriate to point out here that it is very easy to retrieve quality information from the developed countries and institutions, but it is very difficult even to know what is available in one's area of interest in the South Asian countries. Very little information about librarianship and information work in these countries is available to the interested researchers. Therefore, the SAARC Documentation Centre (SDC), New Delhi must play a leadership role in this regard.

South Asia and its Problems

South Asia is characterized by asymmetry, in size, population, economic and military power. India is larger than all other countries put together. South Asia is a split spectrum of a once monolithic political entity consolidated and welded into Indian sub-continent by the British, mainly in the 19th and early 20th centuries. The breakup of this entity into seven independent states has given rise to centripetal as well as centrifugal forces. That is why SAARC (South Asian Association for Regional Cooperation) has emerged as a weak political organization, born of otherwise strong geographical cohesive expansion. The geographical hub of south Asia consists of the great plains formed by the coalescing basins of the Indus, the Ganga, and the Brahamaputra. They contain the nuclei of Pakistan, India and Bangladesh in their basins. South Asia's mountainous peripheral states are Nepal and Bhutan, nesting in the Himalayas on the north. In the south, Sri Lanka is a loose maritime adjunct to the Indian peninsula while Maldives represents the tapering end of the coral leg of this sub-continent, disappearing in the Indian Ocean. India has been so placed in south Asia that she has common borders with all her south Asian neighbours, while none of her neighbours share borders with each other. Such a geographical position creates a peculiar situation with regard to socioeconomic and political as well as geopolitical relations amongst the natives of this region.

There is no denying the fact that diversity present in the earlier conflicts of south Asia remained the major factor that stood as a great impediment to Asian unity. India and Pakistan need to play a key role in this direction, but they have their historic tension over the Kashmir issue. Despite the linguistic and religious diversities and differences in milieu in different parts in south Asian region, there does exist a unique cultural unity in the sub-continent. Unfortunately the nations of south Asia have not had good relations with each other. The entire region is economically backward. The continued existence of problems like unemployment, poverty, inflation, balance of payment difficulties, regional inequality, etc. and continued demographic pressures have forced these countries to resort to massive foreign aid leading to heavy foreign debt burden. This has created a serious problem of debt, which eats away a significant proportion of export earnings of these countries. There is, therefore, an urgent need for these countries to develop self-reliant economies for their sustained economic growth and solution to the other problems. It is ironical that while this region accounts for nearly one fourth of world's population, its growth rate is only 2%, and even the inter-SAARC trade is only 3.4 % of the total global trade of these seven countries. India is easily identified as the giant in south Asia. It occupies 73.2 % of the total area of south Asia, four times larger than Pakistan and eleven thousand times larger than the smallest member Maldives. The growing regional consciousness and trends towards unification of hitherto divided nations are trends which may help to think more seriously about their own regional identity and the need for greater unity among themselves. This unity is now imperative in the context of increasing international pressures both in economical and political terms on the region as a whole. The south Asian nations being in the process of socioeconomic development have to be on guard against any attempt to undermine their sovereign status, be it in the name of human rights, environment, intellectual property rights or security.

The south Asian region has been relatively instable, politically speaking. The countries of this region can be categorized into two categories. The first group consisting of India, Pakistan, Bangladesh, and Sri Lanka, which covers the major part of the region, in terms of area, population, economic development etc. As would be clear in this chapter much of the development in librarianship has also been in the countries of this category, particularly in India. The other group consists of three smaller states of Nepal, Bhutan, and the Maldives. Except for Maldives which has the highest literacy rate (93%) and the highest per capita income ($726) in the region, Nepal and Bhutan are among the least developed countries in the world with per capita incomes $180 and $190, and literacy rates being 27% and 40% respectively. As far as development of librarianship and information work is concerned, these nations have not much to speak of. Nepal, however has made some progress in the field, but the Maldives, in spite of being the most literate of the seven countries, has not made progress in this field parallel to its achievements in its economy.

SAARC and SAPTA (SAARC Preferential Trading Arrangement) are good steps in the direction of regional cooperation and socioeconomic development of the countries of this region. The south Asian countries have decided to move towards building a SAFTA (South Asian Free Trade Area) before 2005, preferably by 2000 AD. SAARC, which came into being in December 1985, reflects the growing trend among regions to accelerate the process of their economic and social development through joint action - encompassing key areas of regional cooperation - arranging from exchange of trade preferences to agriculture and rural development; science and technology to health and population activities; and from telecommunications to infrastructure. In the long run regional cooperation must lead to removal of artificial barriers without in any way damaging the individuality and identity of people. SAARC has made some palpable, if not spectacular, progress in this field. The idea of establishing a SAARC Documentation Centre (SDC) at New Delhi was approved in principle by the Heads of State Governments at the second SAARC meeting held in Banglore in November 1986. It was decided unanimously in this meeting that for the SAARC Documentation Centre (SDC), the INSDOC should be a focal point in India to look after the documentation activities. The work of the SDC will be based on published materials available with focal points, information about which would be compiled into a

SAARC Bibliography. SDC conducts human resource programmes in information management in the SAARC region. It includes short-term courses, seminars, workshops, etc. every year. Participants are drawn from all SAARC nations and the target groups include work professionals engaged in library and information activities. The SDC should facilitate access to all information about Integrated Programme of Action (IPA) for interested scholars and other users. Possibility may be explored for disseminating such information through cyberspace, including the Internet. Establishment of the SAARC Net - The Online Computerized data Information System, headquartered in FICCI BISNET - makes a good beginning.

Conclusion and Suggestions

The countries in the south Asian region display a wide range of disparities, which add to their socioeconomic problems. Unemployment, poverty, illiteracy, inflation, regional inequality etc. are the lingering problems of south Asian countries, which cast their shadows on the growth and development of library and information infrastructure in these countries. Not to speak of other countries in this region, even India has not so far adopted any national policy on library and information systems. Even the National Library of India has not fully internalized the concept of library automation and networking, whereas India is required to provide leadership in resource sharing via networking being the largest country in this region. There are wide variations between and within the countries and institutions in this region. There is perceptible gap between rural and urban settings as far as the provision of library & information resources and services is concerned. Whereas, the number of library schools in India is far more than required, in Bangladesh the situation is totally the reverse. Nepal, Bhutan, and the Maldives have no library schools to make the trained manpower available to cater to their information needs.

The position of academic and special libraries is much better than that of school, public and government libraries. The lack of resources and political will are the main hindrances in the establishment, development and maintenance of public libraries under the clear mandate of law in these countries. Even in India, so far, only ten states out of 26 have enacted library legislation to provide comprehensive public library service to the urban and rural folks. The concept of library automation and networking is being adopted by the academic, particularly university libraries and special libraries in India. There is an immediate need to coordinate and consolidate the resources and services of different types of libraries in south Asia to enhance people's access to quality information in this region. INFLIBNET is an ambitious programme in India to materialize the concept of resource sharing via networking. ERNET, VSNL, and NIC are the three main service providers in India. In fact, there is a clear trend towards library automation and networking in India, Pakistan, Sri Lanka, and Bangladesh. The bye-products of information technology are now visible in the form of indigenous databases and there is also a trend towards electronic publishing. NISSAT (National Information System for Science and Technology), INSDOC (Indian National Scientific Documentation Centre), and DESIDOC (Defence Scientific Information and Documentation Centre) in India have really made perceptible progress in developing their resources and services. Similar work is being done by PANSDOC (Pakistan National Scientific and Technical Documentation Centre) and BANSDOC (Bangladesh National Scientific and Technological Documentation Centre) in Pakistan and Bangladesh respectively. Though in Sri Lanka, a modern technological information system has yet to be realized, even then the planning, coordination and formation of an effective library and information system for the country are the mandatory functions of The Sri Lanka National Library Services Board.

The position of library and information infrastructure in Pakistan, Sri Lanka, and Bangladesh is perceptibly better than in Nepal, Bhutan and the Maldives. Lack of trained manpower, insufficient funds, and inadequate materials are the basic hindrances in the expected development in library and information services in all the south Asian countries. In fact, globalization is a complex phenomena which has resulted in a complicated interaction between "globalism" and "localism", where huge corporations are selling products across national boundaries and creating a globally homogeneous culture of consumption. In this context the slogan given by the ALA, is very significant. All the developing countries in general, and the South Asian countries in particular must formulate their library and information policies and develop adequate infrastructure to provide real time access to their citizens in a cost-effective manner. Efforts must be made to strengthen the SAARC Documentation Centre (SDC) New Delhi and develop connections with the East Asian countries. The international bodies, such as IFLA, FID, UNESCO, IDRC, and World Bank must expand their activities in the South Asian region. At the first instance, the Internet connectivity must be ensured in all the countries in this region, and then the local by-products must be mounted on the main servers of the host institutions in a planned manner. Education and training, and resources consolidation and sharing via various networks is a pre-condition for enhancing users' access to global information resources and services. Otherwise, the so called globalization and the global electronic village will be lip service to the South Asian countries. The real benefit of this process will remain restricted to the industrial countries and the developing countries will continue to be used as consumers only. Real globalization can play a central role in our collective future by its potential to enhance individual freedom, widen opportunities for countries in the South, and increase democratic participation. In fact, the real global electronic village is that where there is equity in resources and equality of access for one and all. For this, there is an immediate need to change the mind-set of the 'haves' and 'have nots'.

References

1. Ahmad, N. (1994) Personnel Requirements in the Libraries of Bangladesh // International Information and Library Review. – 1994. – Vol. 26, N 4. – P. 315-326.

2. Beg, M. T. (1998) Information infrastructure in developing countries / 49th FID Conference and Congress on Towards the New Information Society of Tomorrow: Innovations, Challenges and Impact. – New Delhi: INSDOC, 1998. – P. 27-31.

3. Bhutan // World of Learning. – 45th ed. – London: Europa, 1995. – P. 171.

4. Cronin, B. (1998) Library and Information Science in context / Librarianship and Information Work Worldwide. – London: Bowker-Saur, 1998. – P. 1-17.

5. High. (1997) Level Development Meeting on Asia-Pacific Information Infrastructure // Unisist Newsletter. – 1997. – Vol. 25, N 2. – P. 30-34.

6. IDRC (1997) Corporate Program Framework to the year 2000. – Ottawa: IDRC, 1997. – P. 5-6.

7. INSDOC (1998) A National Information Laboratory. – New Delhi: INSDOC, 1998. – P. 1-16.

8. Ilyas, M. (1998) Librarianship in Pakistan into the 21st Century // Information Development. – 1998. – Vol. 14, N 3. – P. 127-132.

9. Information (1998) Technology Action Plan // Information Today and Tomorrow. – 1998. – Vol. 17, N 3. – P. 10-21.

10. Jagtar S. (1998) Librarianship and Information Work in South Asia / Librarianship and Information Work Worldwide. – London: Bowker-Saur, 1998. – P. 249-279.

11. Kularatne, E. D. T. (1998) Towards a National Information Policy for Sri Lanka // Information Development. – 1998. – Vol. 14, N 3. – P. 137-143.

12. Lievrouw, L. A. (1994) Information Resources and Democracy: Understanding the Paradox // Journal of the American Society for Information Science. – 1994. – Vol. 45, N 6. – P. 350-357.

13. Mahmood, K. (1998) The Technology Challenge and Continuing Education for Pakistan's Librarians // Information Development. – 1998. – Vol. 14, N 2. – P. 84-91.

14. Maldives. (1995) World of Learning. 45th ed. – London: Europa, 1995. – 1005 p.

15. Mangla, P. B. (1993) India. World Encyclopedia of Library and Information Services. – 3rd ed. – Chicago: ALA, 1993. – P. 361-364.

16. Mangla, P. B. (1994) Library and Information Science Education in South Asia: India, Pakistan, Bangladesh and Sri Lanka // Education for Information. – 1994. – Vol. 12, N 4. – P. 399-427.

17. Mangla, P. B. (1998) The Role of Libraries in Global Village with Particular Reference to India // University News. – 1998. – Vol. 36, N 22. – P. 4-11.

18. Meadows, J. (1998) Library and Information Science: the Continuing Transition / Librarianship and Information Work World Wide. – London: Bowker-Saur, 1998. – P. 1-14.

19. Miksa, F. The Cultural Legacy of the Modern Library for the Future // Journal of Education for Library and Information Science. – 1995. – Vol. 37, N 2. – P. 101-120.

20. Mowlana, H. (1999) Globalization of Mass Media: Opportunities and Challenges for the South // CWCR News. – 1999. – Vol. 36, N 1-2. – P. 2, 6-9.

21. Mujoo-Munshi, U., Malayan, I. V. (1998) Information Technology: Concern and Users in Developed Countries with Special Reference to India // Library Herald. – 1998. – Vol. 36, N 2. – P. 69-79.

22. Nepal // World of Learning. – 45th ed. – London: Europa, 1995. – 1047 p.

23. Piyadasa, T. G. (1985) Libraries in Sri Lanka: Their Origin and History from Ancient Times to the Present Time. – Delhi: Sri Satguru, 1985.

24. Queau, P. (1998) Editorial // Unisist Newsletter. – 1998. – Vol. 26, N 1. – P. 3.

25. Rahman, A. (1997) Library Development in Bangladesh // Herald of Library Science. – 1997. – Vol. 36, N 1-2. – P. 52-56.

26. Reid, E. O. F. (1996) Exploiting Internet as an enabler for transforming Library Services // IFLA Journal. – 1996. – Vol. 22, N 10. – P. 18-26.

27. SDC (1998) SAARC Documentation Centre: A Regional Institution under SAARC // New Delhi: SDC. – 1998. – P. 1-8.

28. Swe, T. (1986) Burma. World Encyclopedia of Library and Information Services. – 2nd ed. – Chicago: ALA, 1986. – P. 146-147.

29. Vittal, N. (1998) Information Technology and Library Networking // Delnet Newsletter. – 1998. – Vol. 5, N 1. – P. 5-10.

30. Wedgeworth, R. (1998) A Global Perspective on the Library and Information Agenda // American Libraries. – 1998. – Vol. 29, N 6. – P. 60-65.

31. Wedgeworth, R. (1997) Access to Information // IFLA Council Report 1995-1997. – 1997. – P. 5.

32. Yapa, N. U.(1997) PURNA – AGRINET. Integrated Information System of Sri Lanka // Quarterly Bulletin of the International Association of Agricultural Information Specialists. – 1997. – Vol. 42, N 3-4. – P. 163-167.

MIGRATING FROM THE LIBRARY OF TODAY TO THE LIBRARY OF TOMORROW: RE- OR E-VOLUTION?

Tatiana V. Ershova and Yuri E. Hohlov

Institute of the Information Society – Russia, Moscow, Russian Federation

Abstract

The paper considers the ways of the Library development in the profoundly changing environment arising within the forthcoming Information / Knowledge Society. The role of the Library as a social institution is examined in the context of the evolution of the whole literary and knowledge system. There are presented ideas on conceptual changes to be introduced by the Library in order to respond to challenges of the Information Age. There are offered approaches which could help the Library evolve from an institution to conservate and to provide access to a patrimony towards an inalienable part of a distributed global knowledge warehouse.

The World in Change: Advent of a Knowledge Society

The Information Age has arrived and the rate of change in human society continues to accelerate. This change is ongoing and pervasive - affecting all people, institutions and societies. The change is like a typhoon whose turbulence has spawned not only problems, but also genuine opportunities. Information and communication technologies (ICTs) are the driving forces of change, and transformation is the order of the day. Human intelligence is replacing physical capital as the chief factor of production: intellectual capital becomes the primary factor of growth in the emerging Information, or, according to the latest concept, the Knowledge Society. Access to, and the effective use of information and knowledge, technologies, and various services are essential tools for sustainable economic and social development at the individual, community, national and international levels. Those in possession of all these tools will enjoy a future marked by abundance, but who are deprived of them will be marginalised.

To make the landscape of this society more harmonious, the Global Knowledge Partnership (http://www.globalknowledge.org), a growing network of about 60 public, private and non-governmental organizations from many countries of the world, proposes to focus on three key themes that are important for facilitating the role of knowledge in development: access, empowerment, and governance.

Access involves assuring that there is universal availability of the strategies and tools essential for the effective use of knowledge: it means accessibility to networks, infrastructures and services, as well as the content that is relevant for political and socio-cultural citizenship; it is a facility that enables citizens to communicate with the relevant outside world.

Empowerment can be defined as being the outcome of activities which build the capacity and skills of individuals, community groups, the private sector, governments and institutions, with the aim of enabling them to take part in the global Knowledge Society and Knowledge Economy, and make informed choices relevant to their needs.

Governance is the process through which institutions, businesses and citizen's groups articulate their interests, exercise their rights and obligations, allocate human choices and opportunities, and mediate their differences. This entails exploring ways in which knowledge societies can employ more efficient, transparent, and participatory forms of governance: locally, regionally, nationally, and globally.

In the context of the development of the Knowledge Society [1, p. 4] the following assumptions can be made:

1. Information and knowledge form the basis for decision-making and action, particularly in development.
2. The quality of decisions is dependent upon the quality and quantity of information. Although there is abundant information, the quality of the information must be evaluated.
3. Access to information and knowledge results in an improvement in the Quality of Life, provided that an enabling framework is in place.
4. There will always be inequality in society. Whilst it may not be possible to eliminate inequality, society has a responsibility to strive to reduce it.

All of these assumptions challenge the role of the Library in today's society forcing it to revise its function in order to retain and to strengthen its mission.

Evolution of the Literary and Knowledge System

In addition to these features of today's reality there are three other macro-factors which have a major effect upon the role of the library in society:

- an exponential growth of information;
- the growing complexity of knowledge and of its representation;
- a transformation of the literary system.

Today more and more people (primarily researchers) use new forms of knowledge representation which is not in the form of a linear text printed as a monograph or an article. These new types of publication can include text, images, audio records of a discussion, video records of an experiment, a software source code for calculation of results etc. - all this is impossible within a conventional publication. Furthermore, the more scientific (or, perhaps cultural) information will be created in this or some other sophisticated format, being constantly updated or revised. Now we are witnessing a process that could be defined as the remaking of the "literary system".

Geoffrey Nunberg, a professor at Stanford University, notes that new formats such as multimedia and hypertext take us "beyond the book" by creating new modes of reading and new forms of intellectual and cultural interchange. A dictionary can be linked to an encyclopedia, or an encyclopedia can take us directly into the primary literature. At the limit we may want to think of these forms as the model for the new services and clearinghouses: not as being static compendia but rather as dynamic interfaces to an open-ended discourse. It is not so much a technological revolution (which has already occurred) but, as Carla Hesse puts it, the public reinvention of an intellectual community in its wake. In fact, knowledge is no longer conceived and constructed in the language of forms at all - not as "bodies of knowledge", or a "corpus", bounded and stored, but rather as modes of thought, apprehension, and expression - as techniques and practices.

Digital technologies enable ultrarapid access (via user friendly interfaces and networks) to the richest sources, wherever they are located in the world's collections, and the rapid exchange of commentaries in electronic forums or videoconferences. These new possibilities favour an 'extensive' reading, the comparison of diverse texts and viewpoints, multidisciplinary transversality, a "conversation" between readers. They are beginning to have a considerable impact, as much on the individual mechanism of the appropriation of texts, as on the sociology of reading. True polytextuality - in which diverse types of texts and images, sounds, films, data banks, mail services, interactive networks may mutually resist or interfere with one another - this process of reading generates progressively a new dimension - polymorphic, transversal, and dynamic. We may call it 'metareading', which is becoming a new driving force of culture. Instead of aprioristic strategies that envisage cataloguing every document using a universal classification, hypertextuality prefers a tactic of using small steps, capable of binding them together after the event, whole corpora generated from research and particular points of view. It wagers, in short, on the plurality of the world of documentation. In other words, the ideal of coherent and convergent, unified knowledge (of which the library would be the microcosm). At the same time that it explodes the limits of text, hypertextuality revives one of the founding questions of culture: by what mediations can private experience and collective practices enter into an exchange? [2, pp. 154, 161-162].

By the way, this new architecture of knowledge has given birth to a surprisingly diverse range of recent library architectural projects, e.g. Bibliotheque Nationale de France - a building without walls, a library that is a nonspace; libraries for the new parliamentary bodies emerging in Eastern Europe - a series of globally coordinated satellite networks linking far-flung databases that are not really located anywhere at all except in the hands of their users, the Union Media Center of the Michigan State University are but some examples.

The evolution of the literary and knowledge system has reached the stage when many people are asking the sacred question: What is the destiny of the book in the new era? Two extreme viewpoints are presented by "computer visionaries" (or "technophiles"), and by "bibliophiles", and they run something like: "Printed books, brick-and-mortar libraries ... have been superceded by electronic genres and institutions; where linear narrative has yielded in all of its important functions to hypertext and multimedia" versus "Nobody is going to sit down and read a novel on a twitchy little screen. Ever."

Of course there is no sense in getting into a discussion about these two viewpoints. It is more important to understand which printed genres will survive in the Information Age and what will be superseded by new digital forms.

Nunberg argues along the lines that the types of books whose existence in codex form has no particular cultural significance (catalogs, technical manuals, directories, regulations, legal records, and so forth) are likely to disappear soon. Scientific journals are almost certain to move to electronic distribution, but for popular newspapers and magazines, the conversion is less compelling. CD-ROMs have already cut heavily into the use of print encyclopaedias, but print dictionaries seem largely unaffected by digitization. As for novels, self-help books, political memoirs, critical editions, art books, travel guides etc., it is simply too early to say. Some will probably continue to rest chiefly on printed supports, some will divide their existence between print and digital media, some will definitely migrate, taking their place alongside a variety of completely new digital genres. There will be a digital revolution, but the printed document will be an important participant in it.

From this point of view the most reasonable approach appears to be the one formulated by James Billington, Director of the Library of Congress, in 1994: the new technologies of the multimedia era should be used to "strengthen the culture of the book". Or, on the other hand, we like the idea put forward by Umberto Eco, the renowned modern writer and philosopher: when an integrated multimedia sequence of events succeeds in bringing people back to a non-virtual reality, something new can happen.

The Library in a New Information Environment: Transformation Challenges

Libraries and archives have been created to ensure the long-term accessibility of recorded information. That is what they do now, and that is what they will do in the future. This means they acquire, catalog or process, organize, offer for use and preserve publicly available material irrespective of the form in which it is packaged in such a way that, when it is needed, it can be located and used. This is the unique function of the library, and no other institution carries out this long-term, systematic work. Nothing about this changes in the digital world. But digital technology changes the balance of power among the core functions [3,4].

The change is socio-cultural at least as much as technological. Patric Bazin, Director of the Bibliotheque de Lyon, points out that the growing sophistication of knowledge and that of the methods of information processing appears to be accompanied by an evanescence of stable referents, clearly identifiable and transmittable ones that "the order of the book" (Roger Chartier's term [5]) used to provide. It seems to be natural that libraries should continue to play a very important role, one that will far surpass the simple conservation of a patrimony. But will they be able to become mediators in the Knowledge Society? At this time they are hardly able to perform this role, at least for researchers and specialists in many practical fields who - driven by professional competition - keep up with new technologies and knowledge extraction methods much faster than any library, or other information agent.

Once the notion of a collection is no longer physically constrained, it naturally tends to extend indefinitely. Of course it will include a great deal of what some users will find trivial and ephemeral; when you take down the walls of the library you should not be surprised to find the reading room filling up with street people. The solution, (indicated by Nunberg) is not to try to close off the collection in some arbitrary way, but to help users to thread their way through the maze.

Access to knowledge and culture from a variety of sources (both traditional and the most recent in terms of format and usage), in a variety of languages, views and traditions includes the process of transforming that knowledge into an accessible format. We consider that these problems should be handled within the context of the hybrid / digital library context.

Development Strategy: Towards the Hybrid and Digital Library

One of the major problems that the librarian has to resolve today is how to navigate in a hybrid space of documents, both in printed and digital formats. The motivation behind the concept of the hybrid library is a need to cope with diversity. Diversity is a major problem as libraries struggle to come to grips with the digital information world. The most important question to answer is what new order of knowledge will emerge, and how libraries can participate adapting to the many transformations of the information and research landscapes [6].

Without doubting the everlasting value of the handwritten or printed document or that of the conventional library as a place where people meet to fulfill some of their cultural needs, let us honestly state that more and more information is now emerging as 'digitally born' or digitized for the sake of more convenient use. A very important question arises in this context: who will take the responsibility to carefully collect and store this information to make it available for future use? At the moment it is kept by the creators themselves who constantly update their materials and do not care much about retaining previous versions. So some information currently regarded as being of less value, but probably containing some seeds of unrevealed wisdom, is lost. It is important that a social institute should, sooner or later, accept this function. Will this be the library? We would like to answer this question positively. But for this to happen it is essential that the library of today should be moving towards implementing the digital library concept, making this an organic part of its development strategy.

A digital library can be defined as "a distributed information system ensuring reliable storage and effective use of heterogeneous collections of electronic documents (text, graphics, audio, video etc.) via global data transfer networks in a way convenient for the end user" [7]. Or: "an information service in which all the information resources are available in computer processable form and the functions of acquisition, storage, preservation, retrieval, access and display are carried out through the use of digital technologies" [8].

Digital libraries are able to provide for the preservation and migration of electronic information (both digitally born and digitized) as well as enhanced versions of services we have come to expect from the libraries, for example:

- tools for searching of heterogeneous collections;
- a personalized service based on user profiles representing users' information needs or a user directed summarization system in an information access to help users to decide about the relevance of a document;
- a collaborative infrastructure which allows user groups to index and evaluate documents on specific topics;
- a cross-language information retrieval or interrogation of multilingual databases or a multilingual storage and interface etc., etc. [9, pp. 184, 197, 215, 274, 294, 363].

Today the concept of digital libraries is being realised mainly outside the conventional library world. The main reason for this is not a lack of understanding of all the advances provided by digital libraries (many top library professionals and associations pay due attention to this concept) but simple non-affordability in terms of the costs of equipment and technology. Even the creation of a hybrid environment critically needed to respond to the reality of today is hampered because of such intractable facts as the dependency of digital information on software, hardware, networks, and so forth.

Library Policies for Change

On 17-19 April 2000 Moscow hosted an international conference "Managing the Digital Future of Libraries" which resulted in "The Moscow Manifesto" [10] recognising the following ways in which libraries of all kinds can make substantial contributions in key policy areas:

- Democracy and Citizenship – Publicly accessible libraries have a strategic opportunity to improve the quality of life and democratic opportunities of all citizens by providing free and equal access to high-quality information and ensuring equal access to diverse opinion, helping to overcome inequalities of wealth and location.
- Economic and Social Development and Support for Industry - Libraries support wealth creation by ensuring equal access to information and the opportunities afforded by knowledge. They can be important tools for reducing disparity between the information rich and the information poor citizens of Russia.
- Scholarship, Education and Lifelong Learning – Libraries provide, through their widespread physical network, a cost-effective infrastructure for both formal education and lifelong learning. They support students at all levels of formal education.
- Cultural and Linguistic Diversity – Public libraries are also cultural institutions in the widest sense. They support, preserve and promote directly the written cultural heritage, literature, literacy, authors and publishers. They provide access to knowledge of all forms of cultural expression.

To ensure that this happens it is important to consider and implement at national and international levels policy initiatives aimed at:

- improving conditions for citizens' access to information resources by addressing the legal, technical, economic and policy issues which can enhance access via libraries;
- assisting libraries in meeting the needs of citizens, for example by recommending suitable infrastructures, alliances and training measures [11].

Training implies, among other points, something deep and long-term: nurturing a strong service ethic, building up a new professional culture based on recognising trends and being constantly ready to respond to the pressure for change. Library managers have to ensure that their institutions are user-centred and managed at all times with users' needs being paramount.

It has been noted above that libraries operate most effectively as a network. This sounds especially pertinent in the digital environment where resource and technology sharing becomes a condition for survival and development. Moreover, networking has to be reinforced by integration which implied the efficient co-operation of libraries with other bodies involved in creating and disseminating knowledge and culture - research institutions, archives, museums, publishers, etc. - in terms of using common formats, standards, metadata, protocols etc., and co-ordination of responsibilities.

Expanding institutional borders can bring other practical benefits to the libraries: they can be made more viable economically and attain a high cost-benefit ratio if they adopt some policies which arise from the expansion of the digital environment, e.g.: collecting licence fees for electronic documents, or digitising original materials. The long-term preservation of digital data with transition technologies also provides an additional business opportunity for libraries and firms in the relevant sectors. Libraries are the most important, and sometimes even vital, customers for electronic publishers; they also serve to market the products of multimedia producers, or may attract the attention of telecommunications operators by providing online access to content and information services via telecommunications networks, etc.

Conclusion

The library has to anchor a key role in the emerging Information / Knowledge Society as a place to ensure the preservation and migration of information in order to make it usable for everyone in need of it. This means not only retaining but also considerably reinforcing its traditional mission. What is needed to achieve this ambitious goal in the shortest possible time - Revolution or Evolution? The right approach would involve a combination of approaches, rather than to take one or other alternatives, i.e. Revolution and Evolution.

The revolution the library has to bring about means first of all entering the digital world as a full-value player. This implies - except working with electronic documents which is self-evident – efficient networking with libraries and other relevant institutions, nationally and internationally, i.e. the library has to contribute to the development of a distributed global knowledge warehouse.

In terms of librarianship the revolution means that the library has to become an 'art of passage' instead of the 'art of classification' it traditionally has been. The library of the future must be organized around disciplines like many attractive pools of water whose contours fluctuate, points of view and shifting usages. We find it that it is true that the password of any revolution in the management of library becomes a realignment in terms of contents – which means that a given thematic will have to be able to mobilize around itself all the pertinent holdings, information and tools; it will have to be undertaken from the point of view of all possible uses, whatever the level of each user [2, p. 156-157].

Evolution is acquiring sufficient flexibility to cope with an explosion of documents and technologies coupled with the blurring frontiers between the public and between usages. This includes constant monitoring of constituencies and predicting users' needs via the implementation of advanced methods of user research.

The most challenging aspect is to master the hybrid environment. One of most difficult tasks is to reconcile the fact that, for quite a period of time, the library will have to manage legacy systems while creating and supporting an interface between the old and the new. This means that considerable allocations will have to be permanently invested, but society (since it needs to archive and to use knowledge and wisdom created by mankind) has to bear these costs - as it has done in the past, but traditional libraries were probably less costly institutions.

Libraries must be a meeting point for the many processes and phenomena relating to the Information Society. It is necessary to ensure that they are no less, but even more central now than they used to be in the Industrial Society.

References

1. Report on the Global Knowledge Forum Proceedings: Second Global Knowledge Conference (GKII), Kuala Lumpur, Malaysia, 7-10 March 2000. – 56 p.
2. The Future of the Book / Edited by G. Nunberg, with an afterword by U. Eco. – Berkeley, 1996. – 306 p. – Nunberg: P. 9-20 (introduction), P. 103-138. – Hesse: P. 21-36; Bazin: P. 153-168. – Eco: P. 295-306.
3. Smith A. Digital Preservation Research and Developments // Proceedings of the International Conference "Managing Digital Future of Libraries", Moscow, Russia, 17-19 April, 2000 // Russian Digital Libraries Journal. – 2000. –Vol. 3, N 3. – Mode of access: http://www.iis.ru/el-bib/2000/200003/smitha/smitha.en.html.

4. Ryynänen, M. Report on the Green Paper on the Role of Libraries in the Modern World (25.6.1998; A4-0248/98) // The European Parliament. Committee on Culture, Youth, Education and the Media. – Mode of access: http://www.publiclibraries.fi/publications/report.htm: 8 March, 2000.

5. Chartier, R., Bourdieu, P. Le message ecrit et ses receptions. Du codex a l'ecran // Review des Sciences morales et politiques. – 1993. – N 2.

6. Rusbridge, Ch, Royan, B. Towards the Hybrid Library: Developments in UK Higher Education: Proceedings of the 66th IFLA Council and General Conference, Section on Information Technology Open Session "From Library Automation Systems to Digital Libraries", Jerusalem, Israel, 16 August, 2000.

7. Ershova T.V., Hohlov Yu. E. Russian Digital Libraries Programme: Approaches and Perspectives // Russian Digital Libraries Journal. – 1999. – Vol. 2. – N 2. – Mode of access: http://www.iis.ru/el-bib/1999/199902/ershova/ershova.en.html.

8. Oppenheim Ch., Smithson D. What is the hybrid library? // Journal of Information Science. – 1999. – Vol. 25. – N 2. – P. 97-112.

9. Research and Advanced Technology for Digital Libraries: Proceedings of the Third European Conference, ECDL'99, Paris, France, 22-24 September, 1999 / Ed. by S. Abiteboul and A.-M. Vercoustre. – Berlin: Springer, 1999. – XI, 494 p. – (Lecture Notes in Computer Science, 1696).

10. The Moscow Manifesto: Russian Libraries of the 3rd Millennium and their role in the Global Information and Knowledge Space / Adopted at the International Conference «Managing the Digital Future of Libraries», Moscow, 17-19 April 2000.

11. Policy Development in the Library Area / European Commission. DG Information Society. Cultural Heritage Applications Unit. – Mode of access: http://www.cordis.lu/libraries/en/green.html: March 2000

THE MANAGEMENT OF CHANGE IN ELECTRONIC LIBRARIES

John Akeroyd

Learning and Information Services, South Bank University, London, UK

Abstract

Libraries are in a process of fundamental change brought about by radical changes in technology. This paper charts the changes, which have taken place over the years, and makes some assumptions as to how the future will look. The barriers to increased use of technology are analysed and detailed. Finally the paper looks at what managers need to do to bring about these changes and reviews the relevant key issues.

Introduction

The notion of digital libraries (or electronic libraries or virtual libraries as they are alternatively known) is in some senses long standing whilst in others is still in its infancy. Various commentators have predicted the arrival of digital libraries for some considerable time, but if we argue that traditional libraries comprise more than just data, if we define them as the sum of not only information sources, but also navigational tools, metadata systems such as catalogues, human support systems and a suitable environment within which information is delivered, then we can say that the digital library is still in its infancy. We are only a short way down the road but with no real idea as to where the road might eventually lead. In this paper I want to look briefly at how we have reached this point, and at some of the technical issues which are holding us back. More importantly, I also want to look at the medium term management problems relating to the delivery of digital libraries.

Critical to the current generation of information systems has been the steady progress in computerisation of all or most aspects of library functions, beginning in the early 70's with the development of computerised library catalogues, and moving through the development of circulation systems, to the development of the integrated library systems which appeared in many advanced libraries towards the end of the late 70's and early 80's. These integrated systems use a single, software architecture to manage the core processes of libraries including cataloguing, circulation, acquisitions, and financial control and, with varying degrees, other associated but perhaps less critical functions such as inter-library loan systems and management information. One of the biggest strides over this period was the development of the OPAC which revolutionised catalogue searching and first brought about the notion that libraries could be somehow be distributed and that catalogues did not necessarily represent just the stock held within that particular building.

ILS have continued to develop a mixture of highly sophisticated functions but alongside these has been the parallel emergence of other systems concerned with the delivery of information to the users. Critical has been the development of online information systems delivered initially through stand-alone CD-ROM's, then through networked CD-ROM's and now remote servers. More recently many of these have, in turn, been re-emerging as web compliant databases providing even an average library with the opportunity to search enormous collections of data. As consequence, the ILS has become somewhat less central, particularly if it has been unable to embrace these newer developments.

Perhaps the most recent and significant challenge to the supremacy of the ILS has been the development of the web and web-based resources and access tools. Libraries have had to encompass these emerging services and sometimes embrace them within a traditional library framework. This need - to be able to deal with conventional books and journals on one hand and electronic resources on the other - has given rise to what has become known as the hybrid library[1], the notion being that it must at one and the same time deal with both the plurality of e-resources, often with different interfaces and search engines, with true Internet resources through gateway services i.e. portals, and yet in parallel deal with traditional library books and their circulation. The scale of this challenge is extraordinary. Developed libraries can quote a whole series of discreet services built up over the recent past, which somehow need to be integrated. Chris Rusbridge for example, the Director of the UK electronic libraries program, notes[1] over 18 in one library system, and my own library could quote probably as many and include: the catalogue, several CD/ROM systems (each of which have a different proprietary interface), web based services, internet search engines, gateway services, portals, intranet information retrieval systems, etc. There is a distinct lack of uniformity in the approach so that users are faced with learning a multiplicity of search systems to undertake even a small scale literature search, particularly if they are working in cross disciplinary areas.

Thus there are a number of technical barriers, which stand in the way of the development of the true digital library, and it is to these that I shall now turn. The first is the issue of integration. Digital libraries are increasingly dealing with a distributed environment where users require seamless access to both distributed and heterogeneous resources. What is usually advocated, is a single point of access to a totality of digital library collections, which is adequately scoped to meet the needs of that individual. Such a system would retrieve a relevant set of references together with suitable annotations, be adequately deduplicated and effectively ranked. Much technical effort has gone towards that end and yet you might reflect that it is an unachievable idea. Research suggests that given the choice, users are as likely to look for discreet subsets, for whatever reason, rather than a single integrated source. Some levels of integration have been achieved, particularly through the web itself, although that only offers integration at a rather shallow level. Z39.50 will also permit users to search distributed resources, but this is not widely adopted outside the library sector. A redefinition of Z39.50 in the context of RDF/XML is proposed but success is not guaranteed here either. Meanwhile, we have witnessed the emergence of web portals and harvesting technologies, driven by knowledge management developments, which are capable of harvesting and collating resources into high quality and highly personalised subsets.

A second technical issue, which might be incorrectly considered trivial, is that we do not actually know who the user is. In the electronic domain this is not a simple question. We need assurances as to the fact that users are who they say they are. They must be suitably validated by some other organisation and we must have systems in place, which permit them to do only what we would wish. The first level of that is authentication which is the process of identifying users on the network and is usually brought about by a combination of username/password approaches or IP domain search and restriction. More sophisticated accreditation systems are coming through, but these are currently relatively little used in these areas, and are more common in e-commerce applications. Once we have identified who someone is, there is a secondary process of authorisation, which essentially says what he or she can do once they have access. This is particularly important for the managers of licensed resources and is even more critical in the context of the provision of primary and secondary sources and multimedia. The final challenge is the need for highly effective navigational tools to create seamless logical and understandable routes through the digital library.

Will libraries in the future disappear entirely? Rusbridge[2] argues that libraries can be defined in three ways: as concept, as organisation, as physical space. Though the concept of a library as a collection of information sources defined by certain boundaries will sustain, the boundary definitions will be more complex, deriving as much from consortial deals, usage issues and historical commitments to collections within a building. The digital library will be a more fluent concept capable of continuous change and modification and even defined by the end user as much as by the librarian intermediary.

At an organisational level, licensed resources will still need to be selected and evaluated, contracts negotiated and all placed within context of a suitable navigational system such as a web portal or a learning environment. Moreover even the virtual library must have a context within which it operates which might be the organised corporate context, but might also be the more local context of a research group or a university course or even at an individual level. Bookmarks recorded in a web browser or through personalised environments[3] are in effect personalised digital libraries.

Finally libraries as a physical environment seem on the surface the least likely to exist in a digital future. Access to web services can be got from most places with adequate connectivity which, with the increasing impact of mobile communications, means literally anywhere. Digital libraries will be free of the constraints of delivering audio and graphics and universally portable as individuals become able to access and maintain their own institutional view of the library. The counter arguments to this view are the rather bleak future which centres on the loneliness and isolation that it can engender. The argument goes that we still need spaces where users can come together, even if they are working independently, and which are conducive to long periods of screen use, are ergonomically designed, and have in place support systems and navigational help together with an associated output devices such as colour printers or high definition screens. These centres are already merging as internet cafes, resources centres, learning hubs and so on. Moreover, such centres are likely to coexist with more traditional provision permitting ease of use.

Management of Change

Managerial and change issues encompassing the move to digital libraries are substantial and involve both human and resource factors. Moreover, the changes are often difficult to predict, dependant as they are on the ever-changing nature of technology.

At the economic level, libraries in developed services are already aware of the problems, which derive from the need to maintain dual subscriptions to both electronic and traditional materials during this transitional period, which could last for some years. Users are often disinclined to make radical changes in their use of materials and resent electronic formats being imposed upon them; they also frequently require connectivity, machinery or skills to make best use of what is available. Moreover spiralling journal prices add to the extra cost burden so that any potential savings in labour the library might feel would be brought about by electronic delivery, are often difficult to realise.

Perhaps more positively has been the growth of consortial purchasing of bundled services which, as a consequence, should show some economy in budgets and also serve to democratise resource provision, especially for smaller institutions which can 'piggy back' on larger organisations resource requirements. However, we should be wary of purchasing policies which create redundancy in provision and that such bundled purchasing potentially enables access to large amounts of material which might be little needed. An alternative is that of part-work selling, though at this point there seems to be little enthusiasm at library levels for end user charging or even for libraries to mediate in some similar arrangement. My suspicion is that this will come about in time, at least as a way of providing backup to core materials will enable the shift to happen more quickly.

A third strand is a growth of web publishing at the individual or corporate university level. Such activities may well precede traditional publishing. There is a steady growth of quality material now available on the web and accessible through the main search engines or through the more specialised web portals. Such personalised publishing will, in time, undermine traditionally publishing structures and will most certainly bring down overall pricing mechanisms over a period of time. For the library managers, the economics of digital library delivery are complex and changing but I would argue, the longer term signals are largely healthy in that we may at least seen the end of the spiralling costs of scholarly publishing from a mixture of those resources to which access has been negotiated and those which have been defined as having a requisite level of quality to those which have been self defined by the author including adding in the right descriptions so as to be retrieved through agent or similar technologies.

What then does the library manager need to do to ensure this shift to electronic delivery is as smooth as possible. What are the factors that need to be addressed? I've categorised my own views under four distinct headings which derive from the analysis above. These are strategic change, procurement, IT, staffing and staff development.

Strategic management

To bring about a transition to new forms of library suggest that the library manager should provide clear and articulate vision as to what the service might look like, how it might perform and how it will be evaluated at some future time. It should not be too far fetched or so far beyond the imagination of staff as to preclude its acceptance, but it will be a matter of driving the service forward and ensuring that those charged with delivering the change feel some ownership of it. As importantly it will need to encompass the views of the users, many of whom may with to retain a traditional perspective on library delivery. Strategic plans will need to be sold on to the client base and achieve at least a respectable level of acceptance particularly from the executive, though in the end it may not gain total acceptance of everybody within the organisation. A good example of this might be our own drive towards the delivery of electronic rather than print journals. This has been formulated at the centre but we are having to undertake a program of effectively selling the notion to various schools within the university, to ensure some acceptance of e journals when they duly arrive. This has, to date, proved rather successful and we are now in the position where we are delivering more e- journals than we are traditional journals. The library manager, involved in strategic management must be very focused and the vision should be reinforced to the staff at all levels.

Procurement

The economics of electronic services are described above and in some contexts could well imply a difficult period of increased expenditure so as to achieve medium term economies.

One route through that process is to seek collaborative purchasing with like minded libraries. Such consortial arrangements have become common globally and are not only a way of reducing the expending cost of material provision but can also absorb the load of licence agreements and the legalities surrounding different approaches resulting from electronic libraries. To be effective consortia probably need libraries with similar purchasing power or similar clientele so the charges levied on constituent members begins to be equitable. Consortial approaches can also be used to develop digital content, underwrite the cost of digitisation of material of retrospective conversion and so on and are likely to become more a feature of library services as they become more distributed.

Information Technology

IT can be problematic from a number of points of view. It may for example be without the librarians control in which case one is left with the need to reach sensible agreements with those supporting and delivering IT serves to ensure that the services are reliable and available. Even if there is local control of library related IT, institutional control may not rest with the librarian. In some countries this has become more the case but is still not widespread. Again if IT is without the control of the librarian this can be a factor which hinders overall uptake web based services. There is a need to try to ensure at least a commonality of approach and that basic software such as plugins, etc are available institution wide.

Staffing and Staff Development

Perhaps more critical than any of these is to ensure that staff structures are in place which will meet the new challenges of electronic delivery. This will imply analysing every function within the service and asking the question, is it appropriate to continue to work in this way or there alternatives that will help us achieve the strategic goal of delivery mechanisms? The nature of the core business of a library will change and functions such as cataloguing, which it could be argued has been the absolute foundation of libraries for the past hundred or so, might well be achieved by subsidiary agencies such as National Cataloguing centres or global utilities. Technical services departments may have to find alternatives roles which could imply cataloguing internet resources, though even this begs the question would it be better done co-operatively. It would be foolish to achieve economy in traditional cataloguing methods merely to replace it with another format and the development of the portals render this unnecessary. Many library staff will need to be re-skilled, both to ensure their knowledge and increase awareness of the accent in user support.

In summary we are going through a period of rapid change in the delivery of library services and need to re-think and constantly re-invent what we are. The library of the future will be more concerned with adding value to information resources and providing support and guidance as it will with acting as custodians of print material.

References

1. Rusbridge, C. Towards the Hybrid Library // Digital Librery Magazine. – 1998. – July/August.

2. Rusbridge, C. Of Arms and the Man We Sing. – Mode of access: http://www.ariadne.ac.uk/issue18/rusbridge/intro.htm.
3. Mode of access: http://www.headline.ac.uk/public/diss/nl-pie.pdf

KNOWLEDGE MANAGEMENT IN LIBRARIES IN THE 21ST CENTURY

Tang Shanhong

Library of Chinese Defense Science and Technology Information Center, Beijing, China

Abstract

The knowledge economy is a new concept that has appeared worldwide in recent years. As a sub-discipline of the knowledge economy, knowledge management is a completely new concept and method of management. It works for converting intellectual assets of workers and staff members in the organization into higher productive forces - competition power and new value. Knowledge management requires linkage of information with information, information with activities and information with man - so as to realize the sharing of knowledge (including tacit and explicit knowledge). The conventional functions of a library are to collect, process, disseminate, store and utilize document information to provide service for the society. In the knowledge economy era, the library will become a treasure-house of human knowledge, participate in knowledge innovation, and become an important link in the knowledge innovation chain. In the 21st century, the library will inevitably face the new subject of knowledge management.

Introduction

Knowledge economy is a knowledge-based economy. In the knowledge economy era, the management refers to effectively identify, acquire, develop, resolve, use, store and share knowledge, to create an approach to transforming and sharing of tacit and explicit knowledge, and to raise the emergency and innovation capability by utilizing the wisdom of the team. Since knowledge has become the driving force for social development, the attention of the society to information and knowledge is rising and people's demands for information and knowledge are increasing step by step. This has provided a good environment for library development [1]. Moreover, as information and knowledge has become an important productive factor for the modern economic system, the society will inevitably require intensified management of information and knowledge. How to manage knowledge will become an important subject facing libraries in the near future. Knowledge management in libraries should be focused on effective research and development of knowledge, creation of knowledge bases, exchange and sharing of knowledge between library staffs (including its users), training of library staff, speeding up explicit processing of the implicit knowledge and realizing of its sharing.

Characteristics of Knowledge Management in Libraries

The role of knowledge management in libraries will become more and more important along with the development of knowledge economy. It is a new management mode, boasts the following superiority and characteristics incomparable with conventional management.

Human Resource Management is the Core of Knowledge Management in Libraries

The most important resource in the knowledge economy system is the talents who grasp knowledge. The talent competition has become the focus of market competition in the knowledge economy era. In the knowledge economy era, the libraries will attach importance to vocational training and lifelong education of library staffs to raise their scientific knowledge level and ability of acquiring and innovating knowledge. They also will and fully respect the human value, guide and bring into play wisdom potentialities of library staffs, take developing knowledge resources in the brains of library staffs as an important way for rising work efficiency. An all-round improvement of library staff's quality and positioning of the human value will become important objectives of knowledge management in libraries.

The Objective of Knowledge Management in Libraries is to Promote Knowledge Innovation

Knowledge innovation is the core of the knowledge economy society. As bases for collection, processing, storage and distribution of knowledge and information, libraries represent an indispensable link in the scientific system chain, an important link in the knowledge innovation. Secondly, libraries take part in scientific research process directly. The library work is a component of knowledge innovation. Thirdly, libraries must pay attention to diffusion and conversion of knowledge. They act as bridges for turning the results of knowledge innovation into realistic productive forces. Knowledge management in libraries is to promote relationship in and between libraries, between library and user, to strengthen knowledge internetworking and to quicken knowledge flow. In the knowledge economy era, libraries will carry out researches on development and application of information resources, construction of virtual libraries, protection of intellectual property rights in the electronic era etc., thus founding the base for knowledge innovation [2].

Information Technology is a Tool for Knowledge Management in Libraries

Knowledge acquisition is the starting point of knowledge management in libraries. The application of information technologies enlarges the scope of knowledge acquisition, rises knowledge acquisition speed and reduces knowledge acquisition cost. It is impossible to accomplish such important tasks by using man's brains only in the modern society in which the knowledge changes with each passing day. It will be possible to link closely knowledge sources and knowledge workers by computer networks, thus constructing knowledge networks in libraries based on realization of single-point informatization [3].

The knowledge acquired must be accumulated and converged into knowledge warehouses of libraries. The priority of information technologies in the field of knowledge storage not only finds expression in quantity, but also in retrieval, sorting and security of the knowledge. Information technology is also indispensable in the application and exchange of knowledge and other fields. It functions as a source and tool for knowledge innovation.

Contents of Knowledge Management in Libraries

As a completely new method of management, knowledge management in libraries leaves much to be desired in its theoretical system. In my opinion, knowledge management in libraries should include such respects as follows:

Knowledge Innovation Management

Knowledge innovation management in libraries refers to the management of the production, diffusion and transfer of knowledge as well as of the network systems constructed by related institutions and organizations. It includes three aspects, namely, theoretical innovation management of knowledge, technical innovation management and organizational innovation management.

Theoretical innovation management is to enrich and enlarge the theoretical and practical research fields of library science and information science through pursuing the latest development trends in library science the world over. Technical innovation management is to manage the network systems constructed by institutions and organizations that relate to the full course of technical innovation. In their evolution from conventional libraries to electronic libraries, or digital libraries, Libraries should make technical breakthroughs and progress and build up technical facilities to support knowledge management. Organizational innovation management is to create a set of effective organizational management systems adaptable to the requirements in the electronic library era to support and strengthen knowledge management activities, by optimizing the functional departments and operation procedures of libraries.

In these systems, it firstly requires that leaders who take charge of knowledge management activities should undertake to formulate the management plans and coordinate all knowledge management related activities. Secondly, it requires establishment of special leading groups of knowledge flow for accomplishing all tasks relating to knowledge management activities. Electronic resources committees are established composed of various types of specialists to take charge of evaluating, procuring and creating the electronic resources on the one hand, and coordinating activities of business departments and spurring them on to close cooperation in such fields as procurement and organization of the electronic information resources as well as providing services on the other hand [4].

Knowledge Dissemination Management

Knowledge dissemination is of equal importance as compared to knowledge innovation. Knowledge creators do not have much time and energy to look for knowledge users. Though there are a multitude of knowledge users, it is very difficult to acquire knowledge that already exists in the minds of knowledge creators as restricted by various objective and subjective conditions. Therefore, libraries may play the part of knowledge tosser, use diverse media and channels to disseminate various new knowledge. In the 21st century, the Internet, with its mass information and extensive contents, will provide people with the main approach to searching knowledge and acquiring information. But now there emerge absurd, salacious, false and uncivil information resulting from seeking for commercial profits and political objectives on the Net. Therefore, it is necessary to strengthen knowledge dissemination management in libraries as follows:

1. uninterruptedly strengthening the creation of libraries' own document resources and deepening the development of document information resources;
2. continuously raising the quality of libraries' staffs and strengthening continuous engineering education of working staffs;
3. giving full play to the special role of the expert system in knowledge dissemination;
4. making a comprehensive utilization of all media to ensure security of operation of networks, and prevent online criminal activities and online dissemination of inappropriate information [5].

Knowledge Application Management

In the 21st century libraries should also attach importance to provision of services for people to acquire knowledge and achieve maximum functions and efficiency of knowledge information. Therefore, knowledge services based on high-speed information networks should be carried out by:

1. Setting up virtual libraries or information centers for enterprises, governments, public organizations and scientific research institutions. It is difficult for an enterprise or a social organization to put sufficient manpower, material and financial resources on information gathering, organizing and developing. It is also impossible and unnecessary to spend a large amount of funds on information resources for their own use. Libraries can create virtual libraries or information centers for these organs separately according to their respective information requirements by using abundant information resources on the high-speed information networks.
2. Setting up digitized knowledge services which is actually a development trend of libraries in the 21st century. This presupposes: creating step by step the users-oriented information service systems such as information dissemination, information search and special supply of information; quickening the creation of digitized libraries; studying the methods, means and techniques of information distribution and search with the Internet as the base and WEB technique as the core.
3. Digitizing libraries' resources. The electronic libraries or digitized libraries are the technical modes and development trends of libraries in the knowledge economy era. The knowledge services of libraries in the future will start with creation of databases comprising electronic journals and books in different languages that have discipline features and can operate on high-speed information networks. Great efforts should be made to transform all existing large non-electronic information resources into electronic information and integrate them into electronic libraries.

Human Resources Management

Human resources management takes it as its basic starting point to train high quality specialized talents and to revitalize the library undertaking. In practice, we should pay full attention to diversity and variation of library staffs' requirements, strengthened management of different library staffs by applying contingency management approach. That is, to some people, rigid management method is applied, rigorous supervision and control imposed, and quantity and quality requirements of work according to regulations and procedures are made clear. And, to the rest of people, more flexible management method is applied to let them participate in decision-making and consultation and undertake more jobs so as to bring their management abilities into full play and realize organizational and personal objectives. Doing well in continuous engineering education of specialized staffs, which should not only focus on the theory of library science and related disciplines, but also cover the latest technical knowledge. And strengthening professional ethics education [6].

Technologies for Realizing Knowledge Management of Libraries

One of the aims of knowledge management in libraries is to promote the knowledge exchange among library staffs, strengthen innovation consciousness and abilities, arise the library staffs' enthusiasm and abilities for learning, making the knowledge most efficiently applied to business activities of the library, and rebuilding the library into a learning organization. Therefore, the main train of thought in realizing knowledge management of libraries is a rational design of the organizational structure and business procedures of libraries, and cultural fostering, as well as modernized information support, thus creating an environment and incentive mechanism for innovation, exchange, study and application of the knowledge.

In the Field of Organizational Structure, Business Processes and Culture of Libraries

(1) Introducing the CKO System

The Chief Information Officer (CIO) is a conspicuously high management position that has emerged successively in the government departments and large organizations in Western countries since the 1980s. The Chief Knowledge Officer (CKO) is the highest-ranking person in charge of knowledge management, which has evolved from CIO along with the transition of information research management into knowledge management. The CKO system represents the latest development trends of the information management system of the organizations, and marks the transition of information management from the stage of information resources management to that of knowledge management [7].

(2) Realizing seamless combination of library business management with knowledge management during the business process reorganization of libraries

Knowledge management integrates itself with the whole process of knowledge exchange, sharing, innovation and application of the organization, and becomes the key driving force for the knowledge innovation, exchange and application of the organization. The implementation of knowledge management will inevitably give rise to organization of library business process. This reorganization will also be the process of further combination of library business management with knowledge management.

(3) Rebuilding the library culture by using the theory of knowledge management

Knowledge management will inject new blood into the library cultuie. The main contents include: mutual trust, open exchange, studying, sharing and developing knowledge operation mechanism of libraries, enjoying the knowledge management process [8]. In a word, to make full use of knowledge, it is necessary to foster a new type of library culture suitable to its requirement. This is high level requirement of realizing technology of knowledge management.

In the Field of Information Technology

The main information technologies relevant to knowledge management includes: Internet, Intranet and Extranet; storage architectures; database management systems; metadata; data acquisition and gathering; dissemination, messaging; push and pull; information retrieval; information resources sharing; groupware; middleware; on-line analytical processing; multidimensional analysis and data mining. How to convert data to the object of knowledge management – knowledge is also relevant to some basic information technologies, mainly including data processing, reporting, networked communication, document management, information search and retrieval, relational and object-oriented databases, electronic publishing, work flow and help desks [9].

In addition, because of the differences in architecture, usage and characteristics between information and knowledge, the storage and management of knowledge are more complicated than those of information. The storage architecture technology, database management system technology and metadata are also the key technologies in knowledge management.

Conclusions

Economic environment and information environment is changing quickly today. Knowledge management has become a powerful tool for promoting innovation and realizing reengineering the various walks of life. It occupies very outstanding position in the creation of the knowledge innovation systems of a country. How for the library circles to meet the challenge of knowledge economy and to build the knowledge management systems of libraries is a subject that demands our urgent study and solution.

References

1. Wang Y. Knowledge Economy and the Development of the Library // Library Work & Research. – 1999. – Vol. 6. – P. 17-19.

2. Cao Yi. The Reorientation of Libraries in the Knowledge Economy Era // Library Work & Research. – 1999. – Vol. 3. – P. 24-26.

3. Wang D. The Collection and Processing of Knowledge. – 199?. – February. – Vol. 4. – Mode access: http://www.bsti.ac.cn/bsti_kmchina/gei /048_001.htm.

4,5,6. Sheng X. Knowledge Management of Libraries in the 21st Century // Library Magazine. – 1999. – Vol. 8. – P. 29-32.

7,8. Chen R. Thoughts and Technologies of Knowledge Management // Information Knowledge in Libraries. – 1999. – Vol. 1. – P. 10-13

ICT AND MARKETING CHALLENGES IN LATIN AMERICAN LIBRARIES

Lourdes Feria

University of Colima, Library & IT Division, Colima, Mexico

Abstract

Latin American libraries have experienced an important development in the last two decades. Telecommunications and Information Technologies have been key elements in this process. There are leading institutions with remarkable programs, nevertheless it is necessary to design marketing strategies to improve their benefits. A case study based on a Mexican university library system is presented in order to analyze how ITC applications and marketing techniques have been harmoniously combined. Although every country in the region must find its own solutions, some ideas are presented to emphasize that marketing is not exclusively for businessmen. It is the "science of strategy," and its main objective is client (user) satisfaction, so we librarians are welcome to act enthusiastically on its applications.

Overview

Talking about Latin America is talking about a group of countries which are very close to each other, not only geographically but also culturally speaking. Their libraries can be grouped in 4 different categories: libraries in large countries such as Brazil and Mexico, which have about 60% of the collections in the region, followed by medium-size countries, such as Argentina, Chile, Colombia and Venezuela, which usually share the same library developments as Mexico and Brazil. Finally, there are small countries that can be divided in two groups: countries with a healthy economy, such as Costa Rica and Uruguay, which have a good library development, and countries with more modest economies, such as Nicaragua, Haiti, Honduras and El Salvador, which rarely have academic or specialized libraries (Lau, 1995).

Estela Morales says that the library development is heterogeneous: "within each country there may be excellent services and access to the most sophisticated technology in some places [...] and even a total lack of basic library services in others. However, in general there has been considerable progress, as well as a increasing participation at the international level, where the region has established its own identity and shown it has its own approach and can find its own solutions." (Morales, 1998).

Information Technologies

Today technologies have changed our social and economic life. In the workplace methodologies change, people work home or in the web, with flexible timetables, and more and more virtual communities are emerging in different fields. The large increase of ICTs has supported the multiplicity of global networks. Today people say that the bandwidth is the universal remedy, or that it constitutes a new asset (Ferreiro, 1999), while we are heading, as Negroponte points out, to a new convergence of media.

But 95% of the PCs around the world are located in economically developed countries. USA and the CIS (Community of Independent States) engage with their satellites nearly all geostationary orbits, while the Third World occupies less than 10%. There are more than

6.8 million documents and 80 thousand companies available in the WWW, but 80% of the human race doesn't have access to the most basic telecommunication systems (Ford & Contreras, 1999).

"The Latin American IT market represents 3% of the world market, but growth in Latin American is above the world average" (Callaos, 1999).

Although most Latin American countries have computer networks, there is still much to do in respect to databases and information generated by each place. As J. Soriano says, this turns out because "basically, most countries in the region have not designed policies to integrate two different worlds: the world of technicians who only know how to connect the cables, and the world of users who work with the information. We believe that in the future the next step in the information revolution will come from the potential offered by database developments and electronic edition" (Newsweek, 1995).

We must seriously reflect on the implications, relations and conflicts raised by the information-oriented processes in libraries. In the case of libraries, technologies have made their activities easier, and they have changed them. Among several applications today we want to mention the computing workshops in Mexican public libraries, CD-ROM edition by National Libraries, and the participation in the UNESCO's Memory of the World program. The university libraries "are often the best endowed in terms of budget, professioanl staff and technological infrastructure [...] they offer databases and catalogues on paper, CD-ROM, online or as Online Public Access Catalogues (OPACs) [...] they have been pioneers in the integration and individual development of technologies that have brought users into contact with information either on site or around the world by means of telecommunications, particularly the Internet..." (Morales, 1998)

leading to new initiatives for the integration of Latin American cooperative networks, specially the RedHUCyt (Red Hemisférica Inter-Universitaria de Información Científica y Tecnológica) (Callaos, 1999). Technology has also been a key factor for integration and interaction in the region, and significant efforts have been made by international organizations such as the OAS and the UNESCO, through its Information for Latin America and the Caribbean Cooperative Program (INFOLAC), while the IFLA and the FID have also "helped to bring Latin American and Caribbean librarianship into the global economic and information system" (Morales, 1998).

Challenges and Strategies: the Marketing Role in Libraries

"Libraries in Latin America and the Caribbean have sought to adapt to new technological developments, while their efforts have been concentrated on meeting local needs. Traditionally, however, cooperation initiatives, which are a top priority for modern information services, have been few and far between" (Callaos, 1999).

The extraordinary growth in the use of Internet has definitely improved the cooperation among libraries in these countries. In respect to Internet, Gazitúa (1997) asserts that the technological environment shows how almost all restrictions have been overcome, and that "the main responsibility to advance relies on the information agents rather than with technologies" (Callaos, 1999).

Therefore, reworking our profession to meet the ICTs becomes an urgent issue, giving us the chance to extend the traditional territories from the community library to the global information services, from the territorial library to the virtual library, or a combination thereof (Ferreiro, 1999).

"Social institutions today [including libraries] look vastly different than they did twenty years ago. A variety of forces, most specifically economic changes and technological developments, have reshaped and redefined our notions..." (Cfr. SHAPIRO, 1981 & BESSER, 1998).

Shall we resign to stay in the past? Or are we channeling our efforts to work on specific actions and confront challenges? (Ferreiro, 1999)

- How can we conform mission to technology?
- How can we identify the proper and irreplaceable items of a Library?
- How can we build a strong identity?
- How can we benefit from the "time-space" liberty concept in services?
- How shall we use networks?
- How can we create exciting products and services?
- How can we expand the market?
- How can we develop networks (Internet or Intranet) with primary relation groups?
- How can we speak the same IP language?
- How can we incorporate information?
- Increase the Spanish offering
- Improve the recovery of Spanish expressions (idioms, authorities, thesaurus)
- How shall we face the concentration of digitalized information by large transnational consortiums which have sophisticated recovery mechanisms?

The Latin American region requires specific solutions, and its strengths are the common cultural and language elements leveraged by marketing. Marketing is not only a practice for businessman, it is the "science of strategy" whose main objective is client (user) satisfaction, and we librarians shall know it and apply it as part of our permanent activities in the management and planning processes.

Strategic planning plays a primary role in all these processes: the analysis of Strengths – Weaknesses – Threats – Opportunities, the identification of CSF (Critical Success Factors), and the generation of strategic projects, as well as other elements proposed by Irene Wormell (1996):

- Vision (aim) Where do we want to be?
- Values (beliefs) How do we want to do things?
- Mission (purpose) What is our core business? Who are our customers?
- Objectives (functions) Why are we here? What shall we do?
- Main lines (assurances) What are the results from FDOA/FBE?
- Goals (action lines) Where are we going to?
- Tactics (actions) How are we going to do it?

By putting into practice all these tools we will have the chance to generate new products. Identifying key areas, and evaluating needs through primary strategic group sessions. Among other methods there is the creation of customer and supplier data banks, advertisement, and something very important: our staff, since the main good of a marketable information service are the people who work in it. Promotions and advertisement are part of the success in product marketing, but there are other elements, such as customer satisfaction, the ability to keep customers, and close businesses repeatedly. (Wormell, 1996)

Other authors propose as a complement the development of a corporate image, working in the identification of markets, structuring distribution and promotional systems. In Latin America, we shall mention two additional factors: the generation of results, though small at the beginning, may be a very useful strategy, and a good element to attract the attention of those who make decisions; and the development of alternative actions taking advantage of the creativity of people who work in projects (Feria, 1997).

Case Study: the University of Colima

Countries with a poor infrastructure shall not be limited by their own access to technology resources: what can be done in the Latin American countries to stop this disposition is more than evident... and not only to expand the internal use of information, but also to produce and export information goods.

An example of this is the ICT group, born from a library project in a Mexican university, which has brought together technological applications and significant marketing practices. This group currently works out four programs: the Compact Disc Editing Center, the Educational Multimedia Center, Telematic Services, and Libraries. The project started in 1983. At that time there was much to be done: we didn't have enough personnel, nor financial resources, nor even technology. It was a great challenge. The first step was the creation of a libraries university system: we worked on the services and technical issues. At the beginning we had to recondition classrooms and laboratories; but little by little expressly designed facilities were built.

From its conception, the need to systemize information led us to the development of a computerized program to catalogue and manage libraries, currently known as SIABUC: Integral Automated Library System. Even though it was initially conceived as an internal tool, it is actually used by approximately 500 libraries in Mexico and Latin America. In fact, SIABUC was our access key to computer technology, which give us the chance to start an uninterrupted IT development.

In 1988, the intent to produce for the first time a CD-ROM totally edited by the University of Colima led to the creation of the Cenedic (Compact Disc National Editing Center). From that day on, the production has increased to one CD-ROM every two weeks. But its most important achievement has been the development of new processing and programming methodologies and applications.

After that, the Educational Multimedia Center was established. In this center the latest hypertext, hypermedia, animation and virtual reality techniques are adapted to produce didactic and interactive materials to support education-learning processes. On the other hand, the General Telematic Services Direction has undertaken the installation of a university network to offer distinct support services such as connectivity, access, university web site maintenance, etc. It works in linking programs with private companies. It has highly-trained personnel working on the latest network, data communication, Internet and videoconference developments. In recognition to its achievements, this institution has been recently invited to take part in the Internet2 project.

In addition, the ICT group is working on three projects for the implementation of Digital Libraries: The Digital Library for Latin America and The Caribbean, The Twenty First-Century Library, and Interfaces: Digital Library International Forum.

All this shows that the success achieved by librarians within a corporate environment depends directly on "our ability to perform that function for which we uniquely suited and trained; an that function is the management of information" (Echelman, 1981).

Information services, rather than becoming computer centers, will lead us to rethink the library. They will help us to give an added value to the traditional services, without mistakenly thinking, as some people do, that networks will replace books.

Conclusion

The library development in Latin America is both distinctive and heterogeneous; however, a significant development has been evident in the last two decades. A critical element has been the outstanding development of telecommunications and information technologies. From the 80's the automation of libraries has received a great impulse, and many libraries have introduced more and more equipment and applications, creating their own web sites, generating compact discs, and producing leading projects for some countries in the region. It has provided them with a more refreshing and distinctive touch, giving us the opportunity to conceive new directions (Ferreiro, 1999), such as:

- Increasing the Spanish language offerings in Internet
- Creating Latin American networks for the creation of contents
- Negotiating with consortiums
- Collaborating and contending
- The Library Brand as an Internet offering validator
- The Library as an educational actor
- Technological developer
- Learning on Information Resources
- Integrator of information services
- Information organizer for the www
- Aggressive disclosure of information
- Broker, Specialized Searcher
- Entertainer/ Network, Communities Moderator
- Contents mapping

Finally, it is not worthless to say that every activity requires from the beginning a great deal of perseverance, will and passion. The work done by the information services is an enterprise that requires commitment, and a good disposition to devote time, consideration and love to all these activities, and to become part of the change, delivering and communicating this attitude, converting ordinary things into extraordinary achievements.

References

1. Lau, J. Resource sharing in research libraries of Latin America: A paper for the 13th Annual Research Library Directors Conference organized by RLA and Online Computer Library Center (OCLC) in Dublin, Ohio, USA, 1995.
2. Morales, E. Latin America and the Caribbean / UNESCO. World Information Report 1997-1998. – Paris: Unesco, 1998. – P. 107-123.

3. Ferreiro, S. Internet o morir. Santiago, Chile, 1999: Presentation for the IV Taller Latinoamericano de Redes in Mérida. – Venezuela, 1999.

4. Ford, A., Contreras S. Memorias abandonadas o las brechas infocomunicacionales // Ford, A. La marca de la bestia. – Buenos Aires : Norma, 1999. – p. 117-171.

5. Callaos, N. Latin America and the Caribbean // UNESCO. World Communication and Information Report 1999-2000. – Paris: Unesco, 1999. – p. 241-259; Conexión en Latinoamérica: Interview with José Soriano by David Schrieberg // Newsweek. – Enero 16. – 1995.

6. Shapiro, S. J. Marketing and the information professional: odd couple or meaningful relationship? // The marketing in an age of diversity: ed. by Blaise Cronin. – London: ASLIB, 1981. – P. 102-107.

INTERNET LIBRARIANSHIP: TRADITIONAL ROLES IN A NEW ENVIRONMENT

Kate Sharp

University of Bristol, Bristol, UK

Abstract

This paper looks at some of the potential roles that librarians could adopt in the age of the Internet. It will outline the effect that networked information is having on the library profession. It will identify the new roles that information professionals are performing and shows that traditional professional library skills will continue to provide a good foundation for the sector. The paper concludes with a look at how some of the skills we traditionally associate with librarianship have been applied within the Internet environment.

The Internet is democratising information, empowering the masses and allowing end-users access to a vast array of resources. It is also significantly altering the work of information professionals. This paper will look at some of the roles that information professionals have developed and will suggest that the skills that support these are as relevant as ever in this new networked information era. This paper will go on to consider how these roles and skills transfer into a networked environment with reference to experience drawn from my own work as an Internet Librarian.

Changing Environment

The main focus of this paper will be on the most notable change to affect the working practices of librarians in recent years – the increase in electronic information and communication technologies and in particular networked information.

These network advances have transformed modes of communication and will result in significant changes to traditional library structures to accommodate organised information and access to it. From your desktop it is now possible to "link easily and cost effectively into services, systems and information which were previously either not accessible or not even known" [1]. The characteristics of the environment in which librarians are now working include: greater access to a range of information; increased speed in acquiring information; greater complexity in locating, analysing and linking information; constantly changing technology; lack of standardisation of both hardware and software; continuous learning for users and library staff and substantial financial investment for technology [2].

Traditional Roles and Skills

The information that users require may be accessed differently but the skills information professionals need to manage this information can be adapted from established practices. There is no denying that this is a new global library environment and it is one in which librarians are still finding their way. However, the foundations of the profession and the skills and roles associated with it will help to ensure librarians survival. The core skills traditionally associated with information professionals which include information handling skills, training and facilitating skills, evaluation skills and concern for the customer are all still relevant. These skills cover cataloguing, classification, indexing, enquiry work and user education all functions which if managed by librarians will help to make the Internet an easier place to navigate. Librarians in all sectors have built up roles and library services based on collections and users needs and according to Creth the "values that are the foundation of the library profession should remain the same into the next century...values of service, quality, universal access, and co-operation" [3] It is the way in which these values are translated into operations and activities that will undergo substantial change.

Lancaster correctly states that in order to justify its existence in the electronic world, "the library must continue to perform one of the most important functions it now performs in the print-on-paper world: to organise the universe of resources in such a way that those most likely to be of value to the user community are made most accessible to this community, physically and intellectually." [4].The vast amount of information available in a networked environment suggests that there is more than ever before a role for trained intermediaries with search skills, abilities to analyse and evaluate resources and match needs with sources. The traditional library skills mentioned above should be reassessed and their value to information services in the electronic environment applied. For example, the skills of cataloguing and classification can be used to improve the end users experience of networked information retrieval. The creation of meaningful metadata files based on cataloguing principles can help users find needles in the Internet haystack. The creation of catalogues including electronic resources can ensure access, authenticity, reliability and validity of networked resources.

The increasing amount of information available to users and the ways in which it can be accessed has in theory made it easier for users to get the information they require. However, in practice there is now a danger that they can be overwhelmed by the amount of information they receive making it difficult to locate the exact information they seek as well as overseeing issues of accuracy and authenticity. The role of librarian as both user-educator and intermediary is prevalent in this environment.

The foundations of librarianship, which include skills such as cataloguing and user education are, as explained above, as relevant in an electronic age as they are in a print based one and will continue to provide a solid base of skills.

New Roles and Skills

In addition to the professional skills mentioned, the librarian of the future must be equipped with a wide range of personal and transferable skills in order to manage the changing environment in which he or she works. The importance of transferable skills over information technology skills should be highlighted here. Management and interpersonal skills will make librarians more effective managers of networked resources and services. As Hastings says "it is more important that digital librarians possess particular personal qualities (which are innate) rather than specific technical expertise (which can be learned)." [5].

This is not to say that the way to avoid the electronic age is for library professionals to stick their heads in the sand. The information professional must change and adapt to the new electronic information environment, he or she must learn about new technologies and be aware of the strengths and weaknesses of them. Librarians should not feel threatened by computers and technical developments but should move forward with the new technology and take a pivotal role within organisations. [6].

Information professionals within libraries are playing an increasing role in dealing with information in electronic formats by creating Web pages to promote their services to external customers and choosing automated library management systems. Skills in information organisation are more necessary in this age of information explosion. Library and information professionals have a key role to play in this era. For example, librarians are well equipped to take intranet projects through the various stages of design and maintenance as they understand their users and their organisations information needs and have the range of skills to manage knowledge effectively.

The role of the librarian in this context is to help users find the information they require then provide them with the tools to assess and use the resources for their individual needs. Creth suggests that librarians achieve this by "actively seek(ing) out users in a variety of settings" and by making "full use of information and multimedia technology" by offering instruction in a variety of formats (including Web based instruction and online tutorials). [7].

Working in an Internet Environment

I am project manager for Biz/ed [8] which is based at the Institute for Learning and Research Technology [9], University of Bristol [10]. Biz/ed is an Internet based educational resource for business and economics academic staff, librarians, researchers and students. The management of the Web site itself is a good example of transferring traditional library skills to the Internet environment. Biz/ed itself contains over 4000 static Web pages which have to be organised in a way which will make it easy for users to find the information they require.

One of my main responsibilities as project manager for Biz/ed is to oversee resource discovery in the areas of business, management and economics for the Social Science, Business and Law Hub (SOSIG) [11]. SOSIG is one of the 'faculty' based hubs which make up the RDN (Resource Discovery Network) [12]. The RDN is the UK's 'academic library of Internet resources', supporting academics by offering access to thousands of networked resources.

Cataloguing the Internet

The Internet resources selected by the three information professionals who currently contribute to Biz/ed are entered into an Internet catalogue which is available on Biz/ed or by cross searching SOSIG. The catalogue is a collection of high quality Internet resources located on servers around the world which holds over 2500 records. The catalogue can be searched or browsed and has the added value of resource descriptions which allow users to decide whether the resource is worth accessing. The Biz/ed Internet Catalogue is the Internet version of an academic library. The gateway points to Internet resources but applies many of the principles and practices of traditional librarianship to the collection. Every resource has been selected, classified and catalogued by an information professional. Biz/ed has a collection management policy, quality selection criteria, a classification system, and catalogue records and rules. These methods are widely recognised as being essential for the organisation of printed information, and they translate very effectively to the electronic environment.

Gateways such as Biz/ed can be seen as the electronic equivalent of academic libraries. The librarians submitting resources into this catalogue are serving a similar function to those building traditional print collections based on journals and books.

User Education on the Internet

As the Web is increasingly becoming the first place that students will look for materials the role of information professional as intermediary will also grow in importance. As librarians working with this medium it is up to us to introduce the strengths and weaknesses of the Internet as we would any other library resource during our user education programmes. Just as a traditional academic library offers a programme of "user education" to students and lecturers to maximise the benefit they receive from the library, UK librarians working in the Internet environment in conjunction with the RDN are developing networked user education to help people to get more from this very rich information service. It is our experience that many users do not realise how rich a source the Internet can be and that it can be used to find many research and teaching materials.

Traditional library user education in a university, college or school offers users:

- Library tours – to become familiar with the layout of sections of the library
- Library induction sessions – to learn about the services available and to learn how to use them
- Subject guides – to identify the key information resources for a particular discipline
- Support from subject librarians – to get specialist help
- Information skills development – to learn transferable skills in information handling

By applying a traditional library role such as user education and the knowledge of the best resources available for their subjects in the Internet environment an Internet librarian is well placed to provide a comprehensive Internet information seeking skills induction.

I am currently producing 'Internet Business Manager' for the RDN Virtual Training Suite [13]. The RDN has funding to create ten Web-based, interactive tutorials designed to help students and lecturers develop their "Internet information skills" and to offer a subject-based introduction to discovering, choosing and using high quality Internet resources and materials. The RDN Training Suite will cover the key information skills for the new Internet environment. They will introduce basic ideas, techniques and examples of how the Internet can be used in education within specific subject disciplines. The tutorials will be free to access via the World Wide Web, and will each offer a self-paced lesson lasting around 15-30 minutes. It is also envisaged that these tutorials will help academic librarians who need tools to support their user education programmes

The tutorials will be based on the Internet Detective [14] model. Internet Detective is an interactive, online tutorial that provides an introduction to the issues of information quality on the Internet and teaches the skills required to evaluate critically the quality of an Internet resource. It offers a variety of learning methods, including tutorials, exercises, worked examples and quizzes.

Working on this project I am able to bring my subject expertise, library skills and Internet knowledge together to create a user education programme for Internet users interested in the areas of business and management in effect becoming a subject librarian of the Internet.

This paper has discussed the relevance of traditional library skills in the new era of networked information. It has shown that librarians in all sectors have an important role to play in shaping the Internet through resource discovery and by familiarising themselves with Internet cataloguing standards they can help to ensure consistent records are built. They also have an essential role in teaching their users about critical information seeking on the Internet and assessing the materials they find for quality. If librarians successfully transfer the foundations of the profession into this new medium they will continue to be seen as vital information intermediaries.

References

1. Pantry, S. (1997) Whither the information professional? Challenges and opportunities. The cultivation of information professionals for the new millennium // Aslib Proceedings. – 1997. – Vol. 49, N. 6. – June. – P. 170 – 172.
2. Creth, S. D. (1996) The Electronic Library: Slouching Toward the Future or Creating a New Information Environment Follett Lecture Series. – Mode of access: http://www.ukoln.ac.uk/services/papers/follett/creth/paper.html: 1996.
3. Creth, S. D. (1996) The Electronic Library: Slouching Toward the Future or Creating a New Information Environment Follett Lecture Series. – Mode of access: http://www.ukoln.ac.uk/services/papers/follett/creth/paper.html: 1996.
4. Lancaster, F. W. (1997) Artificial Intelligence and Expert System Technologies: Prospects / Libraries for the New Millennium: Implications for Managers. – London: Library Association Publishing, 1997. – P. 19-37.
5. Hastings, K., Tennant, R. How to Build a Digital Librarian Follett Lecture Series. – November. – Mode of access http://mirrored.ukoln.ac.uk/lis/november96/ucb/11hastings.html: 1996.
6. Medhurst, J. Do or Die: The Librarian in the 21st Century // Managing Information. – 1995. – Vol. 2, N 9. – September. – P. 30-31.
7. Creth, S. D. (1996) The Electronic Library: Slouching Toward the Future or Creating a New Information Environment Follett Lecture Series. – Mode of access: http://www.ukoln.ac.uk/services/papers/follett/creth/paper.html: 1996.
8. Bized. – Mode of access: http://www.bized.ac.uk
9. ILRT. – Mode of access: http://www.ilrt.bris.ac.uk
10. University of Bristol. – Mode of access: http://www.bris.ac.uk
11. SOSIG. – Mode of access:http://www.sosig.ac.uk
12. RDN. – Mode of access: http://www.rdn.ac.uk
13. RDN Virtual Training Suite. - Mode of access: http://www.vts.rdn.ac.uk/
14. Internet Detective. – Mode of access: http://www.sosig.ac.uk/desire/internet-detective.html

TECHNOLOGICAL DISCONTINUITIES IN THE LIBRARY: DIGITAL PROJECTS THAT ILLUSTRATE NEW OPPORTUNITIES FOR THE LIBRARIAN AND THE LIBRARY

Ronald C. Jantz

Alexander Library – Scholarly Communication Center, Rutgers University New Brunswick, New Jersey, USA

Abstract

Our library profession is changing dramatically, largely due to the forces unleashed by major advances in computing, networking, and storage technology. We are at a juncture where the library and librarian must ask how they will embrace and use these new technologies. From a business perspective, we know that the three interrelated concepts of competition, technological discontinuities, and innovation are having more and more relevance for the library. This paper suggests that libraries are losing market share and that we can address external threats from competition through unique partnerships and technological innovation.

Introduction

The concepts of competition, technological discontinuities, and innovation are typically found in a business environment, however these concepts can also be very useful in examining libraries' current practices and establishing new directions and opportunities. Although my framework here is the university and research library, I believe that these concepts will become relevant for all libraries.

Competition

What does competition mean for the library and does the library have competitors? Typically, another institution, business, or person is a competitor if they are taking part of your market share. One measure of a library's market is the number of reference questions dealt with at the reference desk or through electronic reference. We have experience at Rutgers University which indicates that we have handled 23% fewer reference questions in the 98/99 academic year than we did in 96/97 academic year (Boyle, 1999). There are many ways to deal with this problem and, as one approach, reference librarians are pursuing improved methods for delivering reference service (Lipow, 1999). What we are faced with is a competitive threat. In some respects, the threat is very amorphous and difficult to identify and is represented by the millions of Web "publishers" who distribute information on the Internet. Our library users and patrons are finding this information and using it in lieu of the scholarly information available to them in the research library. In other cases, the threat is more clearly and easily identified. What would we do if Amazon.com decided to enter the book lending business? Alternatively, InfoRocket (www.inforocket.com) is a new company which offers reference services through a Web auctioning process similar to eBay. In effect, anyone on the Internet could become an amateur reference librarian. Perhaps closer to home is the assertion by Dr. Michael Kurtz, an astrophysicist at Harvard University. He flatly states that "librarians could not have helped us" to organize and make available the most important research resources to others in the field (Marcum, 1998). The point of these examples is that we do have competition and we need to recognize that there are serious threats not only to the library as an institution, but perhaps more importantly to the users of a library and the quality of information that they are obtaining.

Technological Discontinuities

A technological discontinuity is represented in a new technology or in the re-packaging of a set of existing technologies that results in quickly obsoleting a product or service. An example from the 1960s is the introduction of the electronic calculator. In a very short time, slide rules and mechanical calculators disappeared and, in some cases, the companies that made these products disappeared when they could not adapt to or find ways to use the new technology. Another more recent example is that of using the Internet and the tcp/ip protocol to transport voice calls. This application of the Internet represents a technological discontinuity for traditional telephone companies and provides an opportunity for small entrepreneurs to enter the telephone business with relatively little investment. In general, the Internet and the Web represent technological discontinuities for the library and thus both an opportunity and a threat for the future. As just one example, as we train our reference librarians to do Internet reference using search engines, portals, and web research guides we are finding less use of the Library of Congress classification system, a system which most students find obscure and confusing.

Innovation

Librarians pride themselves on being able to understand user needs, organize information, and provide effective access to information. These skills represent the traditional competencies that are part of what makes a library a success. However, the opportunity that technology offers and the threat of technological discontinuities suggests that we are entering a new era in which it is "more important to know what we don't know than to know what we know" (Berghel, 1999). One way to respond to these threats is by creating an innovative environment within the library that will harness the power of new technology by generating new services. Innovation is an intriguing part of human behavior and it has mysterious and desirable aspects such as creativity. Library administrators should foster more innovation in their institutions, however they may find this human behavior difficult to stimulate and even more difficult to do well. Zairi (1992) provides an excellent definition of technological innovation that helps set the framework and context for this paper: *"Technological innovation is the process by which industry generates new and improved products and production processes. It includes activities ranging from the generation of an idea, research, development and commercialization to the diffusion throughout the economy of new and improved products, processes, and services."*

How does one do innovation? For many years, the concept of "skunkworks" has been a very successful and interesting innovation process within corporations (Bennis & Biederman, 1999). Frequently a *"skunkworks"* operation can be a very innovative process because of the empowered environment, lack of formal processes and the abscence of bureaucracy. Business consultants (Hamel & Prahalad, 1994) have long urged innovators to examine the *"white space"* or the *"cracks"* between traditional markets to find opportunities for new products and services. As introduced in the next section, the

Scholarly Communication Center is examining these *"cracks"* within the context of library needs and competencies in order to prototype and trial new products and services. As in most library endeavors, partnerships are essential.

Projects and Partnerships

At Rutgers University Libraries (RUL), we have established a center in which new technology can be evaluated with the objective of enhancing library services or creating new products and services. The Scholarly Communication Center (SCC) (Collins, Fabiano, et al, 1999) within RUL was officially launched in October, 1997 and has pursued initiatives in teaching, scholarly communications and electronic publishing. Our efforts in the SCC are a catalyst to bring together experts in subject content, technology, and library services in order to forge new partnerships and prototype new services. The SCC has provided a unique opportunity to experiment and innovate and this section will briefly describe four projects which highlight the partnerships, the technology and the lessons learned from our experience.

Medieval Early Modern Data Bank

In the Spring of 1998, the SCC joined with Rudolph Bell, Professor of History at Rutgers, to develop a website (Bell, Jantz, & Khanna, 1999) for finding and retrieving data from the Medieval and Early Modern Data Bank (Research Libraries Group, 1996). The Medieval and Early Modern Data Bank (MEMDB) is a project established at Rutgers University and originally cosponsored by the Research Libraries Group (RLG), Inc. MEMDB is co-directed by Prof. Rudolph M. Bell of Rutgers University and Prof. Martha C. Howell of Columbia University and has an objective to provide scholars with an expanding library of information in electronic format on the medieval and early modern periods of European history, circa 800-1815 C.E. MEMDB contains five large data sets, three pertaining to currency exchanges and two pertaining to prices from the medieval period. Scholars can use this data source in many different ways. For example, by examining prices of commodities from the medieval period, a researcher can show a correlation between prices and major events such as ship wrecks or epidemics. Through this partnership between librarians and teaching faculty, MEMDB is now available world-wide to scholars, students of history and others who will find unique ways to utilize this valuable source of data.

GIS in the Social Sciences

Geographic Information Systems (GIS) tools provide powerful digital mapping capability and can be used in almost any academic discipline. GIS offers social scientists a new tool for conducting and presenting research, yet GIS remains the province of the more traditional geospatially oriented departments such as geography and urban planning. For a state university like Rutgers, there are many researchers who want to develop and analyze data to demonstrate trends, support a developing theory, or to use the technology for instructional purposes in the classroom. The project discussed here demonstrates how the SCC has extended this powerful GIS technology to other departments within the university. In this role, a librarian brings together technology, data, tools and training within a library setting. In this specific project, we discuss a collaboration with one of the political science professors at Rutgers University in order to provide a course entitled "community organization" which focuses on specific cultural, health, and business issues relative to a small urban area in New Brunswick, New Jersey. The political science course referenced here presented quite a challenge as articulated by Professor Michael Shafer. The objective was to teach junior-senior level students to use a powerful GIS tool to map census data about certain urban areas in New Jersey. Four of the course lectures were dedicated to this aspect of the course in which the RUL data librarian presented the essential elements of the mapping tool and how to import and map census data. This experiment in using GIS in a political science course highlighted the difficulties of using sophisticated computer tools in a classroom environment and the delicate balance between the pedagogical aspects of the course and the practical application of technology.

Eagleton Public Opinion Data

Research data is an under-utilized resource in academic settings primarily because of the difficulty in accessing the data and the tools required for effective manipulation of the data. In collaboration with the state premier polling agency, the Eagleton Institute, RUL and the SCC have provided access to New Jersey public opinion data via the Web. To address some of the data complexity issues, the website (Jantz, 1998) has provided the following capabilities:

- Search and browsing the poll database by title, date and keyword.
- Viewing the questionnaires online
- Examining specific question results
- Downloading data files in a file format that can be directly imported into SPSS

Standard web publishing technologies and the statistical tool SPSS were used to generate the question results from the raw data and to present this data on the Web. This feature is especially noteworthy since it enables users who are not familiar with tools like SPSS to actually view and use the data. In addition to providing public access to this valuable set of research data, the Eagleton website was recently used in an undergraduate political science course to introduce students to quantitative methods.

Alcohol Studies Database

This last example represents a collaboration within Rutgers University Libraries and illustrates a new genre of information sources that are delivered through the Web, are subject specific, and continuously evolve as new material becomes available. For some time, a sizable research reference database including journal articles, books and book chapters has been available at the Center for Alcohol Studies at Rutgers University. As in MEMDB and the Eagleton Polls, this database represented a significant research resource that was accessible only through librarians at the Center for Alcohol Studies. The database of over 50,000 citations is now available through the Web (Page, Jantz, and Mead, 2000). The search interface presents thesaurus terms in three categories of physiological aspects, social aspects, and drug terms in order to provide a standard vocabulary and effective searching to the user. Sophisticated boolean operations can be easily constructed using pick-lists and the search can be limited by special categories such as populations or audience. To publish this database on the Web, we have used standard database technology and a database publishing tool called ColdFusion (Allaire, 1999). In order to streamline this publishing process, we have also developed a reusable platform that consists of the software technology above and a repeatable process that uses a website template and a standard bibliographic database definition. The database definition and website template can be quickly customized to highlight the specific content and unique characteristics of the specific database.

The "e" Connections

We are continuing to explore new and exciting possibilities that we believe will help the Library discover innovative and valuable services. Although we are inundated with the commercial jargon that prefixes many of our products and services with the notation "e-" (e-library, e-journal, e-encyclopedia, e-book), these areas all represent potential technological discontinuities for the library. In another emerging project with Professor Rudy Bell, we are contributing organization, design, and technology enablers as part of a new history honors course on medical advice in the medieval period. Students will search, find, and download to a local SCC archive electronic books (e-bocks) from a vendor's site. Since the books are from the medieval period the text cannot be easily character recognized and thus the books are represented as digital images. As part of this course, the students will have an opportunity to use e-book appliances for the book images rather than print a copy of the book. The e-book is a perfect example of the "cracks" between traditional library services and it represents a potential discontinuity for the library. Here is a book with no permanent content so how does one catalog such a product. One can easily imagine library servers that enable users to download books to their portable reading devices, yet there is at present no institutional framework to handle a device such as an e-book. And, as one might expect, there are a variety of vendors offering e-book products, some of them clearly thinking about the library market as a potential source of revenue. Through this technological innovation, we stand to lose another part of our traditional product base or we can aggressively pursue approaches to using this technology in the library.

There are many other opportunities that are emerging for the librarian and which also represent potential discontinuities. Internet reference offers the capability to deliver reference service "anytime, anyplace" and is a service that our users are demanding. With technologies such as voice on the Internet and streaming video, we can imagine sophisticated and effective internet reference. As indicated in the introduction, commercial vendors are already entering into this arena by auctioning reference service and producing web-based research guides.

Conclusion

This paper has described several endeavors in the Scholarly Communication Center that illustrate how librarians can undertake technology oriented projects that benefit both research and the classroom and which illustrate how we can address the threats from technological discontinuities. The projects demonstrate that:

- Prototyping is an effective tool to understand potential new services.
- Reusable platforms reduce time to market.
- New technologies in combination with traditional librarian competencies offer the opportunity for new services.
- Platforms offer ways to encapsulate knowledge so we don't lose it.

As learning and education are transformed by the digital revolution, we can expect a further dissolution of the traditional structures of the library. The research library must transform itself to keep pace with this revolution and to fully utilize the innovations in network and computing technology. In undertaking this transformation, as Lynch points out (1999), "we've chosen to emphasize extrapolation rather than identify and understand emerging discontinuity." We will no longer be able to provide effective service by using analogies to what we have done with our print resources. Librarians can deal with the impending technological discontinuities by learning about and becoming experts in the competencies of innovation and partnership. Innovation suggests that we look for totally new paradigms to provide information service and that understanding what we don't know might be more important than relying on what we know. Partnership competencies suggest that we strive to understand how the professionals in our respective subject areas conduct their research and teaching and how we can become part of their team. Bringing together special competencies and new technology in an innovative environment can result in new products and services in the library that will provide tremendous benefits to our users.

Some time ago in a reference to the challenges of innovation, Steele (1983) described the "gauntlet of innovation" as a process that has many barriers. To successfully negotiate the technological revolution in libraries, we need not only new ideas and a stimulating environment in which they can grow, but we also need people who believe in new products and who will undertake the difficult tasks of building them. These people are the champions of new ideas and they will need lots of support to flourish in an environment steeped in tradition. Innovations will be lost without these champions.

References

1. Bell, R., Jantz, R., Khanna, D. (1999) Medieval and Early Modern Data Bank. – 1999. – Mode of access: http://scc01.rutgers.edu/memdb. Research Libraries Group. –1996. Medieval and Early Modern Data Bank.
2. Bennis, W., Biederman, P. (1999) The Skunk Works / Organizing Genius: The Secrets of Creative Collaboration. – New York: Addison-Wesley Publishing Company, Inc., 1999. – P. 117-130.
3. Berghel, H. (1999) The cost of having analog executives in a digital world // Communications of the ACM. – 1999. – Vol. 11, N 42. – P. 11-15.
4. Boyle, J. Annual Report, 1998/99. Public Services and Communications: Rutgers University Libraries. – 1999.
5. Collins, B. at al. (1999) Building a Scholarly Communications Center. Modeling the Rutgers Experience. – Chicago: American Library Association, 1999.
6. Hamel, G., Prahalad, C. (1994). Competing for the Future. – Boston: Harvard Business School Press, 1994.
7. Jantz, R. Eagleton Public Opinion Polls. – Mode of access: http://scc01.rutgers.edu/eagleton: 1998.
8. Lynch, C. On the threshold of discontinuity: The new genres of scholarly communication and the role of the research library // Racing Toward Tomorrow: Proceedings of the Ninth National Conference of the Association of College and Research Libraries / Thompson, H. (Ed.). – Chicago: Association of College and Research Libraries, 1999. – P. 410-418.

9. Marcum, D. Educating leaders for the digital library // Council on Library and Information Resources – 1998. – Vol. 6. – November/December. – P. 1-4.

10. Page, P., Jantz, R., Mead, V. The Alcohol Studies Database. – 2000. – Mode of access: http://scc01.rutgers.edu/alcohol_studies.

11. Steele, L. Managers' misconceptions about technology // Harvard Business Review, 1983. – November/December. – P. 133-141.

12. Zairi, M. Managing user-supplied interactions: Management of R&D activity // Management Decision. – 1992. – Vol. 8, N 30. – P. 49-57.

LIBRARIES AND LIBRARIANS IN INDIA ON THE THRESHOLD OF THE THIRD MILLENNIUM: CHALLENGES AND RISKS

Kalpana Dasgupta

Central Secretariat Library, New Delhi, India

Abstract

The information era with its electronic facilities will come with many challenges in all the sectors of development since information is the base for all developmental activities. Libraries and information centres and librarians will have their share of challenges and risks to partake in this major activity. To bring about this change India will need to have a vision for the 3rd millennium and each sector will have to adopt the latest developments in information technology. This includes change in the functions of the library to make it service oriented rather than collection building oriented; preservation and access may be considered as vital; marketing of information and library service development of library professionals to cope with new environment and to deal with the management techniques for dealing with the new objectives and prepare a national policy for libraries and information centres keeping in mind the needs of the different sectors within the field of Indian librarianship.

Introduction

The information age is here with many challenges and risks for the information generator and the information disseminator. The challenges before libraries and information centres are manifold. The main challenge will emerge from the expected change in the very nature of future libraries and information centres.

Library Scenario in India

The diversity of the Indian library scenario is an important aspect for consideration while speaking about a vision for the 3rd millennium, since different library sectors in India are in various stages of development and no single solution or approach will be relevant in the Indian situation.

Indian library and information sector can be divided into five major areas: the National Library sector; Academic library sector; the Special and Scientific library sector, Government library sector; and the Public library sector due to various factors the scientific and special library sector is much more developed and modernized than the other four sectors.

The challenges which Indian libraries and librarians will encounter in the 3rd millennium are manifold but the most important challenge will be the change in the very nature of libraries and librarians i.e., the libraries must change from collection oriented institutions to service oriented organisations and librarians have to change from custodians of books and documents to information managers and disseminators. In this changing scenario IT will play the most important role. While taking advantage of the different components of information technology the libraries of each sector will have to ensure the following:

1. take stock of the actual need of the library and its users;

2. bring about change in the functions of the library to make it service oriented rather than collection oriented;
3. resource sharing and networking of libraries;
4. consider both preservation and access as vital components of library service;
5. marketing of information and library services;
6. development of library professionals to cope with the new environment;
7. utilization of management techniques for dealing with the new objectives.

At the decision-making level India will need a National Policy for libraries and information centres within the changed socio-economic environment keeping in mind the new requirements of the different sectors within the field of librarianship. It will now be worthwhile to analyze the present Library and Information scenario before preparing a vision for the 3rd millennium in each sector of librarianship in India.

The National Library Sector

The National Library sector in India can be divided into two types of libraries. The first one comprises the National Library, Calcutta and the recipient Public libraries under the Delivery of Books Act i.e., Delhi Public Library (DPL), Connemara Public Library, Chennai and the State Central Library, Mumbai. These are the depositories of the printed cultural heritage of India under the Delivery of Books Act.

The depository libraries are a very important part of the National Library sector because India is a very vast and multi-lingual country with rich linguistic heritage. The 3rd millennium will have to see the cooperation between all these four libraries with the National Library at the apex. This can only be implemented if all these libraries are modernized at the same scale and have compatible systems to ensure resource sharing and networking. As these are financed by the Department of Culture (DoC) of the Government of India (GoI), the standards for modernization laid down by the DoC will be applicable to all these libraries.

The other part comprises the National level subject specific libraries such as National Science Library, National Medical Library, etc. In both these parts the National Library stands out as the largest single library which acts as the depository as well as the repository of all published material of India. The 20th century saw the development of all these national level libraries in isolation. The main challenge in the 3rd millennium in the national library sector would be to bring about close coordination between all these national level subject libraries and the National Library of India.

Academic Library Sector

The Academic library sector comprises school and college and the university libraries. While evolving a vision for university libraries for the millennium, the main focus should be on the role of the existing university library in addressing the national issues. Since most university libraries in India work in isolation some information need to be collected and collated before preparing such a perspective plan.

1. Data regarding the actual functioning of the library, its collection, user approach, library facilities, IT application status, library manpower status, etc.
2. A national agency may be identified for undertaking this work.

A major aspect of the new millennium will be cooperation at all levels starting from the local to the global level. Cooperation is a pre-requisite for all types of networking for resource sharing. Therefore, the following must be ensured before preparing the plan for linkages between university libraries.

1. Institutional commitment to accept the given measures.
2. Fund and support resource sharing solution.
3. Attitudinal changes in library staff to undertake additional responsibility in resource sharing environment.
4. Training of library staff to understand and appreciate the changed situation.

If these pre-requisites are made available the university libraries could plan for resource sharing programmes, apprenticeship in libraries for learning new skills and IT training programmes, consultancy in retro-conversion and in developing IT infrastructure. All these put together will be the basis of preparing a perspective plan and evolve a vision for university libraries in the country.

School and College Libraries

Excepting very high brow private schools, most schools in India do not have a library per se in the present situation. This area of librarianship is very neglected and needs immediate and continuous attention. As regards college libraries, most colleges have libraries but other than very well known colleges in each state, the ordinary colleges do not run libraries of any consequence. Therefore, India faces the challenges of actually preparing a perspective plan from scratch i.e., from collection development to networking through IT solutions, and will need a complete blueprint to develop these two types of libraries during the coming centuries.

India has set up the Information and Library Network (INFLIBNET) under the University Grants Commission (UGC) as the inter-university agency on library modernization to take the initiative and address the issues required to implement the perspective plan for the Academic sector. Each university and its affiliated college libraries also should be part of the overall scheme of development.

Distance Education

India has developed a well organized distance learning system through the Indira Gandhi National Open University (IGNOU) to achieve a high percentage of educated citizens as a prelude to an ultimate knowledge based society. The diversity and geographical distance of India need a strong, well-planned distance learning system for all citizens of the country. To make distance learning worthwhile the information base of the library sector will be equally responsible to be able to cater to the information need of Indians different societal levels. IGNOU has started some unique services for students with the help of IT but unless the rich collection of reading material available in different libraries in India are accessible to the younger generation the aim of distance learning gets nullified. Therefore, the academic sector has to be so inter-connected that it will also cater to distance learners.

Public Library Sector

The Public library system in India has developed over the years for more than a century, initially under the patronage of the aristocracy. However, the new independent India which developed a democratic society, recognised the need for public libraries which will work for the common good and will build a strong foundation for a democratic set up.

According to the Constitution of India, Public library development is a State responsibility. Therefore, all states are vested with the mandate to set up libraries within the state at different levels. But due to the diversity in the level of state-wise development, the Department of Culture, Government of India has set up Raja Rammohun Roy Library Foundation (RRRLF) to act as a nodal agency for development of public libraries in India.

Though library legislation is almost a pre-requisite, all the Indian states have not yet passed the library legislation. Therefore, RRRLF is also working towards a model Public Library Bill which may be able to encompass all the facets needed for development of public libraries to suit the new changing environment. Moreover, in the rural sector the local governments have been made responsible and accountable for the development of public library facilities through new constitutional amendments. Also, the Central Government is taking well-considered steps to make dissemination of information the main activity in all sectors which deal with rural and social development. The 3rd millennium will see a drastic change which will ensure cooperation and collaborative efforts between the information generating agencies (whether government or NGOs) and the libraries and the information dissemination sector. The government is seriously considering to bring about conceptual change in the rural library sector by coordinating its activities along with the continuing education schemes of the National Literacy Mission (NLM).

The RRRLF has also been given the responsibility of resource mobilization for modernisation of the state and district central libraries, the development of infrastructure and training of personnel. The Department of Culture through the Central Secretariat Library (CSL) has laid down standards for library development software and networking as well as for bibliographic description to ensure standardization both in infrastructural development as well as retro-conversion of library catalogue in machine readable format.

Government Libraries

Government libraries in India were developed mainly during the British period to cater to the needs of the decision-makers and the bureaucrats. These libraries have always been institutionalised within the departments of the government. All these departmental and ministerial libraries have collected government documents mainly of their respective department/ministry and have restricted their acquisition to the need of the departmental staff alone. The Central Secretariat Library (CSL) has, however, worked within a broader spectrum being the main library in the ministerial and bureaucratic set up.

During the last 50 years some of the government libraries have been developed into well-organised collections which can cater to an informed clientele. Since government information started being handled by the National Informatics Centre (NIC), the use of information technology became the key word in the government sector. The Department of Culture, which is the nodal agency for library development in India, has taken viable steps towards resource sharing and networking of the libraries under its supervision. This includes the National Library, Calcutta, Central Secretariat Library and National Archives of India library, libraries under the Archaeological Survey of India and the Anthropological Survey of India, etc.

Special and Scientific Libraries

The special libraries and the libraries under Science and Technology group are in a much better developmental stage compared to the other four sectors. A good number of these libraries use current IT products and systems like computers, email, CD.ROMs and on-line storing and retrieval. Libraries and information centres of research institutions such as those under Council of Scientific and Industrial Research (CSIR), Defence Research and Development Organisation (DRDO), Indian Council of Agricultural Research (ICAR), Indian Council of Medical Research (ICMR), Department of Atomic Energy (DAE), Indian Space and Research Organisation (ISRO), Department of Science & Technology (DST) and Institutes of higher learning like the Indian Institutes of Technology (IITs), Indian Institute of Science (IIS), Indian National Science Academy (INSA), Indian Institutes of Management (IIMs), are modernized and have been given the necessary resources for development.

Library Networks

Other than INFLIBNET, there are a number of networks which have developed in the past decade. These are either city networks or activity subject specific networks. Developing Libraries Network (DELNET), Calcutta Library Network (CALIBNET), Madras Library Network (MALIBNET), Management Library Network, etc., are important and useful ventures for networking and resource sharing. Future of Library Development and the Challenges in the 3rd Millennium The details given above actually picturizes the latest situation encountered by Indian librarianship till the end of the last millennium.

The main challenge in the Indian situation is to visualise the present situation and bring about changes so as to nullify the observations made in the World Information Report, 1997-98, which are as follows:

- The bulk of the population is not information-dependent in day-to-day work and living.
- A large proportion of the population cannot consume information, especially if it is delivered in written form.
- The vast majority of the population does not have the means to access information.
- People in general are not accustomed to pay, cannot pay or are unwilling to pay for information. In fact, information does not even figure in their list of wants.
- The existing pattern of economic activities does not favour a growth in information consumption.
- The countries do not have sufficient capacity to invest in infrastructural development

Therefore, the future of Indian librarianship lies in descending from its ivory tower of catering to only a select few and the literate minority and to create a system which will penetrate into the actual information need of the majority of Indian people. So, there has to be a major paradigm shift to deal with the information needs of the vast majority of the population who at present do not have means to access information. Specially, the public library system in the country needs to be rejuvenated and re-modeled to cope with the present situation and the future trends.

There will be need to change the following on a broad-based basis in all types of libraries:

a. Library environment
b. Fragmented and isolated services
c. Organisational structure
d. Library collection
e. Information based infrastructure
f. Information and knowledge management

The first step towards this direction has been taken to a certain extent as the Report of the Working Group of the Planning Commission on Libraries and Informatics for the 9th Five Year Plan 1997-2002 addresses some of the challenges which confront Indian librarianship The Challenges and Risks for Librarians and Information Specialists in the 3rd Millennium The biggest challenge for Indian librarianship is to bring about attitudinal change among both library staff and users. Libraries and librarians are still the lowest priority in the decision making process and the librarians are the least visible persons. If this main challenge is confronted by librarians and libraries in real earnest it is only then that one can expect all the necessary changes within the system itself.

Libraries will also have to cope with the initiatives developed in the society in the changed IT environment. Libraries can no longer afford to remain institutionalized passive spectators. All the activities will now have to be tailored to give long distance and often home delivered information.

Opportunities and Risks

The new millennium will open up unprecedented opportunities for information professionals. Employers will no longer look for the traditional career requirements but a flexible work force which can take on different roles and responsibilities as and when required. In this context the following changes are to be brought about in India:

1. Change the teaching curricula in the field of library and information science.
2. Utilize the traditional expertise and apply them effectively in the new situations by understanding the actual requirements and applying these skills.
3. Content generation to suit the new fields of study with the help of IT.
4. Play the role of information managers by utilizing the new technology to give access to the rich resources available in libraries.

Tomorrows information professionals will be knowledge navigators instead of information collectors. In the Indian situation the new generation of librarians will have to face these challenges and risks to remain in the information business in all the sectors. Inter-changeability and capabilities to adjust from one sector to the other will be the biggest challenge for Indian librarians.

National Policy for the New Millennium

To fructify all that has been stated above there is a felt need to frame a National Policy of Libraries and Information Systems and Services, suited to the new environment. The DoC had framed a National Policy on Library and Information System (NAPLIS) during the late 1980s which is a very good foundation for preparing a new policy which will encompass the futuristic viewpoints for the library sector as a whole. It has to spell out all relevant issues, challenges, threats and opportunities which are envisioned for the new millennium.

India is on the threshold of major changes which will be possible only if a worthwhile and modern information system is set up at the right time, with the help of right infrastructure and is administered by the right type of qualified people.

References

1. 50 Years of Library and Information Services in India; edited by M.K. Jain and others. – Delhi: Shipra Publications, 1998.
2. Abell, A. Skills for the 21st Century: editorial // Journal of Librarianship and Information Science. – 1998. – Vol. 4, N 30. – December. – P. 211-214.
3. National Seminar on Challenges before the University Libraries in India in the 21st century / Indian Library Association. – Vadodara, Delhi: ILA, 1999.
4. Library Vision 2010: Indian Libraries and Librarianship in retrospect and prospect: ILA Conference // Indian Library Association: 45 th. – Delhi; ILA, 1999.
5. World Information Report: 1997/98. – Paris: UNESCO, 1997.

USE OF NEW TECHNOLOGIES FOR BETTER LIBRARY MANAGEMENT: GIS (GEOGRAPHIC INFORMATION SYSTEM SOFTWARE) AND PDAS (PERSONAL DIGITAL DATA COLLECTORS)

Christine Koontz and Dean K. Jue

Florida State University, GeoLib Program, Allahassee, FL, USA

Abstract

New technology for any discipline is frequently technology that is not necessarily new from the broadest perspective, but technology that is finally capable of being widely adopted within the discipline. Two such technologies are currently available and can now be used in the library and information discipline: GIS (geographic information system software) for library market profiling and location analysis; and PDAs (palm pilot type instruments) with built in bar code scanners, for better collecting in-library use. This paper describes and discusses applications and technologies.

Introduction

"New technology" for any discipline is frequently technology that is not necessarily new from the broadest perspective, but technology that is finally capable of being widely adopted within the discipline. The lag time from the initial development of the technology to its adoption within a discipline may be caused by a variety of factors, such as costs, difficulty of usage, or lack of required support services. Two technologies that fit into this "new technology" description that are in existence presently, for well over a decade, but can now be widely used in the library discipline, are geographic information systems (GIS) and portable data collectors (PDCs) or personal digital assistants (PDAs).

Geographic information system software was developed in the early 1960's. However, up until the early 1990's, the use of GIS required a computer configuration that would cost well over $100,000 USD. The GIS software was command line driven, (code and number language) making it difficult for casual users to easily understand and use. As a result, a dedicated support staff was often needed. Finally, data for the software was expensive to either buy or to develop in-house. Today, GIS software can cost less than $1000 USD and be run on PC-compatible computers costing less than $2000 USD. Many GIS software vendors provide several data sets as part of the initial purchase price of the software, further lessening costs.

A study funded by the U.S. Department of Education combined bar codes representing pre-defined in-library use data attributes with bar code scanners to collect such data in a manner that is more detailed than previously available. ("Handheld..." 1999). The study involved 100 public library branches in over 40 library systems within the U.S. The general categories of in-library use in which data were collected were in-library material usage, library assistance, and library user activities. Refer to the web site http://www.geolib.org for a detailed look at the level of data details that could be derived from the collected data.

Although the initial study involved public libraries, there is no reason why similar methodology could not be adopted in other types of libraries (e.g., academic, special). The rapid pace of technology has meant that the technology used in the initial study is now even more affordable and can be collected using hand-held devices running the Palm or Window CE operating systems.

In March of 2000, the in-library data collection methodology was presented to the Federal-State Cooperative System, the group responsible for setting library data collection standards within the U.S. In addition, the methodology was adapted to both the public and academic library situation within France. As the value of better measurement of in-library use becomes better know, it can be expected that the use of PDCs and PDAs in libraries will become standard library practice.

Personal digital assistants and portable data collectors have been widely used in warehousing applications since the late 1980's. New technology have made these PDAs and PDCs even more portable (e.g.. Palm Pilots which can be held in the palm of a hand). These PDAs can now be easily integrated with built-in bar code scanners to help standardize data collection in a variety of library environments that were traditionally ignored within the U.S. (e.g., in-library usage). Today, PDAs can be bought for well under $1000 USD, including application generator programs that can be used to develop custom library data collection programs on the PDAs.

This paper will discuss the applications of these two technologies in a library environment.

GIS: Geographic Information System Software Applications for Libraries

For retailers the two basic functional uses of GIS are market profiling and location analysis. Marketing requires a detailed breakdown of the socio-economic and demographic status of immediate locales, the surrounding population, and subsequent estimation of the geographic market range. These types of retail applications are useful for libraries – as libraries share the "travelled-to" characteristics of many retail outlets (Koontz, 1997, 112).

Library Market Area Measurement

There are five ways to measure geographic markets that illustrate the dynamism and versatility of GIS ("Using..." 1996, 187.) A market area is the geographic area from which a library draws most of its users. Maps based upon US geographic and political boundaries are provided to illustrate these concepts.

1. Assigning each library branch a certain number of census tracts or block groups. Block groups are smaller divisions within a census tract. These can vary from country to country, e.g., Scotland population districts are called cachement grids.
2. Determining a branch market through overlay of zip code (or postal) boundaries. These zip codes are based upon customer/user address data.
3. Determining branch markets by assigning equal portions of the population to the nearest existing facility. This is a modeling technique, location allocation which simply assigns each member of the population to the nearest facility.
4. Determine a branch market by assigning a certain mile radii to be served. This is a standard and more general approach used to compare key features.
5. Determining the actual market area by geocoding user address data. This is by far the most accurate.

Market Profile

In the US, US Census Data provides hundreds of variables that describe the population and is collected every ten years. Research in the library field (Koontz 1990) recognizes certain broad variable groups that are strongly associated with library use. Nine broad groups include: 1) population; 2) sex; 3) race/ethnicity; 4) age; 5) family life cycle; 6) owner occupied housing; 7) income; 8) education; 9) vehicles per housing unit. These are strictly US based, and relevant to the US environment. Within the US there will of course, be important population differences that the library manager must be aware of in their own locale. These of course, will be different from country to country and within countries.

Once the important population characteristics are identified, the library manager can identify who resides within the geographic market, to better determine what products and services may be desired.

Further analysis can be performed by GIS to provide more precise information. Several examples include: 1) analysis of overlaps and gaps in library service; 2) market areas that have over 50% college graduates, or under 30% children (any variable can be input and displayed); 3) identification of which library market has the highest per capita circulation; and 4) new site analysis, including distance of new facility from other branches, population growth, and a review of major topography.

The power of GIS to have many data sets collapsed and viewable in one environment, provides a powerful dynamic digital tool for library managers.

Other Applications

There are other uses of GIS that may be of interest to library managers. For example, because GIS allows one to view many geographic data sets in one environment, the software also permits research and analysis into aspects of regional or national library policies that may be difficult to perform in other analytical environments.

A recent political issue in the United States has been the difficulty of providing computer access (and, by extension, information access) to individuals with low income or in poverty. The public library and its many branches have been held to be one of the key solutions to this problem. But this assumes, among many other assumptions, that individuals with low income or in poverty are located near a public library outlet.

To research this, GIS was recently used to estimate the geographic market area being served by each individual public library outlet in the United Stales (Jue, et. al., 1999). The market profile of each of these market areas was analyzed to estimate how many people in the estimated geographic market areas of existing public library outlets were in poverty. In addition, an estimate could be made on how many people were in poverty that were completely outside the estimated geographic market areas of all existing public library outlets. From these analyses, it was determined that there may need to be regional policy differences in the funding of public library outlets if the original goal of improving information access to individuals in poverty through public libraries was to be realized. In policy issues of providing information access over a geographic area, whether it is local, regional, or national, the power of GIS may prove to be quite useful and the results enlightening.

Finally, as GIS becomes more affordable and easier to use, the software itself may become a new service that a library manager may want to provide. It is quite common for libraries to provide access to computer software such as word processing, spreadsheets, and databases. GIS is simply computer software that manages and analyzes data that have a geographic component to it.

There have been attempts to introduce GIS software within both academic and public libraries since the early 1990's in the U.S. ("Implementing..."). This effort was hampered significantly by lack of inexpensive geographic data, especially local data. Today, as local governments develop local data sets and want to provide easy access to this information, libraries may find that they can be a vital local institution in providing information access to all.

PDA Application for Collecting In-Library Use Data

Libraries collect materials circulation data because those materials are cataloged and, consequently, their movement out of and back into the library can be automated. This has not been the case, however, for materials that were used but never left the library at all. Because library user activities have also been difficult to collect in an automated manner, good data on this aspect of library usage is also difficult to find. Today's technology has provided an answer to these problems, however. The non-collection of in-library use data today is not due to the inability to collect such data in an automated manner but because of the up-until-now lack of habit of doing so and the lack of widely-accepted standards for what types of in-library use data to collect.

References

1. Hand-held computers check out library usage // Automatic IDNews. – 1999. – June.
2. Implementing GIS in the Public Library Arena. Jue, D. K., a chapter in Geographic information systems and libraries: patrons, maps, and spatial information: paper presented at the 1995 Clinic on Library Applications of Data Processing, 10-12 April 1995. – University of Illinois at Urbana-Champaign: Graduate School of Library and Information Science. – 1996.
3. Jue, D. K. at al. Using public libraries to provide technology access for individuals in poverty, the hope and the reality: a nationwide analysis of library market areas using geographic information systems // Library and Information Science Research. – 1999. – 21 p.
4. Koontz, Ch. M. Library facility siting and location handbook. – Westport, CT.: Greenwood Publishing, 1997.
5. Koontz, Ch. M. Market-based modelling for public library facility location and use-forecasting. Unpublished doctoral dissertation. – Tallahassee: Florida State University, 1990.
6. Koontz, Ch. M. Using geographic information systems for estimating and profiling geographic library market areas. / Geographic information systems and libraries: patrons, maps, and spatial information: paper presented at the 1995 Clinic on Library Applications of Data Processing, 10-12 April 1995, University of Illinois at Urbana-Champaign: Graduate School of Library and Information Science. – 1996.

TOWARDS THE HYBRID LIBRARY: DEVELOPMENTS IN UK HIGHER EDUCATION

Chris Rusbridge and Bruce Royan

Information Services, University of Glasgow, UK and Scottish Cultural Resources Access Network, Scotland, UK

Abstract

The real world in which information professionals struggle to provide high quality services is not the simple world of most so-called "digital library" services, but rather is characterised by complexity and diversity in almost all aspects of the information access chain. Dealing with diversity is the real problem for providers interested in offering quality services, and for users seeking to access relevant sources to answer their information problems.

This paper outlines the efforts of the UK Joint Information Systems Committee (JISC) to help UK Higher Education Institutions deal with this growing diversity of information resources. These efforts are based on two strands: the Electronic Libraries Program and the development of the JISC Collections. These strands are now coming together as JISC concentrates on developing a Distributed National Electronic Resource (DNER), and encourages organisations to harmonise and facilitate access to this and a plethora of other resources, digital and conventional, through the model of the Hybrid Library.

This paper contains material presented at the VALA Conference in Melbourne Australia, in February 2000.

Introduction

The term "Hybrid Library" conjures up an image of some triumph of Genetic Engineering; part bookhouse, part scorpion, with a dash of eye of newt. To continue the metaphor, it describes a specie of library adaptive to today's increasingly complex and turbulent information environment. The term is not necessarily synonymous with Organizational Convergence, since it describes a process of service provision, rather than administrative structure. Less elegant perhaps than its US equivalent the "Gateway Library", it nevertheless conveys a Janus-headed service driven by a recognition that despite the burgeoning of the internet and digital publication, the vast majority of useful information resources in academic libraries are and will remain print based. The Hybrid Library, by exploiting both access and storage, Clicks and Mortar, seeks to provide the end-user with, in Ian Winkworth's phrase, "a managed blend of traditional and electronic resources".

Follett report

The development of Hybrid Libraries in the UK had a somewhat unlikely start. The abolition in 1992 of the "binary divide" between the older universities and the polytechnics approximately doubled the number of universities. Library provision in the former polytechnics had been chronically under-funded, and there was serious concern at the potential impact of having to upgrade all these libraries to "research quality".

This issue was the genesis for the Joint Funding Councils' Libraries Review Group, which in November 1993 produced its findings in the "Follett report", as it is colloquially referred to after the Chair of the Committee, Prof. Sir Brian Follett. This Report was one of the most influential of recent years, if measured by the amount of spending on its recommendations. Chapter 7 of the Report related to the use of IT to alleviate library problems. The implementation of this part of the Report was delegated to the HE Funding Councils' Joint Information Systems Committee (JISC), with a budget of J15 million over 3 years. Within JISC, this implementation was handed to a newly created sub-committee, the Follett Implementation Group for IT, with the splendid acronym of FIGIT.

eLib Phases 1 and 2

FIGIT's response to the agenda laid out in Chapter 7 of the Follett report was to call for proposals for what became the Electronic Libraries Program, or eLib. Two calls were made, and the resulting Phases 1 and 2 of eLib comprised almost 60 projects http://www.ukoln.ac.uk/services/elib/

It is impossible to sum up the results of 60 projects in a few sentences, but a few points are worth noting here in view of later developments:

- A low technology, distributed document delivery co-operative was set up (LAMBDA), providing both price and performance competition with British Library's Document Supply Centre, without however challenging the latter's entrenched position. Our ambitions for user-initiated document delivery remain un-realised as yet due to a variety of factors including delays in software delivery.
- Non-destructive digitisation is extremely expensive, particularly for older material (especially pre-19th century). It is not easy to justify on space-saving grounds, although it can be eminently justifiable in terms of accessibility. Copyright material, particularly when including many pictorial images, remains a serious problem.
- Providing extracts of key texts on demand in print or especially electronic form is a valuable support for learners. Publishers began to understand and even accept this practice, and some economic factors are better understood. However, without support in copyright law for fair use in this area, copyright clearance and then digitisation activities (especially when OCR is used to convert to text, because of the proof-reading overhead) introduced such delays into a time-critical process, that the system is unlikely to work for institutions acting alone.
- The change towards producing parallel print and digital versions of journals *increases* costs in the short term. While new journals with no print equivalent can be created, those which make full and effective use of the new medium (eg *Internet Archaeology*) are also very expensive. Meanwhile the economic models for freely accessible electronic journals remain unclear, while the technology for subscription-based electronic journals is much more intrusive than in the print world.
- Librarians respond extremely positively to the pressure for change, driven by a strong service ethic. Some academics also grasp the opportunities for change, but careful co-ordination with the academic cycle is essential (and often difficult to achieve). Many academics do not have the time to experiment in their use of technological change. Some academics are distinctly techno-phobic, at least in their teaching practice. Cultural change by retirement may be an important factor!
- Dissemination is therefore a major issue, and one that is too often insufficiently stressed. If the goals of a program include cultural change in a community, it is not enough to report on results via web pages, conference papers or journal articles. There needs to be a sustained dissemination program.

The comments above are reflections of the current authors, rather than the results of the independent summative evaluation of eLib recently completed. Though they appear somewhat negative, we believe the program had enormous impact in changing the direction of library provision towards the digital domain, including:

- A sea-change in attitudes in and towards the LIS community.
- A change in direction for JISC from being a network provider with a bit of information to a realisation that it is committed to the information enabling business.

eLib Phase 3 and the Hybrid Library

When contemplating what should come after the first 2 phases of eLib, it was time to think beyond the bounds of the Follett report. Phase 3 was concerned with converting successful Elib projects into self-sustaining services, building a distributed national union catalogue, working towards a national policy for digital preservation, and in particular, exploring the feasibility of the Hybrid Library. As explained above, the motivation behind the hybrid library program area was a need to cope with diversity. Diversity is a major problem as real libraries struggle to come to grips with the digital information world:

- Results from eLib Phase 1/2 projects, and from other programs internationally, were extremely varied, but there had been little study of the impacts of bringing in several of these technologies to play in real library environments.
- As a corollary to the above, many "digital library" projects (especially those from the US National Science Foundation's Digital Libraries Initiative) had been expressed in terms quite independent from real library environments. Digital Library projects often appear to be "single topic" services without the needed breadth. We felt libraries had a continuing value in HEIs, whether or not the domain was print or digital. In particular, libraries have roles in selection, presentation and mediation of resources, although they deal with them in very format-specific ways. So diversity already exists within the library; one view of the library is as imposer of order on diversity. Even for existing or legacy digital material, mostly CD-ROMs and bibliographic or full-text datasets, the interfaces which are offered are extremely varied, not to say idiosyncratic; specialisation and differentiation of interfaces have occurred as vendor marketing tools. The result is a hodgepodge of different approaches which the would-be user of information must navigate. In truth these different approaches are barriers to the user; they are sustainable only while there are small numbers of digital resources but will not be as these numbers increase.

The idea of the hybrid library program area developed from these and related thoughts. As is usual, the final program to emerge from the proposals presented in response to the call may not have explored these areas as deeply in some areas as we would have liked. Nevertheless the program outlined below is producing some very interesting results, which indicate that much can be achieved with some careful thought and modest investment.

Agora

Agora is working with a commercial vendor to develop a standards-based broker system (based on a 3-tier architecture with thin, web-based client, intelligent brokers based around library policies, and distributed resource providers) suitable for hybrid library use. The architecture is based on the MODELS Information Architecture (Gardner, Miller and Russell). The broker aims to provide levels of integration across diverse data sets mainly through the use of Z39.50, and expects to integrate more than 40 Z39.50-based resources. This project has been adversely affected by difficulties experienced by their commercial partner.

Agora supports the aggregation of resources in groups called "information landscapes" which can then be searched. The same idea appears again in HeadLine, below, and Agora has worked with other Phase 3 projects to develop collection level descriptions (Brack), to help define the information landscape. Agora provides a complete process for the user from discovery of a collection through to a document request and delivery.

BUILDER

BUILDER is working in an institutional context, and aims to exploit all the synergies possible in the institutional resources available to them, to deliver innovative services.

Although BUILDER appears to have focused on products, this is because of its belief that demonstration is better than explanation. Their cycle could be described as "think far, build near, try out and evaluate." Much of this work has centered on toolkits for their particular local environment: Talis for the library management system, and IIS with SiteServer for the web server. These tools are linked together in clever ways to produce a whole variety of demonstrator products which can be viewed on their web site.

Probably the most popular service is the exam paper service, which has been formally evaluated (Dalton and Nankivell). It was initially restricted to on-campus access for legal reasons, but this year being extended off campus with added authentication. To this end they have explored authentication approaches linked to their Novell LAN and also to their particular OPAC's borrower identification system. They have also looked at the integration of electronic journals, and of local and remotely digitised resources. They have run a pilot electronic short loan system involving over 60 documents including 4 complete books; once again this has been formally evaluated (Dalton and Nankivell).

HeadLine

"The information landscape" is a term used to refer to the set of information resources of interest at any one time to a user. HeadLine is particularly concerned with tailoring information landscapes. To this end HeadLine is constructing an interface based around a *Personal Information Environment* (PIE) which allows groups of users to be presented with initial views from their teachers but subsequently to adapt these to suit their own needs. Authentication and authorisation are critical for this work, as are links to MIS systems so that the initial requirements of students can be assessed automatically. Building these links has been found to be considerably more complex than was expected.

The project has also completed a significant analysis of library information service enquiries, and has prototyped a system called SHERLOC to help users find documents on the physical shelves (*Shelfmark & Resource Locator*). They are investigating a document delivery service between the partner sites, of the kind useful to a multi-campus institution.

HYLIFE

HYLIFE is interesting in demonstrating the wide variety of solutions which may be appropriate for different groups of users. It is our most "geographically challenged" project, including Plymouth in the south and the University of the Highlands and Islands Project in the far north, with several partners in between. Some aspects of the project are already being brought into service at the University of Northumbria at Newcastle.

Interesting findings from HYLIFE include evidence that students view information retrieved electronically as intrinsically more valid than print sources. Given widespread concern in the LIS community at the difficulty in distinguishing garbage from good digital information, this emphasis emphasises the need for guidance on quality.

The HYLIFE annual report for 1999 also raises concerns at issues related to what it calls "the convergence of book and gown" (chapter 3). It is getting less possible to clearly distinguish and separate the educational, academic process, managed by faculty, from information provision, managed by the library. Information delivery becomes an intimate part of the educational process. Although HYLIFE is concerned at a perceived threat to funding independence for the library, there is also clearly value in being an increasingly irreplaceable part of the whole process.

MALIBU

MALIBU has also made progress on many fronts, but two in particular are worth noting. The first is a pre-prototype searching agent allowing cross searching of web sites using HTTP (sometimes disparagingly referred to as HTML scraping) (Harris). The advantage of this implementation over rivals is claimed to be the ability to bypass the target's state while maintaining its own state as a broadcast search. Although it is potentially high maintenance, this approach may prove extremely valuable in the short to medium term.

The other major development in MALIBU is the pair of complementary models of the Hybrid Library (Wissenburg). The first is a user model and the second is a technical services model. Forming models of the hybrid library was one of the tasks for the projects.

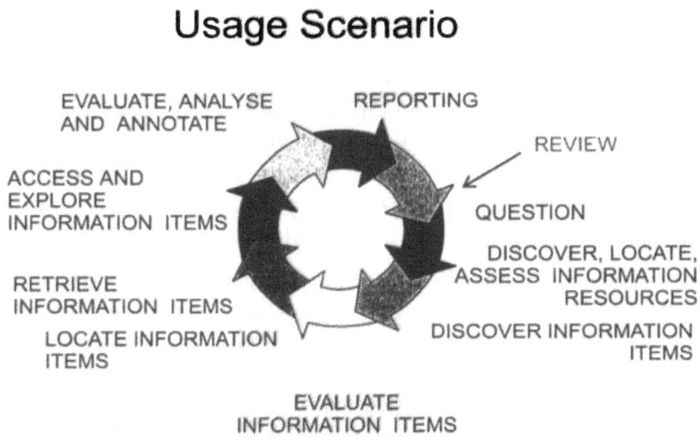

Figure 1: MALIBU Usage Scenario model

The user model shows the stages a user goes through, often iteratively, in discovering, evaluating and using information. The model above starts from the user having some kind of question.

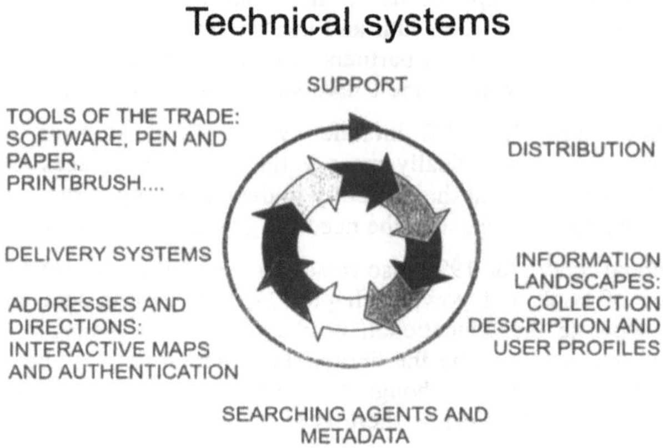

Figure 2: MALIBU Technical Systems model

The technical services model shows the services that are needed to support these user stages. See the MALIBU documentation for further ideas on the applicability of these models. The key here is the extent to which the use of information has to be closely linked to - or embedded in - the delivery of the information.

The hybrid library seems to have been an idea whose time had come; in addition to the eLib projects reported on above, several unsuccessful bidders nevertheless decided to continue with their hybrid library plans, albeit on a reduced scale. And all the hybrid library work in the UK has proceeded in step with, and informed by, JISC-funded contributions to nationwide electronic resource discovery

The Resource Discovery Network

One of the successes of eLib Phase 1 was the set of subject-based Internet gateways (eg ADAM, EEVL, OMNI, SOSIG etc), which provided quality-tested access to collections of Internet-based resources. This idea was worth extending, but it was not easy to see how this could occur fairly across the subject spectrum. The decision was taken to establish a networked organisation, the Resource Discovery Network (RDN), which would integrate and extend this work, seeking additional financial and other support.

The RDN is organisationally based on the model tested with the Arts and Humanities Data Service, with the RDN Centre running common services, interoperability standards and systems. A range of "faculty-level" hubs addressing a larger subset of the subject spectrum are located in institutions with strong links to the subjects embraced by the hub; this subject-linkage is seen as one of the strengths of the approach. Each faculty hub may have a number of subject-level gateways associated with it. Initial hubs have been created based on eLib projects covering social sciences, business and law; engineering, maths and computing; and medical/biomedical. Additional hubs are being established covering humanities and physical sciences. At least 3 more hubs are needed, but the funding is hard to find.

The JISC Collections

Meanwhile, JISC was continuing to develop its portfolio of digital collections. Initially, these had been presented to users through home grown and proprietary interfaces. The prime example of this was the ISI Citation Service, delivered by Bath Information and Data Services (BIDS). Later services began to develop from this base, providing a family resemblance for users. Services were established at 3 Data Centres. Then, as always, the limitations of proprietary in house developments began to emerge, and there was pressure to use commercial interfaces which the student might encounter later in the real world. This extended to the point where one dataset (INSPEC) was offered with a choice of interfaces from 6 data hosts, a separate choice by the library once the decision to subscribe was taken. While this approach gave some benefits, it started to increase the diversity problems already referred to.

Now the collection extends to over 40 datasets covering areas such as statistical and geospatial data as well as bibliographic and full text.

An important development has been the development of a JISC "Collections Policy" (*An integrated information environment for higher education*), describing the framework in which collection and retention decisions will be made.

The DNER

The Distributed National Electronic Resource was initially the expression of two simple ideas. First was the notion that the provision of digital resources should be physically distributed for redundancy and avoidance of single points of failure. Second was the belief that the collections offered should fit within a national framework, the JISC Collections Policy.

Over time this approach to the DNER began to develop, spurred by the increasing diversity of the resources being offered and by concerns about the sustainability of this diversity:

- The location of resources was determined more by historical "accidents of negotiation" than by logic (at least as far as the user could determine). This was in keeping with the distributed idea, but it turns out that different Data Centres have their own differentiation (more diversity). Also, it appears that users have a greater sense of "network place" than we had expected.
- The diversity of interfaces has already been noted. It is not so much the diversity itself (since fitness for purpose will always drive some diversity), but the wanton use of diversity as a market differentiation tool, which is of concern. We believe in different interfaces, oriented to the needs of particular user groups.
- There was beginning to be a diversity of authentication approaches. As the idea of the DNER moved in concept from a small set of individual resources towards resources as components of a whole, the problem of authentication and authorisation was thrown into sharp relief. Bluntly, users did not want to remember more usernames and passwords. The response to this was ATHENS 3, about which little more can be written here, other than that it is very valuable, far from perfect, possibly inadequate for the task, a triumph of pragmatism, and/or a disaster in the making. Take your pick!
- There was an increasing need to be able to "join up" different services, so that when a bibliographic reference is discovered from a search of an abstracting and

indexing dataset, the location of the journal could be discovered from a union catalogue, and the article requested via ILL or document delivery. This joined up integration was impossible with the diversity of interfaces. A dataset independent protocol such as Z39.50 appeared potentially a most important component.

Any particular user group will have interests in a range of datasets from different data providers. The DNER allows a user group to provide access to this range of resources, independent of the data provider, in much the way that a library's books are arranged by subject but not by publisher.

The DNER plans the construction of *portals* to facilitate user-centered access to the resources. Portals are envisaged to be standards-based web-fronted brokers (probably using Z39.50 and other appropriate protocols), similar to the hybrid library broker in Agora, capable of multiple types of integration. This integration would include:

a. Integration of access to existing services, through a variety of entry points tailored to appropriate communities rather than to the data owners, data suppliers or even data types.

b. Integration through enabled cross-searching; the ability in one search to access several datasets (we call this breadth rather than depth searching, as only the common data features will be searchable and some of the functionality will be lost).

c. Integration through linking to value-added services such as ILL, document acquisition transactions, etc, especially in a "joined-up" way where information is carried across appropriately and does not have to be re-keyed.

d. Integration across domains, eg searching across different media types, curatorial traditions etc.

e. Access to a wide range of sources through non-traditional interfaces.

So we have again a 3-layer architecture: a set of resources at the bottom, a set of portals based on brokers in the middle, and the users through web browsers at the top. There would be many cross-linkages between the layers.

The set of portals might include:

- One central, JISC portal: a starting place for anyone, especially those who have not yet identified a specialist portal which suits their needs.
- A set of subject-oriented portals; these are seen as natural extensions of the RDN faculty-level hubs and their associated subject gateways.
- An extension of the hybrid library idea to encompass local portals to the DNER. Local portals could support access to non-JISC resources licensed by the institution. A local portal could even be extended as "personal portals", including access to resources which an individual has subscribed to.
- More specialised portals further into the future. First and simplest of these could be portals dedicated to particular media types such as still images, and time-based media such as movies or sound, or maps.
- Portals with specific world views, such as a geo-spatial portal.

Out of this will emerge the idea of different views of the same data appropriate to different groups of users.

Conclusion

To conclude, the eLib program has developed from a diverse set of projects in Phases 1 and 2 to a rather more focused set in Phase 3, in which the hybrid library projects represent a particularly important strand. The idea of the DNER has developed from simple beginnings to a complex concept of "joined up services". Underlying infrastructure issues including access management, middle-ware and standards have been tackled. A significant portfolio of datasets has been amassed. The future holds increasing attempts to control the increasing diversity by coupling national provision of a DNER, with an institutional emphasis on making digital resources more accessible for learning and teaching.

References

1. AGORA. (1997) University of East Anglia. – Mode of access: http://hosted.ukoln.ac.uk/agora/: 1997.
2. Arts and Humanities Data Service. – London: Kings College, 1995. – Mode of access: http://www.ahds.ac.uk/: 1995.
3. ATHENS. Access management. – NISS. – Mode of access: http://www.athens.ac.uk/: 1997.
4. Brack, V. e-Lib Collection Description Scheme, ver 1.0 / University of Sheffield. – Mode of access: http://www.shef.ac.uk/~riding/cld/cldschem.html: 1999.
5. BUILDER. University of Birminghamm. – Mode of access: http://builder.bham.ac.uk/main.asp: 1997.
6. Dalton, P., Nankivell, C. The University of Birmingham Exam Paper Database: an analysis of user accesses and feedback from 19 December 1998 to 25 June 1999. University of Central England. – Mode of access: http://builder.bham.ac.uk/reports/pdf/exam.pdf: 1999.
7. Dalton, P., Nankivell, C. The University of Birmingham Pilot Electronic Short Loan Service: an analysis of user access logs between 1 January 1999 and 30 June 1999. University of Central England. – Mode of access: http://builder.bham.ac.uk/reports/pdf/esllog.pdf: 1999.
8. Dalton, P., Nankivell, C. Analysis of the questionnaire survey concerning the use of the University of Birmingham Pilot Electronic Short Loan Service. University of Central England. – Mode of access: http://builder.bham.ac.uk/reports/pdf/eslquestionnaire.pdf: 1999.
9. CEDARS. (1998) Consortium of University Research Libraries. – Mode of access: http://www.curl.ac.uk/projects.shtml.: 1998.
10. CLA and the Digitisation of Text. Copyright Licensing Agency. – Mode of access: http://www.cla.co.uk/www/digital.htm: 1999.
11. COPAC. Consortium of University Research Libraries. – Mode of access: http://www.copac.ac.uk/copac/: 1996.
12. The DNER: Description of the DNER. Joint Information Systems Committee. – 1999. – Mode of access: http://www.jisc.ac.uk/pub99/dner_desc.html: 1999.

13. eLib: Electronic Libraries Programme. UK Office for Library and Information Networking. – Mode of access: http://www.ukoln.ac.uk/services/elib/: 1995.

14. Gardner, T., Miller, P., Russell, R. The MIA Logical Architecture. Draft 0.3. UK Office for Library and Information Networking. – 1999. – Mode of access: http://www.ukoln.ac.uk/dlis/models/requirements/arch/:1999.

15. Harris, St. The MALIBU Pre-prototype: broadcast searching disparate HTTP targets. – London: Kings College, 1999. – Mode of access: http://www.kcl.ac.uk/humanities/cch/malibu/reports/searhttp.htm.

16. HeadLine. London School of Economics. – Mode of access: http://www.headline.ac.uk/: 1997.

17. The HeadLine Personal Information Environment (PIE) / London School of Economics. – 1999. – Mode of access: http://www.headline.ac.uk/public/diss/nl-pie.pdf.

18. HERON. University of Stirling. – Mode of access: http://www.stir.ac.uk/infoserv/heron/: 1998.

19. HYLIFE. University of Northumbria at Newcastle. – Mode of access: http://www.unn.ac.uk/~xcu2/hylife/: 1997.

20. HYLIFE Annual report. University of Northumbria at Newcastle. – 1999. – Mode of access: http://www.unn.ac.uk/~xcu2/hylife/Annrephome.html: 1999.

21. Internet Archaeology. (1996) Council for British Archaeology. – Mode of access: http://intarch.ac.uk/: 1996.

22. JISC Circular 5/99. Joint Information Systems Committee. – Mode of access: http://www.jisc.ac.uk/pub99/c05_99.html: 1999.

23. Imesh Toolkit. UK Office for Library and Information Networking. – Mode of access: http://www.imesh.org/toolkit/: 1999.

24. An integrated information environment for higher education: developing the Distributed, National Electronic Resource (DNER). Joint Information Systems Committee. – 1997. – Mode of access: http://www.jisc.ac.uk/cei/dner_colpol.html.

25. Joint Funding Councils' Libraries Review Group: Report. – Bristol: HEFCE. – 1993.

26. Lunau, C., Miller, P., Moen, W. E. The Bath Profile: An International Z39.50 Specification for Library Applications and Resource Discovery: (draft) / UK Office for Library and Information Networking. – 1999. – Mode of access: http://www.ukoln.ac.uk/interop-focus/activities/z3950/int_profile/bath/draft/stable1.html.

27. MALIBU. (1997) London: Kings College. – Mode of access: http://www.kcl.ac.uk/humanities/cch/malibu/: 1997.

28. National Electronic Site Licence Initiative. University of Manchester. – Mode of access: http://www.nesli.ac.uk/: 1998.

29. Newton-Ingham, G., Palmer, D, Kay, D., Smith, N. Agora Hybrid Library Management System (HLMS) requirements catalogue: release 1 specification / University of East Anglia. – 1999. - Mode of access: http://hosted.ukoln.ac.uk/agora/documents/agora_spec_public1.doc.

30. Powell, A. The Resource Discovery Network (RDN) architecture / UK Office for Library and Information Networking. – Mode of access: http://www.ukoln.ac.uk/dlis/models/models9/presentations/rdn.ppt: 1999.

31. Resource Discovery Network. – London Kings College, 1999. – Mode of access: http://www.ukoln.ac.uk/dlis/models/models9/presentations/rdn.ppt.

32. Shelfmark & Resource Locator (SHERLOC). – London School of Economics. – 1999. – Mode of access: http://decomate.lse.ac.uk/john/cgi-bin/sherloc/sherloc.cgi.

33. Wissenburg, Astrid. MALIBU: Hybrid Library Models version 1. – London: Kings College, 1999. – Mode of access: http://www.kcl.ac.uk/humanities/cch/malibu/reports/modv1.htm.

THE RELATIONSHIP BETWEEN NATIONAL AND INSTITUTIONAL ELECTRONIC LIBRARY DEVELOPMENTS IN THE Uk: AN OVERVIEW

Stephen Pinfield

Academic Services Librarian, University of Nottingham, UK

Abstract

National co-ordination has been an important feature of electronic library development in the UK university sector. This paper looks at the issue of national co-ordination and how it affects local institutions in four main ways. Firstly some of the main features of national co-ordination are identified. Secondly, the impact this has had on institutions is analysed. Thirdly, some of the key issues associated with the relationship between national agencies and local institutions are discussed. Fourthly, the possible future impact of the increasingly important policy agendas of 'regionalisation' and 'globalisation' are highlighted. The paper discusses major services delivered on a national basis and also major research and development programmes, such as eLib (the Electronic Libraries Programme). It emphasises the importance of the co-ordinated approach to electronic library development now being taken as part of the DNER (Distributed National Electronic Resource) initiative. It is argued that, based on the UK experience, national co-ordination of developments can result in considerable benefits but that the benefits rely on the national strategy remaining in touch with the needs of users in local institutions.

Introduction

One of the important features of electronic library development in the UK university sector has been national co-ordination. This paper focuses on the issue of national co-ordination and how it affects institutions in four main ways:

1. some of the main features of national co-ordination of UK electronic library developments over the last ten years are identified
2. the impact it has had on individual institutions is analysed
3. some of the key issues associated with the interface between national agencies and local institutions are discussed
4. the increasingly important regional and international agendas in the UK are highlighted.

It will be argued here, based on the UK experience, that national co-ordination of developments can result in considerable benefits but that the benefits rely on the national strategy being in touch with the needs of users in local institutions. National co-ordination should not be an end in itself: it is only 'a good thing' when it helps to get the information to the users.

The issues are viewed in this paper from the perspective of a manager within an institutional library service with previous experience of working on a nationally funded electronic library project. However, it is hoped that the discussion may be of interest to others, including those not based in the UK. Some of the points raised may have relevance for those involved in regional co-ordination and consortia-based developments elsewhere.

Background

The ways in which national co-ordination can be achieved (if at all) depend to a large extent on the wider national context. The UK has a tradition of national co-ordination of many kinds – political, economic, legal. The structure of UK government has traditionally been well suited to UK-wide initiatives. Such initiatives are also common in the general library world in the UK, quite apart from electronic library developments. For example, the British Library provides a national inter-library loan system which satisfies the vast majority of traditional ILL requests in the UK.

National co-ordination is also a feature of the funding arrangements for the UK university ('higher education' or HE) sector. National co-ordination of HE electronic library development has been achievable in large measure because of this. As Figure 1 illustrates, all universities in the UK (with one or two notable exceptions) are funded by central government through the Department for Education and Skills (although some research grants are provided by other government departments). The DfES works through the Higher Education Funding Councils (there are separate funding councils for England, Wales, Scotland and Northern Ireland) which allocate funds directly to institutions. The funding councils also place some HE funds in the hands of national co-ordinating bodies, one of which is the Joint Information Systems Committee (JISC). JISC is jointly supported by all of the funding councils, and carries out work centrally for UK universities. It is the JISC (or its predecessor equivalents) which has been responsible for much of the co-ordinated electronic library development in the UK.

Figure 1: The funding structure of national developments

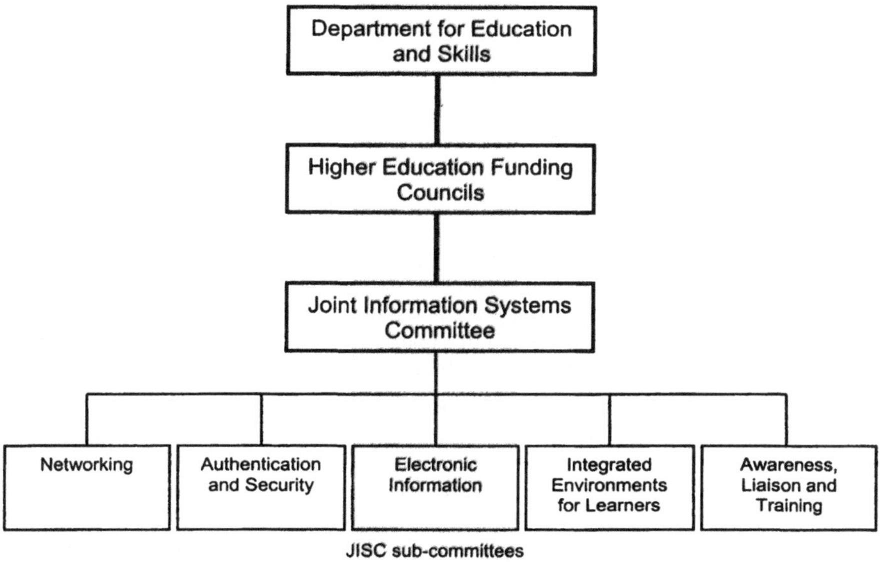

The mission of JISC is "to stimulate and enable the cost effective exploitation of information systems and to provide a high quality national network infrastructure for the UK higher education and research councils communities" [1]. The basic rationale for JISC activity is that it "should demonstrably add value beyond that which could be achieved by institutions acting individually or collectively." At the time of writing, JISC attempted to achieve this aim through five sub-committees: networking, authentication and security, electronic information, integrated environments for learners, and awareness, liaison and training [2]. These sub-committees represent a wide range of interests and activities, many of which have some impact electronic library developments. Of course, JISC is not the only body to provide funding for national electronic library developments. Other funding has come from the European Union or from commercial organisations; but JISC is the most significant.

Features of National Co-ordination

The fact that most co-ordinating activity is being carried out by one body has not meant that national co-ordination in the UK is monolithic. On the contrary, it has occurred in different ways at different times and has therefore had differing impacts on institutions. The differing forms of UK national co-ordination may be summarised as follows:

- National infrastructure services
- Communications services
- Content services
- Negotiating services
- Middleware services
- Research and development funding
- Advisory and expert services
- Standards and guidelines
- Training and awareness services

These are discussed in turn with most attention being given to content services and research and development funding.

National Infrastructure and Communications Services

The most significant service in the infrastructure area is the Joint Academic Network (JANET) [3]. JANET is a high speed network linking universities to each other and the outside world via the Internet. It has been in existence for well over a decade and been continually upgraded. The latest version of SuperJANET (as it now known) is expected to be upgraded to be a 20Gb core network in 2002.

JANET has provided the foundation for electronic library developments. For institutions, it has meant that access to the Internet has been heavily subsidised at national level. Institutions have to fund their own local area networks, and moderate charges for transatlantic traffic are in place, but Internet use is still very inexpensive to institutions. Costs for transatlantic traffic have been kept to a minimum by the introduction of other complementary services, the national cache and the national mirror. Together these services are clear examples of the systemic coherence of service provision that is possible with national co-ordination.

For users in institutions, the Internet has always been free at the point of access. This has created a culture in UK HE of high Internet usage – an ideal climate for the development of networked electronic library services. JISC itself has attempted to encourage network usage of all kinds. For example, users have been encouraged to use the network for communication by the establishment of national services such as Mailbase and its successor service, JISCmail, which have run e-mail discussion lists for the UK university community [4].

As well as providing the network and encouraging people to use it, JISC has also funded the development of three National Data Centres to manage content on it. The Data Centres, BIDS, MIMAS and EDINA [5], are housed in the Universities of Bath, Manchester and Edinburgh respectively. Between them they provide the national organisational infrastructure for electronic content provision. Since the establishment of the first Data Centre, BIDS in 1991, a wide range of significant datasets has been made available on the network, first via telnet then on the web.

Content and Negotiating Services

Large amounts of JISC investment have been concentrated on creating or delivering electronic content. This content has taken a large number of forms: "scholarly journals, monographs, textbooks, abstracts, manuscripts, maps, music scores, still images, geospatial images and other kinds of vector and numeric data, as well as moving picture and sound collections" [6]. The content has been provided in different ways which have led to a variety institutional responses.

The main ways in which national content has been delivered are:

1. JISC (or a JISC-assisted service) has funded the production and delivery of content
2. JISC has acquired externally produced content and then
   i. managed and delivered content with its own user interface, or
   ii. managed and delivered content with the publisher's interface
3. JISC has negotiated access to the publisher's site
4. JISC has provided content for institutions to deliver.

Firstly then, some content has been provided by JISC (or JISC-funded services) where JISC has financed the production of the data itself and also its delivery (category 1 above). Examples of this are the Internet subject gateways, such as SOSIG, OMNI, and EEVL [7]. These services provide searchable metadata for quality web resources in defined subject areas. They are based in various university institutions in the UK. For example, OMNI, the medical and health sciences gateway, is based at the University of Nottingham. The first group of these gateways were set up as projects under the eLib programme (see below) but are now run as mature services. More recently, they have been grouped together within the JISC strategy into the Resource Discovery Network (RDN) and their work co-ordinated by a national team [8]. Gateways have been brought together into subject discipline clusters (so called 'hubs') and encouraged to expand their activities into major subject portals. New hubs have also been set up to plug subject gaps. Action has also been taken to ensure that they all interoperate and have compatible collection policies.

The great advantage for institutions of these services funded and delivered by JISC is that they are free at the institutional level. JISC has often provided services which are of considerable value to institutional users, some of which would not have been provided by commercial suppliers. In some cases they have been taken up and used enthusiastically in institutions. In others, it must be said, take-up has been patchy. It has become clear that making resources available is one thing, getting people to use it is quite another. Sometimes the problem lies with the services. Many were developed as projects on tight budgets and it has taken them time to achieve a critical mass of material. Sometimes it is a problem of marketing. National services have often relied on institutions to market them to local users. This has not always happened.

As well as providing its own content, JISC has also provided access to the content of other (often commercial) providers. Sometimes a Data Centre takes a publisher's data and provides access to it via an interface developed by the Data Centre (category 2i). Perhaps the best known example of this is the BIDS ISI service, which between 1991 and 2000 provided access to the ISI citation indexes. This service has had a major impact on UK HE. It has played an important role in encouraging staff and research students in particular to use electronic information.

The take-up of BIDS ISI during the 1990s was remarkable [9]. In the early days, it was one of the first self-service online resources. Institutions were charged at a fixed annual rate (rather than 'pay as you go'), which meant that they have been able to encourage end users to carry out their own searches without having to worry about the bill. The system was designed by BIDS with UK HE in mind and was regularly improved in line with feedback from the community. It also produced high quality documentation and marketing material. All of this created a sense of ownership within the UK university community – this might not have been the case with a simple commercially provided resource. More recently, other services have been designed along the same lines. BIDS has spun off a commercial service, Ingenta (which aggregates full text e-journals from various publishers), and EDINA has developed its own range of services, such as Digimap (which delivers UK mapping data).

However, some publishers have been unwilling to hand their data over in such a way and have preferred to deliver it through their own branded interface (category 2ii). This is now the case, for example, with the ISI indexes. BIDS ISI has now been replaced by the ISI Web of Science service which has the standard ISI user interface. It is still a JISC-supported service and is now served from MIMAS. Similarly, EDINA provides access to a number of Ovid datasets, using the Ovid user interface. JISC has been involved in negotiating deals of this sort with a wide range of publishers of electronic information.

On occasions, the role of JISC has been limited to negotiating access on behalf of the community and has not taken direct responsibility for delivering the data (category 3). JISC negotiates access to a service but the publisher still manages the data at its own site. An example is the Oxford English Dictionary online service. It is also true of a large number of e-journal deals for which JISC has set up a negotiating agency. JISC is now also negotiating with e-book suppliers. The advantages for institutions of JISC-led negotiations are obvious but very important. A nationally negotiated package often results in a better deal for each individual institution. There are usually standardised licenses and access agreements. These factors have been crucial in encouraging UK universities to invest in electronic library services. However, there is a downside. This and the preceding model of national content provision mean that JISC has little control over the presentation of the data itself. Wide disparities of user interface and access method have often resulted.

The final form of JISC-supported content provision is a relatively new one. Here a JISC service produces digital content which is delivered at an institutional level (category 4). This category refers specifically to HERON (Higher Education Resources On Demand) [10], a service which acts as a national clearing house for copyright permissions for course readings. In particular, it was set up to deal with electronic copyright permissions. Once copyright permission has been obtained for material, HERON offers a digitisation service and then supplies institutions directly with digitised files. Institutions then mount the files for their own users [11]. Although institutions pay a fee for this service, the signs are that this is considerably cheaper than each institution seeking permissions individually. Whether it is still cheap enough remains a moot point.

These various categories of national content services in the UK are not watertight but they are indicative of the range of possibilities. Other models of content delivery may emerge, especially in relation to images and moving images, in the future. The current models range from the position where institutions are consumers of free services to where they are purchasers of commercial services. Sometimes institutions benefit from free high quality data, sometimes from a tailored interface, sometimes from a better price. There are normally economies of scale and avoidance of duplication. National co-ordination does normally play to institutional advantage.

Take-up of content services offered on a national basis has however varied considerably. For reasons of price alone, take-up in any one institution of the range of services is only ever partial. On occasions, institutions have complained they are not aware of the range of resources available to them. Even when an institution does take a service there may be a problem of take-up *within* the institution. There are marketing responsibilities here. JISC has to market services to institutions and institutions have to market services to users. Both are essential if national provision is to be successful. Both could be improved.

Content Coherence and the DNER

There is still a major problem. The problem of incoherence. It is a problem at both national and institutional levels. At a national level, it is clear that the range of services offered are to a large extent separate and self-contained. They are available in different places with different interfaces and different access methods. At an institutional level, the problem of incoherence is compounded by the fact that there is a wide range of electronic services (JISC and non-JISC) plus services in other formats. Institutions find it increasingly difficult to present users with a coherent view of the wide range of different resources available to them – local and remote, printed and electronic. What can be done?

At a national level, there are a number of important developments. Perhaps the most significant of these is that national content services are now being managed at a strategic level in a more co-ordinated way. The concept of the Distributed National Electronic Resource (DNER) has been formulated to give these various national services a coherent identity. At the same time, JISC has appointed a DNER directorate to give the developments a strategic direction. JISC strategy documents characterise the DNER as "... a managed environment for accessing quality information resources on the Internet which are available from many sources." As such it encompasses the work of the Data Centres, RDN subject hubs, and JISC-provided and JISC-negotiated datasets. The DNER directorate has as one of its strategic aims to bring "coherence out of chaos". It has now developed a collection policy and a technical strategy and these are beginning to be implemented [12]. The latter involves the whole question of interoperability and interconnectivity – attempting to get services to release their value to a greater extent by enabling them to be used in a more integrated way. The possibilities of developing common user interfaces (using, for example, Z39.50), or of linking between bibliographic and full-text services are currently being considered. The amount of control the DNER team has over the data and its presentation varies, but it is hoped that by operating on a national scale the community can where necessary use its market power to influence data providers.

It is envisaged that the DNER will be accessed through various portals – based perhaps on subject or community, but institutional entry points into the services will always be amongst the most important. In providing these entry points to the DNER, institutions themselves are also addressing the issue of coherence. Most are currently taking a pragmatic view of the situation by trying to construct information landscapes for users based on their web sites. These information landscapes have to provide users with a view of the range of information resources available to them. DNER resources are only one part of the picture. At the University of Nottingham, we have designed the Library Services web site to act as a gateway to the range of resources available to users [13]. The site provides access to the web OPAC (Aleph) and two other web-enabled databases. The latter provide access to 'Subject Resources' (a collection of key resources in all formats – web resources, CD-ROMs, printed materials and so on) and e-journals [14]. The site is based on a subject approach. Rather than listing material by format or source, users are encouraged to look at material by subject. It is hoped that this will enable users to obtain a more coherent view of the resources available.

This kind of pragmatic approach is important, but only partial. Further research needs to be carried out on how institutions can tackle this problem in the medium term. The DNER directorate has already begun to make efforts to help institutions provide access to data over which it has direct control by local means. The new pilot service, RDN-I, allows institutions to cross search all of the subject gateways simultaneously, providing the search form and results from within the institutional web interface. This is an interesting early example of where national and institutional efforts to achieve coherence are coming together. At the same time, research is being carried out on the potential of the new generation of products on the market which address the coherence issue. These include Ex Libris' MetaLib/SFX, OCLC's WebExpress, and Fretwell Downing's VDX.

Middleware Services

Another way in which the problem of coherence from the user perspective is being addressed is in the development of middleware initiatives. Perhaps the most significant of these is the national authentication service, ATHENS. ATHENS provides an important standard authentication front door to the DNER. As many as 70 services now have ATHENS authentication. Because of the growing importance of the ATHENS service, many commercial data providers have made their services ATHENS-compliant. The service has been taken up enthusiastically by institutions. There are now 700,000 ATHENS user accounts in 300 institutions. Although this is a national service, much of the administration is devolved to institutions. This is however considered to be acceptable (at least in the short term) simply because the benefits to the user are significant. Users can access a wide range of resources using only one username and password. In the medium term, ATHENS will be replaced with a more flexible system which has been given the working name of SPARTA.

R&D Funding

As well as providing a series of 'hard' services (the network, content, authentication), JISC has also supported a number of 'soft' initiatives to complement the services. One of these is research and development (R&D) funding. Perhaps the most significant programme in this area has been eLib, the Electronic Libraries development programme [15]. This programme was launched in 1994 and was completed in 2001. It was a nationally co-ordinated programme with a central directorate which provided support for projects and monitored their development. Projects were carried out within individual or institutions consortia, but these were funded centrally by JISC with some institutional contributions. Institutions went through a competitive bidding process for the available funds and bids had to be focused in broad areas defined centrally [16].

The first phases of eLib (phases 1 and 2) concentrated on a number of different areas:

- Electronic publishing: including projects developing e-journals, pre-prints, electronic short loan, on-demand publishing, digitisation, digital images, quality assurance.
- Resource access: including document delivery, access to network resources.
- Training and awareness.
- Supporting studies.

In total there were about 60 projects, accounting for £15 million between 1994 and 1998. The third and final phase of eLib built on many of the emerging lessons of phases 1 and 2. In particular, it attempted to address the issues of information coherence and service implementation. How could these separate technologies and services be taken forward in a more integrated and mature way? Phase 3 had the following strands:

- 'Hybrid libraries': aiming to set up models and exemplars of how libraries can be given coherence.
- Clumps': implementing Z39.50 to create virtual union catalogues.
- Digital preservation: investigating issues, promoting awareness and making recommendations.
- Projects to services: allowing selected phase 1 and 2 projects to continue their services until they could become self-supporting.

In all, there were 20 phase 3 projects, funded to the tune of £5 million. Most of these projects reported in 2001 but their work was already beginning to have an impact on the technical development and strategies of JISC and of individual institutions before this. Aspects of DNER strategy have for example clearly been influenced by eLib.

The impact of eLib on institutions still needs to be systematically analysed but it is certainly clear that it has had a profound effect at a local level. Since over 100 higher education institutions have been directly involved in eLib projects, the impact has also been widespread. Some of the consequences of eLib at the institutional level can already be identified:

- Many successful JISC services (such as subject hubs and HERON) grew out of early eLib projects.
- Many of the projects proved to be genuinely valuable to the institutions which housed them by enhancing local services.
- eLib concentrated on practical development work rather than pure research. This meant that many technologies could be quickly applied by others and were scalable.
- eLib has acted as a catalyst for electronic library development in institutions outside the projects themselves. Many of the concepts involved and many of the learning outcomes from projects have filtered into library organisations. eLib projects had a brief to disseminate their work as widely as possible. Many have done this successfully and have become exemplars for other local initiatives.

- eLib had the effect of creating new technical and managerial skills and a newly skilled group of staff in UK HE who have been of great benefit to institutions.
- eLib had a major impact, amongst all staff, on the culture of organisations and the academic library and information profession.
- It has often been a useful focus for library and computer service staff to work together often in multi-skilled teams.
- eLib has had the effect of improving project planning and working in institutions.
- With externally funded projects comes bidding, it is noticeable that a bidding culture has also developed.
- Because some institutions become good at bidding and others do not, eLib did in some respects lead to the development of 'haves' and 'have nots'. Some institutions were successful in attracting funding and running multiple projects, others were not.
- Many eLib projects were implemented by consortia. The programme has encouraged partnerships between HEIs.
- eLib has also enabled institutions to engage in a dialogue with commercial suppliers. Some have participated as partners in projects, others have simply monitored technical outcomes. In either case, eLib has helped to affect their agenda and has influenced technical directions.

Some have argued that eLib activity might have been even more closely co-ordinated. Amongst the projects, work was sometimes duplicated. There were, for example, several similar 'electronic short loan' (e-reserve) projects. However, it is worth noting that some projects working in the same areas were more successful than others. Funding a number of projects in the same areas has led to the opportunity to make evaluative comparisons. More co-ordination might have been achieved in other areas, however. At a central level, eLib was run in parallel with another JISC R&D programme, JTAP (JISC Technology Applications Programme). It is ironic that although both programmes were co-ordinated nationally and both had a great deal in common, they were run by different JISC committees and were never fully co-ordinated with each other! It is encouraging that the recent JISC calls for programmes which succeed eLib and JTAP have involved more explicit co-ordination.

The importance of directed R&D is set to continue. Although the name eLib has been dropped, major new R&D projects to enhance the DNER are now being funded by JISC. [17]. JISC has invested £14 million for the period 2000 to 2003. There are DNER development projects in the following areas:

- Learning and teaching: including access to learning and teaching resources, enhancing JISC data services, images, moving images and sound, museum content.
- Infrastructure projects: including Z39.50 development, RDN development, the join-up between references and full text.
- Special studies: including investigation on the link between the electronic library and learning technologies.
- Evaluation.

These projects, being carried out in institutions throughout the UK, are taking the practical development approach adopted by eLib. They are extending electronic library research into new areas to support research, learning and teaching.

Other National Services

As programmes like eLib progressed and as institutions launched their own electronic library initiatives, it became clear that similar issues were being raised in many places. Partly in response to this, JISC has funded (or partially funded) a number of advisory and expert services to serve the national community. These include the HEDS (Higher Education Digitisation Service), TASI (Technical Advisory Service on Images) and UKOLN (UK Office for Library and information Networking) [18]. These services have different remits but carry out research, produce documentation, act as consultants, and in some cases carry out practical work for institutions. Many of these services are free to institutions.

Linked to this, JISC has also supported the development of a series of national guidelines and standards. For example, JISC has produced guidelines for the production of institutional information strategies [19]. Various JISC agencies have also been active in contributing to international standards such as Dublin Core and Z39.50 [20]. Finally, JISC agencies have been set up to carry out training and marketing activities. One example of this is Netskills [21]. Initially an eLib project but now a stand-alone service, Netskills is an Internet training organisation, producing online training packages, documentation and carrying out training activities.

Once again these services have supplemented and supported institutional provision. Often they have provided a valuable way of avoiding duplicating work or have saved institutions money by providing expert assistance at subsidised rates. These services have begun to play a significant role in embedding nationally co-ordinated services in local implementations. Local implementations are however going at different speeds and with different emphases. The relationship between the central and the local can always be strengthened to improve this.

National and Institutional Issues

Having discussed national developments and their immediate impact on institutions, it is now possible to draw together some key issues. There are key benefits at the institutional level of nationally co-ordinated developments in the UK. Institutions benefit from a wide range of services (infrastructure, content, middleware, expert support and so on) which are inexpensive or even free. These services are often tailored to local needs. Institutional provision is usually simplified by standard national licences and access agreements. These are significant benefits, but a number of issues remain which require further discussion.

Perhaps most importantly, institutions and co-ordinating bodies need to maintain an awareness of the limitations of co-ordination. It is not a panacea. It will not solve all of an institution's problems. It should aim to solve some of them and should always be designed to support and enhance institutional provision. As such it should stay in touch with the needs and concerns of institutions.

Any attempt to build a national electronic library collection in particular needs to have institutional requirements at its centre. For example, there is little use in striving for a coherent, self-contained collection at the national level when access to it by users in institutions will always be partial and when nationally provided resources will only ever be part of the totality of information resources available to users in their institutions. The national collection should be built to ensure it can be used in the way institutions need to use it. Institutions should be assisted in various technical and organisational ways to give their users access to national services.

The issue of coherence should continue to be seriously addressed at both the national and the institutional level if users are to take full advantage of resources available. There are signs that this is beginning to happen at the national level as well as locally.

The problem of incoherence is not one that can be solved by the higher education community alone, of course. It requires the responsiveness of commercial providers, many of whom operate at a multinational level. How far should a national agency go in trying to intervene in the market? Should national co-ordination simply be involved in negotiating deals on behalf of institutions? Should it act as a corrective to the market by setting up services which the market will not? Should it fund research and development work which may then be used by the commercial suppliers (or does this amount to doing their work for them)? Should it encourage commercial suppliers to provide certain services (such as Z39.50 or OpenURLs) which they may not otherwise do? JISC has certainly answered in the affirmative to many of these questions; if it is to continue to be as active there has to be a clear strategy and sufficient funding.

If national agencies are involved in setting up non-commercial services, the issue of sustainability becomes crucial. JISC has attempted to encourage some services, like the subject gateways to become self-supporting (through sponsorship and advertising). But the success of this has been variable. A humanities service will always find it more difficult to gain commercial sponsorship than say a business studies one. If a resource is worth having, is it not worth funding? If so, who should fund it? Many institutions would claim that implementing nationally funded projects or housing nationally-assisted services actually results in substantial hidden costs locally which are difficult to justify within the institution.

This is not just a financial question. In many other ways the demarcation line between the national agencies and the institutions is unclear. Who is responsible for what? At present, for example, who is responsible for developing e-print archives? Should institutions wait for this to be co-ordinated at a national level or should they begin investing locally?

Some have argued that too much national co-ordination stifles local innovation. It has been suggested, for example, that there is a danger of a 'vision gap' developing amongst some senior library managers in institutions. Instead of seeing what needs to be done and driving developments themselves, they may be inclined to sit back and wait for things to happen or at least be told what to do. National agencies need to guard against this over-reliance on their work by ensuring the agendas of national bodies are kept in synchronicity with institutional needs. Strategy should be formed by a process that is as much bottom up as top down. Of course, national agencies, such as JISC, are largely composed of representatives from institutions but they need to ensure that they put in place clear mechanisms for communicating with institutional policy makers more widely.

This is particularly important now since institutional library managers increasingly need to ensure that electronic library strategy fits in with other institutional aims. For example, there are pressures in most UK institutions at present to develop sophisticated virtual learning environments for students. The question of how the electronic library fits into these learning environments needs to be addressed. Once again, national strategy needs to ensure that these institutional concerns are taken into account.

It has already been pointed out that providing information resources is one thing, but getting them to be used is quite another. National initiatives have often suffered from patchy implementation in institutions. As well as ensuring that communication between institutions is enhanced, marketing to users also needs to be improved. This applies at both a national and an institutional level. National services are however best marketed at an institutional level. Strategies need to be put in place by national agencies to assist institutions in marketing services to their users.

The complexities of national co-ordination need to be managed carefully if it is to be successful. In the UK considerable progress has been achieved through national co-ordination, but the balance between national strategy and institutional implementation needs to be kept under constant review. This can only be achieved where institutions and national agencies are working in partnership to serve users.

The Future: Regional and International Developments

The JISC strategic aims for 2001 to 2005 include "regionalisation" and "globalisation" of its activities. It is yet to be seen precisely what these aims will mean on the ground, but they could potentially have a profound effect.

The regional agenda is one which is affecting all aspects of UK society at the moment. Greater powers have been devolved to the different countries of the UK (not strictly 'regions') and the regions of England. JANET has increasingly become based on a series of Metropolitan Area Networks which are supported regionally. Regional co-operation in library development of all kinds is becoming more common. Many regions may soon be able to lead on developments which may benefit their particular user communities. There is the distinct possibility that the 'evenness' of national provision at present may be affected as different parts of the UK advance at different rates. It will be interesting to see how the national and regional agendas interact.

Whilst there are pressures to devolve some activities to a regional level, there are equally others to operate on an international level. Many aspects of electronic library development do not know national borders. Technical standards, for example, need to be worked out on an international basis. JISC is already active in this area. Partnerships in research and development, and service delivery are also already beginning to happen [22]. Since many of the advantages of national co-ordination may also apply to international co-ordination these developments should be encouraged. It should be emphasised however that the needs of users in the institutions must be at the centre of these developments. The success of the developments should be judged by their impact on the working lives of university staff and students on the ground.

Conclusion

User needs should be at the heart of electronic library development. In the UK, major initiatives at a national level have enabled institutions to improve the service they provide to their users. With a co-ordinated DNER strategy, this is set to continue. It is important that this strategy does not just involve enlargement of the collections but also improvements in the ways national agencies assist institutions to market and deliver the services to users. The relationship between the national agencies and institutions is crucial, but even more important is the relationship between users and service providers, institutional and national. The national-institutional partnership is only worthwhile if it is used as a way of improving services to users.

Acronyms

ATHENS – UK HE authentication service

BIDS – Bath Information Data Services

DfES – Department for Education and Skills

DNER – Distributed National Electronic Resource

EDINA – Edinburgh University Data Library

EEVL – Edinburgh Engineering Virtual Library

eLib – Electronic Libraries Programme

HE – Higher Education (university level education)

HEI – Higher Education Institution

HERON – Higher Education Resources On Demand

JANET – Joint Academic Network

JISC – Joint Information Systems Committee

JTAP – JISC Technology Applications Programme

MIMAS - Manchester Information and Associated Services

NESLI – National Electronic Site Licence Initiative

OMNI – Organising Medical Networked Information

OPAC – Online Public Access Catalogue

R&D – Research and Development

RDN – Resource Discovery Network

SOSIG – Social Science Information Gateway

UKOLN – UK Office for Library and Information Networking

Acknowledgements

This paper was originally published in the IFLA conference proceedings under the title 'Managing academic libraries in a digital world: institutional, regional and national developments in the UK' (*Proceedings of the 66th IFLA general conference*, Jerusalem, Israel, 13-18 August 2000, available at http://www.ifla.org/IV/ifla66/papers/130-132e.htm). A number of details in the paper have been updated here but it remains substantially unchanged. A previous revision was published in the *New Review of Academic Librarianship*, 6, 2000, pp. 3-20. Thanks to Taylor Graham, publishers of NRAL, for permission to re-publish the article. Thanks to Reg Carr and Lorcan Dempsey for their comments on the original conference paper.

References

1. Mode of access: http://www.jisc.ac.uk.

2. The structure of JISC of course changes from time to time. The names of national committees have also changed. This paper will refer to JISC where this is taken to include parts of JISC, JISC-assisted services or their predecessor equivalents.
3. Mode of access: http://www.ja.net.
4. Mode of access: http://www.jiscmail.ac.uk.
5. BIDS (Bath Information and Data Services). – Mode of access: http://www.bids.ac.uk; MIMAS (Manchester Information and Associated Services). – Mode of access: http://www.mimas.ac.uk; EDINA (Edinburgh University Data Library). – Mode of access: http://edina.ed.ac.uk.
6. Adding Value to the UK's Learning, Teaching and Research Resources: the Distributed National Electronic Resource (DNER).' JISC working paper. – 1999. – October. – Mode of access: http://www.jisc.ac.uk/pub99/dner_vision.html.
7. SOSIG (Social Science Information Gateway). – Mode of access: http://www.sosig.ac.uk; OMNI (Organising Medical Networked Information). – Mode of access: http://omni.ac.uk; EEVL (Edinburgh Engineering Virtual Library). – Mode of access: http://eevl.ac.uk.
8. Mode of access: http://www.rdn.ac.uk.
9. For a discussion of the success of BIDS ISI see: Morrow, T. 'BIDS – the growth of a networked end-user bibliographic database service': Program. – 1995. - Vol 29, N 1. – P. 31-41; Stephen Pinfield 'The use of BIDS ISI in a research university: a case study of the University of Birmingham': Program. – 1998. – Vol. 32, N 3. – 225-240.
10. Mode of access: http://www.heron.ac.uk.
11. Mode of access: http://builder.bham.ac.uk/documentation/electronicshortloan/esl-heron/index.asp.
12. For the DNER collections strategy. – Mode of access: http://www.jisc.ac.uk/dner/collections/strategy.htm; For the technical architecture. – Mode of access: http://www.ukoln.ac.uk/distributed-systems/dner/arch.
13. Mode of access: http://www.nottingham.ac.uk/library.
14. See: Gardner, M., Pinfield, S. Database-backed library web sites: a case study of the use of PHP and MySQL at the University of Nottingham // Program. – 2001. – Vol. 35, N 1. – P. 33-42.
15. Mode of access: http://www.ukoln.ac.uk/services/elib.
16. Rusbridge, Ch. Towards the hybrid library // D-Lib Magazine. – 1998. – July/August. – Mode of access: http://www.dlib.org/dlib/july98/rusbridge/07rusbridge.html.
17. Mode of access: http://www.jisc.ac.uk/dner/programmes.
18. HEDS (Higher Education Digitisation Service). – Mode of access: http://heds.herts.ac.uk; TASI (Technical Advisory Service on Images). – Mode of access: http://www.tasi.ac.uk; UKOLN (UK Office for Library and Information Networking). – Mode of access: http://www.ukoln.ac.uk.
19. Mode of access: http://www.jisc.ac.uk/info_strat.

20. Mode of access: http://www.ukoln.ac.uk/interop-focus; UKOLN. – Mode of access: http://www.ukoln.ac.uk/metadata.
21. Mode of access: http://www.netskills.ac.uk.
22. For example: in 1999 JISC funded a number of R&D projects jointly with the National Science Foundation in the USA.

GLOBAL KNOWLEDGE: A CHALLENGE FOR LIBRARIANS

Christopher Edwards

Information Services, the British Council
United Kingdom

This paper describes how the information and communication technologies are creating the knowledge society, which will impact upon developing and transitional economies as well as developed nations. It argues that librarians have an important role to play in overcoming the digital divide, and makes reference to the Global Knowledge Partnership.

The so-called law of IT which states that computers double in power each year, and halve in price is well known. What's essential, as Nicholas Negroponte has stressed, is that the growth is not linear but exponential, and in any exponential curve, most of the gain comes right at the end. After fifty years of innovation, the curve is almost vertical and we are in the midst of a revolution - or, if you are more optimistic, a renaissance - made possible by Information and Communications Technologies. What we couldn't imagine yesterday is possible today, and will probably be done tomorrow.

Defining a revolution-in-progress is like mapping the larva flow from an active volcano - well neigh impossible and extremely dangerous. Almost every aspect of our lives seems to be changing; and it does feel as if many of the familiar economic, political and social structures of the 20th century are being eroded, and reformed for the new millennium. It can be difficult to determine cause and effect, but I think it is plausible to say that the rapid development and convergence of communications, computing and digital content is enabling the globalization of production; stimulating enterprise and creativity. This is what is meant by the "knowledge driven economy", recently defined by the British government as "one in which the generation and exploitation of knowledge plays the predominant part in the creation of wealth. It is not simply about pushing back the frontiers of knowledge; it is also about more effective use and exploitation of all types of knowledge in all manner of economic activity" [1]. In fact, knowledge-based goods and services already make up over 60% of OECD countries' wealth production, and the knowledge economy - which includes information & communication technologies, publishing, media and research - is the fastest growing part of the global economy.

But the changes are not just economic. One reason for this is that we are also seeing the globalization of expectations. These can be material expectations, but they can also be political, cultural and educational, and these expectations are beginning to challenge the role and sovereignty of the nation state. So to does the fact that knowledge-based industries are highly mobile and distributed, and thus not easily regulated within national borders.

However, the shift of power is by no means all upwards. ICT also empowers local communities (and geographically distributed virtual communities, too): we see this most clearly in the UK right now, as the Westminster government cedes authority both to the European Union and to a new parliament in Scotland).

And the knowledge society enables (perhaps requires?) more participative democracy and stronger civil society institutions - for if the key commodity is knowledge, then such values as openness, trust and legitimacy are crucially important. I should, of course, include Library Associations amongst the fundamental civil society institutions.

This knowledge revolution - or renaissance - is not just a matter for the richest countries, for the fifth of the world's population which consumes 84% of its total income. The Information and Communication Technologies have the potential to improve the lot of the most disadvantaged. There is now wide recognition that information and knowledge are key in the fight against poverty. As Kofi Annan put it back in 1997:

Information and knowledge are expanding in quantity and accessibility. In many fields future decision-makers will be presented with unprecedented new tools for development. In such fields as agriculture, health, education, human resources and environmental management, or transport and business development, the consequences really could be revolutionary. Communication and information technology has enormous potential, especially for developing countries and in furthering sustainable development.

How might this happen? The UN Human Development Report 1999 suggested three principal ways:

- Firstly, by providing information - that is to say, for example, by allowing doctors in isolated hospitals, teachers in under-funded universities to access a wide range of current and desperately-needed information and distance-learning materials without having to meet the huge infrastructure and running costs of traditional libraries.
- Secondly, by empowering small players to compete in the global marketplace. The internet gives small and medium sized enterprises the ability to cut administrative costs, respond quickly to changes in demand, and supply world markets - in other words, to begin to challenge the big corporations. The emergence of India as a world player in the software industry demonstrates this, and there are plenty of smaller, non-technical successes stories too - such as Tropical Whole Foods, as UK company selling fairly traded fruits from co-operatives and small businesses in Africa which has been transformed by the ability to co-ordinate marketing and production information using e-mail, thus preventing stockpiles and shortages in a way which not long ago would have only been feasible for multinational corporations with integrated data networks.
- Thirdly, in the political arena, the internet can empower poor countries. In 1990 more than 90% of the data and the debate about Africa was held in the US and Europe, largely inaccessible to African policy-makers and academics. The internet can change that - but not just for governments. Non-Governmetnal Organizations have gained increased power and influence over the last decade largely because they can quickly generate global campaigns using the web. And of course threatened minority groups world-wide - for example in Indonesia and Yugoslavia - have made very effective use of the net to ensure that their voice is heard. The Internet is a major factor in the political shift away from non-interference in other countries internal affairs, which has characterised global politics over the last decade.

So, we find James D. Wolfensohn, President of the World Bank said to the UN just last month:

"Don't let people talk to you about Internet being a luxury. While it is not an alternative to bread, it gives us the opportunity of bringing knowledge and opportunity to people at all levels throughout the world. It is time to grasp that. It is time for us to pledge to each other in international institutions...the private sector, civil society and [government] to come together, and make sure that this new age, not the agricultural revolution, not the industrial revolution, but the digital revolution, gives equity to poor people throughout the world" [2].

But realising this opportunity will, before anything else, require a huge investment in connectivity. Is it really going to happen?

In a bid to leapfrog stages of development, some transitional economies are investing heavily in building up information age infrastructures. Malaysia's 2020 vision, for example, is a clear attempt by its Government to create within the next twenty years an information rich society, which they hope will confer on the country the status of fully developed nation [3].

In fact, as far as IT infrastructure is concerned, there is some ground for optimism. Thanks to the rapidly declining cost of wireless and fiber-optic networks, and supportive government policies, huge investment in several key countries does mean that the gap between the most developed nations (which already have more than one phone line per household) and the rest is narrowing fast. China, in particular, is showing phenomenal growth in telecommunications. In the 60 countries which account for 90% of the global telecommunications markets, 400 million new subscribers were connected between 1998 and 1998 - twice as many as in the preceding three years [4]. So dramatic is the change that, in 1998, the UN's Commission on Science and Technology for Development could say:

"It is remarkable that...the rates of growth of the telecommunications infrastructure are sufficiently rapid that convergence is foreseeable for the majority for the world's population" [5].

Globally, we can see near exponential growth in Internet use, too. Accurate numbers are more difficult to obtain, but probably close to half a billion people are already connected, and the UN expects the figure to reach 700 million next year. And remember just how quickly the web has developed - radio took 38 years to gain 50 million users, and television 13 years, but the web took just four [6]. And, whilst it's true that the typical web user has been a rich, highly educated, English-speaking white man, it is encouraging that 35% of users are now women (up from 15% in 1994) and that by 2003 non-English material will account for over half the content on the web" [7].

Of course, there remains a close correlation between connectivity and GNP per capita, and UN forecasts confirm that a developed world telecommunications infrastructure remains a dream for very many countries, particularly in Africa. However, we must factor in the added impact of community-based telecommunications. I don't need my own private line to make a call, or my own PC to access the web. I'd like to share with you a couple of inspiring stories:

- The Grameen Village Pay Phone scheme is bringing the information revolution to the rural people of Bangladesh and is generating a new breed of entrepreneurs: village women. The women, having first taken a loan from the Grameen Bank to set themselves up in business, make a living by providing a mobile phone service to their neighbours. This enables them to earn an income, which is usually higher than the national average. The scheme is also popular among local people who find that the new service is making their lives easier and more secure [8].
- People in remote and disadvantaged communities in South Africa are gaining access for the first time to the Internet and other information age services via telecentres. These outposts of the Information Society, often community-owned and run, support local economic and social development by providing a wide

range of information goods and services such as e-mail, fax, telephones, information on markets, weather conditions, crops, and access to public services such as distance education, telemedicine etc. South Africa's strong commitment to increasing the availability of information and knowledge for its historically disadvantaged peoples has put its telecentre policy at the forefront of international good practice [9].

With initiatives like these, it is quite feasible that the majority of the world's population will have telecommunications access within the next 15-20 years, and that this will deliver data, as well as voice, at affordable cost.

The knowledge society, then, is upon us. It has the potential to be a powerful tool for development - perhaps the key tool. But there are formidable challenges. Developing the appropriate skills and content will be far more difficult than building the telecommunications infrastructure. There are real risks:

- Will there be wide and equitable access? Or a growing divide between the information rich and information poor - both between countries and within individual countries - and, overall, a worsening north-south information gap, possibly leading to political conflict?
- Will content be varied and appropriate? Or will it be controlled by a small number of monopolies, meaning that certain content is marginalised? Remember how much global consolidation there has been in the publishing and media industry over the last decade, and the fact that in 1996 there were 5,300 database vendors in the US, and just 8 in Africa [10].
- Will all user communities have the necessary skills? Or will information illiteracy be the new sign of exclusion?
- Will the values of the knowledge society encourage participation by civil society, promote open access, and respect a multiplicity of cultures? Or will the values be determined entirely by business? Or will dominant ideologies restrict debate?
- And finally, the knowledge society will require partnerships between governments, the private sector and civil society. Will we have the right partnerships in place?

Put together, these risks - or challenges - constitute "The Digital Divide". Alongside debt relief, organised crime, GM foods, AIDS and the environment, the digital divide featured prominently on the list of topics discussed at the Okinawa G8 summit a few week ago. The leaders of the eight most industrialised democracies have pledged themselves to pursue the aspirations of the Okinawa Charter on the Global Information Society and to find ways to bridge the digital divide [11]. A Digital Opportunities Task Force has been set up to develop recommendations for global action in this area. It is unfortunate that criticism of the G8 summit's policy on debt relief - for example the ritual buring of a laptop at a recent demonstration - has damaged its important message about the digital divide [12].

G8 is by no means the only body committed to ending the digital divide. A few years ago, the World Bank began exploring the complex relationship between knowledge and development and made a case for the need to address information problems as a way to eradicate poverty and improve people's lives. The findings, which were later published in the groundbreaking 1998/99 Knowledge for Development report, were the subject of an international conference in 1997 in Toronto.

The conference resulted in the establishment of the Global Knowledge Partnership, a grouping of over 60 international organisations, united in their commitment to ensure that developing countries benefit from appropriate and sustainable investment in ICTs. The membership is drawn from government, donor agencies, NGOs, the media and the private sector. Prominent members include the Government of Malaysia, the European Commission, USAID, UNDP, UNESCO, Cisco, Sun Microsystems and the British Council. The World Bank Institute in Washington currently hosts the secretariat [13]. The GKP defines its purpose as "to work in partnership to help people access knowledge and harness ICTs that will help them improve their lives". It plans to help communities:

- Acquire knowledge, information and technology that can improve their lives
- Obtain the tools of knowledge such as telephones, radio, television and computers
- Use modern technologies, especially computers and the Internet, to increase opportunity for sharing and learning together.

The Partnership is currently developing a plan of action, which will bring partner organisations together to work on a portfolio of projects. The plan comprises over twenty projects addressing the partnership's three priority themes - access, empowerment and governance - and four crosscutting issues - youth, the media, gender and local knowledge.

IFLA has recently submitted an application to join the Global Knowledge Partnership. This is a welcome development, one that will highlight the pivotal role the information sector - libraries, publishers, information providers and content creators - play in the Knowledge Society. It is also an opportunity for us to reflect on the opportunities and challenges which face us, the library and information profession, in this new age.

In talking about the Knowledge Society I have focused on the digital divide as an issue in world development. I've done this because I wanted to tell you about the Global Knowledge Partnership, and tempt you to get involved in its debates and projects. But I also wanted to stress that the knowledge society is not just an issue for librarians in California, Cambridge or Kuala Lumpur. The digital divide exists within nations as well as between them, and the solutions must be global.

So, what can libraries and librarians offer?

Well, quite a lot. As it happens, our traditional contributions -

- Providing access
- Working in partnership
- Structuring knowledge
- Imparting skills
- Preserving heritage
- and inspiring trust

all remain crucial in the knowledge society.

Providing access to information has traditionally been about buildings, based around institutions offering services to on-site users. Building tomorrow's libraries will not simply be a matter of installing rows of computers with Internet access: our users will increasingly expect to be able to access material from where they live and work. Providing access will increasingly be about developing electronic information services such as Internet portals and acting as a broker between content providers and remote users. At the same time, I believe that even in the most wired communities there will still be a demand for physical spaces where people can not just access knowledge but can discuss, learn from and support each other. In less advantaged communities, the knowledge society simply won't happen without public access.

Librarians have been surprisingly good at working in partnerships. We have a strong communitarian instinct. In the past we have needed to work co-operatively because no one library could have everything. That is less true in a digital world: in the future our key partners won't be other libraries but content providers and ICT companies. And we shall need to think of our users or customers as our partners too, because we shall be in the business of creating knowledge as well as providing information. For example, in universities we could be acting as electronic publishers; in companies we should certainly be acting as knowledge managers, capturing and sharing internal as much as external content; and in public libraries I believe our greatest value will be in strengthening communities by providing learning and networking opportunities.

The need to structure knowledge is as important now as it ever has been. Accessing the web today is like entering a large library, where there is no catalogue but where a deranged janitor has assembled in the lobby a few pages torn from the indexes of randomly selected volumes. We know, as information professionals, that this just won't do. Of course, we also know that traditional catalogues are not the answer. BrightPlanet estimates that, when all the content stored in databases in taken into account, the web is more than 500 times larger than the pages which can be found by popular search engines [14]. Highly sophisticated retrieval software using language pattern recognition can offer users a dynamic and personalised view of networked content. We'll need to understand and apply these technologies - and be aware of their limitations and dangers. My guess is that despite the application of Artificial Intelligence to content management, real users in the real world are going to find the librarian's skills in selection and quality assurance invaluable for some years yet.

In this context, imparting information skills might well emerge as our most valuable role. Information illiteracy will be a key threat to prosperity and social inclusion in the knowledge society. Helping our communities to become critical consumers, confident learners and accomplished creators of knowledge will be a crucial task.

We will continue to be custodians of our cultural heritage, a role we share with archivists and museum curators. Our preservation role has already extended beyond paper-based materials to cover a multitude of different media, all with their own conservation problems. There is now a real danger that vast quantities of our history, recorded electronically, will be lost forever. Solutions to the preservation of digital content must be at the top of our agenda.

Finally, the matter of trust. It is perhaps naive to talk of a professional code of conduct for librarians - we work in various cultures, for public and private employers each with their own values and objectives. But what we do have in common is our role as intermediaries working on behalf of the consumer. The trust we have earned doing this will be difficult to retain, as we get more involved in complex dealings with content providers and in the manipulation of increasingly fragmented information. But if we can succeed, then the librarian brand will be in world-wide demand.

This paper has been nothing more than an overview. Our conference programme is ample evidence that librarians everywhere are actively engaged in finding practicable solutions to the challenges of the digital age. Yet most will admit that our role the knowledge society is neither fully recognised nor understood. All too often major initiatives bypass the library sector, and the skills we have developed over generations are marginalised. It is time for librarians to stand up. We need major public relations campaigns to raise awareness of what we can offer, and we need to have a voice in the debate about the digital divide at community, national and global level. IFLA's involvement in the Global Knowledge Partnership is a major step towards that goal and I wish it every success.

References

1. United Kingdom Department of Trade and Industry. – 1999
2. Wolfensohn J. D. Statement made at the United Nations 2000 Economic and Social Council on 5 July 2000.
3. Mode of access: http://www.wawasan2020.com/vision/.
4. Carl D. et al Republic of Korea: Transition to a Knowledge-based economy Washington / The World Bank, 29 June 2000. – Report N 20346-KO. – 22 p.
5. Mansell R. When U. Knowledge Societies: Information Technology for Sustainable Development Oxford University Press for The United Nations. – 1998. – 25 p.
6. The Economist. – 1998.
7. Mode of access: http://www.techserver.com.
8. Mode of access: http://www.grameen.org.
9. Mode of access: http://www.centratel.com.
10. Haves, B.W., Nots, H. In the Information Age Rutgers University Press. – 1996.
11. Mode of access: http://www.g8kyushu-okinawa.go.jp.
12. Mode of access: http://www.summitwatch.net/ story.php3?type=ok&id=10.
13. Mode of access: http://www.globalknowledge.org.
14. Mode of access: http://www.completeplanet.com/Tutorials/DeepWeb/index.asp.

BUILDING SMART COMMUNITIES: WHAT THEY ARE AND HOW THEY CAN BENEFIT BLIND AND VISUALLY IMPAIRED PERSONS

Stan Skrzeszewski

ASM Advanced Strategic Management Consultants
London, Ontario, Canada

E-mail: asmstan@attcanada.ca
http://asm-consultants.com

1. Introduction

Smart community initiatives offer the potential to enhance social, cultural and economic development for blind and visually impaired people that no one could have imagined as recently as a few years ago. For the first time in history blind and visually impaired people can hope to receive the level of information services that the general population takes for granted. However, this potential can only be realized by creating smart communities by and for blind and visually impaired people. This can be done in two ways. One way involves creating a public policy framework that supports the appropriate technology requirements and is based on a service base provided through charitable institutions. The second way is to tie the needs of blind and visually impaired people to the commercial, infotainment sector and take advantage of the power of commodification. The first way represents the status quo. The second way requires a radical break in established norms. Both ways are based on the development of smart communities for blind and visually impaired people.

2. Definition and Description

Smart communities are a new and evolving concept. "Smart communities" are defined as:

> Communities that provide an advanced communication and information infrastructure and that enables residents and organizations to make good and independent use of these technologies. To be "smart" the use of technology must be interactive or must lead to a transaction, that is, on-line activity must be more than a passive act. The members of smart communities must be able to use the technologies to transform information into knowledge.

The definition of a smart community for blind and visually impaired persons would be expanded to include:

> Communities that enhance the new technologies by:
>
> > * including the use of adaptive technologies and the requisite standards that enable the creative use of technology through the conversion of electronic files to the alternate formats, such as reading machines that can convert printed text to spoken word or braille, and screen readers that can read online books from the Internet or from computer disks.

The key elements of a smart community are:

- Technology: the tool that enables a smart community to function.
- Digital Content: the building material.
- Relationships between people: the glue that holds the smart community together.
- Interactive/Transactional applications: the processes that give smart communities a purpose.

The success of a smart community initiative is dependent on:

- the rethinking of community

  Smart Communities must think of "community" in a different way. Local communities must see themselves as largely self-governing and they must see themselves as "part of an interlinked global community." Blind and visually impaired people must approach smart technologies as a unified, self-governing and interlinked global community.

- an effective information/innovation interface.
- a high level of education.
- the capability to self-educate long after the formal education process has been completed.

A smart community is animated by:

- the free and open flow of information
- the able, creative and extensive use of advanced digital information and communications technologies.
- extensive interpersonal communications
- the connectedness of information-skilled people to each other
- global communications

  Global communication networks have enabled us to communicate on a regular basis with other people around the globe. Global communications have expanded our social, cultural and economic circles. Both large and small companies that in the past conducted their businesses in limited, local environments are now doing business around the globe. Social, cultural and economic globalization will continue.

- multi-partner approaches

  Smart community initiatives must be approached in a collective and coordinated way. This is particularly true of the blind and the visually impaired community. Individually, the blind community or the visually impaired community does not have the resources to successfully initiate a smart community initiative.

  If the blind community approaches smart community development in a fragmented, competitive way, it will not be able to benefit from them. The coordinated, multi-partner approach to dealing with information technology trends is one of the defining characteristics of the smart community movement and one of the major tasks of any smart community initiative.

  The blind community must partner with the visually impaired, learning disabled, and physically disabled community at a minimum in order to initiate a successful smart community initiative.

3. Applications

Smart Communities are built upon a foundation of exciting, life-enhancing smart applications that use existing and emerging technologies. These technologies are most typically applied to the areas of:

- Health/Medicine
- Environmental Management
- Employment: Telework and Telecommuting
- Education and Learning
- Transportation Information
- Social Services
- Law and Public Safety
- Housing
- Tourism
- Access to Government
- Community Networks
- Resource Sectors

One word about employment in the smart community. "More than 60 percent of the new jobs in the future will be computer and Internet related, and without computer skills, minorities and other marginalised people will become even more estranged from opportunities that help define one's quality of Life." Employment for blind and visually impaired people rests with smart technology.

4. Barriers

The major barriers to the development of Smart Communities of blind and visually impaired people are:

- that people who could use technology in an interactive way are being denied access to it because their needs are not fully considered in the IT society. Limiting technologies such as graphical user interfaces and mouse-driven systems reduce access.
- lack of awareness and information about assistive technologies
- lack of skills; lack of sources of specialized instruction
- lack of sufficient understanding of the potential of the technology
- inadequate access to high bandwidths
- cost

5. An Action Agenda for Building Smart Communities

The building of smart, connected communities is a dynamic and ongoing process. Each community is different in terms of background and priorities. Built on solid local infrastructure and partnership arrangements, smart communities bring people together to solve mutual problems and support and build on existing relationships.

The following action agenda will help with the development and sustainability of smart community initiatives.

5.1 Vision: Develop and Communicate a Clear Vision

The Blind and Visually Impaired Community must agree upon a new and clear vision that will guide the development of a smart community. The new vision should include:

- full and equitable access to library services for blind and visually impaired people.
- the products and services provided for and by the smart blind and visually impaired community are of use and value to other communities

5.2 Community Engagement

Engagement is the process of collectively identifying community strengths and weaknesses, matching solutions with problems and sharing expertise with others toward the goal of ensuring that a significant percentage of community members will benefit from any Smart Community initiative. Individual blind and visually impaired people must approach smart community development as members of a larger, engaged community. No one else can do this for you, and it cannot be done for you by a select, representative group. It requires significant community participation.

5.2.1 Conduct an Inventory/Needs Assessment

Conducting a needs assessment is one of the fundamental elements of developing a Smart Community. The collective expression of need by the community must be analyzed in order to set priorities for the Smart Community initiative.

A new smart community initiative should begin by:

- conducting an inventory of what is, with an emphasis on accessible web sites and accessibility products,
- conducting a needs assessment to determine what people want from a smart community initiative. Needs assessments determine the content and applications that people, companies and organizations need to be connected to and the content that should be created to enable people to benefit from the smart community.

5.3 Smart Services

Smart services are services that are informative, interactive, innovative, improving and international in scope. Smart services enrich the lives of members of a Smart Community by enabling them to meet the business and personal challenges of the information age through the use of information and communications technology. Smart services provide networked communities with interactive software and multimedia content that is delivered through secure and private in-home, at-work or community access facilities to improve the overall economic, social and cultural well being of a community.

Each community will have to develop a suite of smart services or applications that accurately reflects the developmental priorities of the community.

Smart Services for the Blind and Visually Impaired should be:

- commodified and taken out of the charitable sector. They could be provided by the nonprofit or social sector.

- turned into mass market products and services (digitized voice)
- based on sensory-rich production, which includes the senses of hearing and touch, and high level of entertainment (broad marketability).

The Internet and the Web have become commodification and commercialization drivers. Although much of the early discussions around the Internet involved the concepts of equity and empowerment through public policy and government legislation, this has changed considerably in the past few years. The focus is on commercialization and commodification of information-based products. If the Blind and visually impaired community wants to be a smart community and take advantage of the new paradigms offered by the new technologies, the community will have to focus on commercializing their requirements rather than presenting arguments for equity based on a concept of public obligation or responsibility.

To commercialize and commodify the requirements of the blind and visually impaired smart community will take a great deal of imagination and innovation.

The innovation must include seeing the smart blind and visually impaired community in much larger and different terms. For example, this smart community must include other groups of challenged individuals such as those with dyslexia or physically limiting disabilities. The blind and visually impaired community must partner with other communities that have the same or similar requirements from the new technologies. This smart community must see itself in global terms, rather than one restricted to a national area. It will be important to create the critical mass necessary to build a market that will support commodification and commercialization. I think that the key will be to convince enough sighted people, especially at the executive level, that they don't want to have to type in everything they wish to communicate and that they don't want to suffer ongoing eyestrain from the continuous reading of material on screens. Some of the current overwhelming information flow in print must be redirected to the audio and tactile senses.

Of course, there is likely to be strong opposition from the established nonprofit industry and bureaucracy that has been established to serve the blind and visually impaired. The commercial approach represents a radical departure from the current charitable approach, but then the Internet has radically changed the approach to how we do things in many ways.

5.3.1 Principles for Smart Services

Smart Services should be based on the following six principles:

Principle 1: Smart services result in transactions; content must lead to transactions. In this context, a transaction is defined as a series of web-based interactions that result in the completion of a process. A transaction is more than interactivity. For example, being able to check a library catalogue on-line and verify the location of a book is an interactive service. Being able to actually order the book and have it delivered is a transaction, or a 'smart' service.

Principle 2: Relationships drive transactions

Principle 3: Smart Communities give away/share information

Principle 4: Smart Communities must facilitate community transactions / interactions

Principle 5: Smart services are cross-sectoral, that is, they are not restricted by functional, organizational or jurisdictional borders.

Principle 6: Smart services provide services or information at the level required by the user, which drill down to the required information level, and they provide the level of service detail that is required by the user.

5.3.2 Accessible Web Portals

Smart communities should increase the ease and equity of access to timely, well organized (simple, clear, user-oriented) comprehensive applications and content resources and services. In a web-based environment the best way to provide easy access to information is through Web Portals.

The Portal should:

- provide an easy-to-use index to existing resources
- provide access to web sites with full-text
- be easy to update and change so that organizations can amend their information and links without substantial technical expertise
- be based on universal design principles that "are usable by people with the widest range of abilities, operating within the widest range of situations (environments, conditions, and circumstances)."
- be governed by established policies that address ethical, liability and copyright issues. For example, policies regarding Terms of Eligibility and Appropriate Use will be essential.

5.4 INFRASTRUCTURE: Build an Accessible Information Technology Infrastructure.

"Infrastructure" includes the computer networks, systems and hardware and software necessary for a smart community. Smart infrastructures combine high-speed, two-way communications capabilities with an Internet Protocol (IP) network and sufficient bandwidth to support the services needed by a community.

5.4.1 ACCESS - Provide Equitable and Affordable Access

Smart communities for the Blind must ensure that everyone who is blind or visually impaired:

- is connected and has access to the new computer and adaptive technologies. Home access must be the goal.
- has the opportunity to learn the information technology skills they need.
- has access to accessible Internet access sites with adaptive technology if they do not own computers, have connectivity etc.
- has access to technology that is not dependent on using a mouse
- has access to assistance with access and connectivity.

5.4.2 Adaptive Technology

Readily available computers and adaptive technologies are essential if blind and visually impaired persons are going to create smart communities.

The term 'adaptive technology' refers to any device, computerized or mechanical, that enables blind or physically disabled people to use printed or digital information.

Adaptive technology includes:

- screen readers (software) interfaced with voice synthesizers (hardware)
- braille printers/braille display
- screen magnification systems
- magnification systems
- voice recognition systems/ speech synthesizers
- breath-controlled typing and point and click systems
- closed captioning
- audio descriptioning

Wherever possible smart community development for blind and visually impaired people should rely on off-the-shelf hardware and software.

5.4.3 High Speed Connectivity Plan

Smart communities must build a high speed data and Internet Protocol (IP) network that serve the community.

A High Speed Connectivity Plan should include recommendations regarding:

- high speed backbone which will provide affordable access to public and private institutions
- sufficient bandwidth to deliver audio products and teleconferencing; tele-conferencing capabilities will enable services, such as, distance education offerings, virtual job interviews, virtual medical consultations or tele-health
- fibre-optic, wireless, and satellite-based connectivity options
- scalability, compatibility, integration
- extending high-speed data access lines throughout the community especially in those areas that currently don't have high speed access
- linkages to major institutions
- building the technological capacity that will encourage business and economic growth in the new economy in the area. This economic growth will result in an increase in the number of good quality jobs that are available in the knowledge-based economy.

5.5 Training and Education: Train people to use the information technologies in creative and innovative ways

Smart Communities should ensure that basic training in the use of the Internet, World Wide Web and information technology is available and affordable. When possible, and in certain economic circumstances, basic training should be free. Formal training programs located in accessible technology learning centres should be supplemented by volunteer mentors and onsite trainers that would be available to help people at public access sites. A regional help desk should be established to help people with basic connectivity problems.

5.6 Strategic Partnerships: Build a Coordinated, Multi-member, Community-wide Partnership.

Smart Communities should be built on a foundation of trust and mutual benefits through cooperative ventures and strategic alliances. The partnerships should include current connectivity initiatives so as to avoid duplication of database and web site development.

Smart Communities must mobilize all the municipalities and the numerous groups and organizations that will be required to implement this initiative. Partners are needed that:

- can contribute significant resources to realizing the vision
- are already engaged in connectivity and digital content projects
- can provide access to those who do not own their own computers
- can engage people in the Smart Community project

5.7 Identify Smart Community Champions

Individuals who can take charge, with high public profiles, influential, non-political and with cross-sectoral interests should be identified to champion and implement the Smart Community initiative.

Smart Communities for blind and visually impaired persons should consider a regional approach. In a regional initiative regional leaders should be identified. Regional leaders should work to connect their assets through collaborative initiatives.

Create a Smart Community Leadership Committee. A representative, cross-sectoral Leadership Committee should be created to:

- seek agreement on the vision (mission, values, action plans)
- coordinate community-based development
- develop a collaborative and consensual approach to finalizing and implementing an Action Plan.

5.8 Develop a Business Plan for the Smart Community

A business plan will be required for grant submissions and to gain buy-in from the community, especially the business community. A budget should be developed to support the action plan. Smart communities must look at new approaches and sources for funding.

Conduct Coordinated Research Into, and Develop Applications for, Potential Funding Sources Potential multiple-funding sources will be maximized through a coordinated approach to funding. Coordinated research should be conducted to identify sources of funding that will support connectivity.

6. CONCLUSION

Smart Communities are about creating a community based on a new ethic of cooperation and collective action, shared resources and information. The essential players will include governments, educational institutions, nonprofit organizations, social institutions, local businesses and visionary individuals. Through the power of cooperation and shared knowledge the Smart Community will increase the quality of life and the competitive capacity of the area. Smart Communities are an innovative response to the social and economic changes that have occurred as a result of the dramatic development in information and communications technologies.

A Smart Community is a work in progress that will depend for success upon imagination and commitment.

> "Smart communities require an act of the imagination and what must be imagined is the idea of the smart community itself."

(Adapted from Benedict Anderson's Imagined Communities)

APPENDIX A:

Examples of Smart Community Developments

A Municipal Model ? Grande Prairie CyberCity, Grande Prairie, Alberta, Canada
www.city.grande?prairie.ab.ca/home_cy.htm

Grande Prairie CyberCity is a good example of a smart city initiative that is driven by the municipal government. It began as an effort to integrate and share information among municipal departments. The original purpose of the project was to enable the City of Grande Prairie to discharge its part of the responsibility government has in the development of electronic communications.

The initiative has three principal thrusts:

- X Cooperative deployment of shared high-speed equipment, systems and software providing universal interactive access to data and information,
- X Generation of awareness throughout every segment of the community concerning the opportunities and challenges of living and competing in the Information Age, and
- X Assurance of affordable, managed, interoperable equipment and network connections which are reliable, expandable and secure.

Grand Prairie is using information technology to aggressively promote local economic development. Fibre-optic links installed in all public buildings are enhancing the community's connectivity, allowing the transmission of text, images and multimedia presentations to attract potential developers and investors to set up businesses and create jobs.

A Community-Based Model ? The Lanark County Community Info Net, Lanark County, Ontario, Canada
http://www.lccin.on.ca

The Lanark County Community Info Net (LCCIN) is a not-for-profit corporation with a mandate to

a. undertake public education and provide public access points to allow all citizens of rural and urban Lanark County the use of up-to-date electronic communications and multi-media information systems;
b. improve communications and promote networking among social service agencies, organizations, businesses, schools and special interest groups of Lanark County in order to promote County activities and to avoid duplication of effort;
c. promote and provide funds for education, including continuing education, and promote the development of technical skills to increase opportunities for the development of a highly skilled work force within Lanark County.

Starting in 1995, LCCIN has significantly raised the level of awareness regarding the potential of telecommunications among all sectors of the population in Lanark County and through its promotional activities has caused a greater and earlier use of use of computers and associated technology to occur.

Parthenay, ville numérisée. France
http://www.district?parthenay.fr/sommaire.htm

Parthenay, capitale de la Gâtine, est surtout connue pour son patrimoine monumental qui forme un ensemble cohérent et particulièrement représentatif d'une ville médiévale: château et fortifications, maisons à pans de bois, églises romanes et gothiques.

Le projet "Parthenay, ville numérisée" est né d'une dynamique préexistante de développement local. Depuis 1996, plusieurs espaces numérisés mettant à disposition des ordinateurs connectés à internet et à l'In-Town-Net (District de Parthenay) ont été mis en oeuvre. On y trouve des informations sur la vie de la commune, celle des associations. On y commande un acte d'état civil. On y consulte le cadastre.

Plusieurs espaces de ce type ont été créés dans différents quartiers de Parthenay. Chacun dispose d'animateurs multimédia, spécialistes du domaine abordé, dont le but est de permettre aux utilisateurs d'être autonomes. Particuliers de tous âges, grands parents entraînés par leurs petits enfants, associations, entreprises, administrations les fréquentent. Ainsi, la Maison de la citoyenneté active accueille des chômeurs qui apprennent à rédiger un CV, à rechercher des annonces sur le Net, des informations sur des entreprises, etc.

Parthenay, capital of Gâtine, is known for its monuments which are particularly representative of a medieval city: castle and fortifications, wooden houses and Romanesque and Gothic churches.

Parthenay, the digital city consists of digitized spaces connected to the Internet and the Town-Net (District of Parthenay). Information is provided on the life of the village, organizations. Several on-line services are also provided including access to marital records and a land registry.

Several electronic spaces of this type have been created. Individuals of all ages, including parents and children, associations, companies and government agencies use these sites. For example, the House of the active citizenship provides information for the unemployed who learn how to write CVs, find job ads on the Net, locate information on companies, etc.

Craigmiller Community Information Centre, Edinburgh, Scotland

The Craigmillar Community Information Service (CCIS) is a community-based team project, situated on the East side of Edinburgh that provides information network services to the local community. – Mode of access: http://www.ccis.org.uk.

Teleport is the new EEC-FUNDED arm of CCIS The aim is to provide good basic grounding in computer & IT skills. Teleport trains users in basic software packages and skills - word processing, spreadsheets, databasing, desktop publishing & desktop presentation. Teleport also prides IT-based conference & presentation services. Designed for use by both local community groups and businesses, the conference space is comfortable, spacious, fully IT equipped & available to rent. – Mode of access: http://www.teleport.org.uk.

References

1. Harris, B. Rethinking Community // Government Technology. – 2000. – May. – P.7.

2. Simani, J. Atlanta fills the void for what is needed – computer access // Government Technology. – 2000. – Vol. 13, N 8. – June. – P. 18.
3. Mates, B. Adaptive Technology for the Internet. – Chicago: American Library Association, 2000. – 13 p.

THE DIGITAL SOCIETY'S CHALLENGE TO THE LIBRARY FOR THE BLIND

Elsebeth Tank

The Danish National Library for the Blind, Denmark

Abstract

The information technology community poses challenges to libraries for the blind all over the world. Technology is on our side. As a result of technological advances it is now feasible to establish true equality between visually impaired and sighted people. To benefit from the brand new possibilities the libraries for the blind have to go through a range of changes and development processes. This paper comments on new strategies and potential roles for the libraries for the blind.

Introduction

During the past two years The Danish National Library for the Blind (DBB) has dedicated a lot of effort to formulating a new strategy for the institution's work. This new strategy stemmed from an analysis of DBB's own needs, the requirements of DBB's users, and last but not least the possibilities and barriers in DBB's surroundings.

Simultaneously with defining the new strategy, DBB has initiated an all-encompassing process of change that is intended to enable the organisation to optimise its performance; to function in a modern manner and to progress at all levels.

Unlike most other libraries for the blind across the world, DBB is a national and publicly financed library. This means that DBB can base its activities on a stable and known economy, knowing that the Danish State supports the organisation. Several aspects make the function of DBB manageable. These aspects include the nationwide status of the library, the country's infrastructure and size - geographically as well as demographically. When compared to libraries for the blind in other countries, DBB has quite comfortable working conditions. Considering our unique basis for business at DBB, colleagues from other countries may find it difficult to directly emulate our situation and the way we work. On the other hand, it is my hope through this paper to be able to inspire you and give you food for thought for further discussions on the challenges posed by the information technology community to libraries for blind and visually impaired all over the world.

Characteristics of the Information Community

So what exactly is the community we come into contact with? the digital? the electronic the information technology world? Perhaps the most important in this context is a community where the flow of information is incomprehensibly expansive and is still growing exponentially.

It is a society in which the overview of and the access to information has a defining influence on the individual citizens possibilities. A society in which the individuals capacity to comprehend and process the content of the information has much significance.

It is also a society in which the development of information carrying media occurs at an outrageous pace; a society in which the choice of media forms is vast. Through the use of interactive media, the user chooses and rejects information at his or her whim. Through multi-activities the user's senses are stimulated or bombarded by a plethora of impressions. That and an abundance of other new technological refinements have become everyday phenomena in the lives of many people.

Many old borders have been superseded both virtually and literally. The global village was an expression much talked about in Denmark just a few years ago.

This phrase bears witness to the simultaneous existence of globalisation and localisation. The concept of the global village also illustrates the inherent need for seeking roots, for feeling safe, for social companionship and togetherness; traits that would be accorded a premium position for many when defining a balanced life.

In the current discussion globalisation is of special interest because globalisation also deals with the plethora of information inundating us - often electronically; crossing all borders via the Internet and satellites.

The Task of the Library for the Blind in the Digital Reality

Information Equality Between Handicapped and Non-Handicapped

When defining major features of the digital community, we can also identify the role of the library for the blind. The fundamental goal of the library for the blind is not much different today than in former times - but then again quite different. The digital technology brings a whole new set of possibilities and therewith greater expectations of the results Technology is on our side. As a result of many advances in technology; digitalised texts, internet connections, PC's hooked up to a network, cheap scanners, dedicated screen readers, synthesized speech and braille; for the first time in the history of mankind it is now feasible for us to establish true equality between visually handicapped and sighted people. It is this groundbreaking vision that changes the world, and must be ultimate basis for our future aspirations.

Lobbyist, Inspirer and Watchdog

So far the libraries for the blind have primarily been an information source for the visually impaired. The libraries for the blind have carried out the production of audio books and braille publications, a production which has been enhanced during the past couple of years with the introduction of electronic texts.

Even though the libraries for the blind have thus accomplished a major task, it has never been possible to acquire sufficient finances to support the production of audio and braille publication on a scale that would equal the amount of publications in society at large. On the contrary, despite acceptable allocations of funds for a small language area as Denmark, it has not been possible to produce audio publications of more than about 5% of the market's books, and only between 1 - 2% in braille of the total number of books published. Even though a far larger number of books is published in the l major languages in the form of audio and braille, it is still not possible for these countries to even come close to emulating the amount of publications on the market.

The libraries for the blind continue to have a future as publishers and producers of alternative formats. However, in-house production alone is far from sufficient. The technologies carry the promise of a new potential.

Only by encouraging other information providers to think about multiple forms of accessibility will it be possible for the libraries for the blind to increase the amount of useable information sources on a much larger scale than possible with only in-house production.

Hence, a major crusade for the libraries for the blind would be to motivate information providers to take responsibility for enhancing accessibility.

Therefore the libraries for the blind should take upon themselves the role of inspirer, lobbyist and watchdog. In Denmark we assume that role primarily towards other public libraries but also towards commercial information vendors, who develop and sell library systems.

Information Directly at the Source

The libraries for the blind can take part in creating a direct contact between information vendors and the visually impaired by means of lobbying and the increasing knowledge of the problems of access by visually impaired readers. Together with other groups, DBB strives to encourage commercial information vendors to take handicap accessibility into consideration when planning their electronic products or services.

Alas, the desire to make profits far outstrips consideration that should be paid to access for all.

The solution is information, information and yet again information. Those not normally involved with producing publications for the visually impaired often consider the demand for accessibility as a cumbersome and costly affair. We cannot accomplish this mission on our own; but we can contribute by participating in concrete co-operative projects with commercial information vendors. And by doing so, show that handicap accessibility is a stumbling block in the path of functionality neither does it offend the aesthetic value so much coveted by the sighted.

Standards and Universal Design

A prerequisite for our crusade of keeping abreast of developments in society is that we base our solutions on common, well-known standards in combination with standard and mainstream products. Hence DBB firmly supports the Daisy consortium's concern for standards. This applies to the standard for the digital audio book and for the e-book, moreover for the lobbying for achieving accessibility standards in web-designs.

The same applies to playback devices. DBB strives, as far as possible, to rely on products that currently exist on the market. To what extent that will be possible is a question we hope to find the answer to within the next couple of years.

Competency Development

All the things I have so far mentioned show that there are many tasks that need to be handled by the libraries for the blind. What is more, if the visually impaired are to reach the same level of communication as other members of society, it is of paramount importance that these goals be achieved in the foreseeable future. That alone constitutes a big challenge - at least for DBB.

At DBB we have enjoyed a very traditional and steady existence, where changes and developments happened upon us in a calm and controlled manner. But times have changed. The organisation's 100 employees have been there for many years. When they started their carriers at DBB, demands were simpler and fewer.

If we continue in the same tempo, our users will lag far behind in the general development of society. Therefore, we give high priority to encouraging the ability and desire for change. It is not an easy process, but small successes foster hope in the organisation and convince the individual participant that he/she has a place and a role to play in creating the ongoing success of DBB.

The tasks are more complex than ever before. Highly advanced knowledge and development takes the place of, or supplements the old production model. In step with the development of society in general and the users own development in particular, more demands are placed on the communicating of materials and information. This means, at DBB, that the communications unit acquire whole new assignments, e.g. to act as co-navigators for the users on the Internet.

The situation requires completely different forms of work and co-operation than we have known and used so far. Therefore we see the need for the continued development of qualifications on a professional as well as on a personal level.

The growing need for knowledge intensive competencies is not only a prerequisite for the libraries for the blind. It is a condition that influences many societies and institutions in general. Hence we are open to inspiration from other parts of the society in helping us proceed with the development processes we have initiated. At DBB we have developed a competency development programme "unchain your values" which we will go ahead with over the next couple of years provided that we obtain the finances we need. The process consists of four modules that deal with the following aspects:

- Development of communication skills
- Technological shift from analogue to digital production
- Strengthening the personal competencies that make it possible to work in a flat structure organisation that empowers the individual as much as possible.
- Strengthening of management.

Reorganising the DBB

As part of the process of change initiated at DBB, we have redesigned our organisation. The changes were brought about in order to support the general objectives of DBB. In practice this has meant that 8 departments have been merged into four areas. For instance the sound and brail production departments have been merged into one production unit. We strive to align as many work processes as possible from the two productions in order to free resources that can be channelled to increased development and larger production. Another focus for DBB is to break out of the isolation that has influenced the organisation's relations with the outside world. DBB has had its determining focus on the world of the blind, nationally and internationally. Thereby knowledge of and cooperation with other parts of the Danish society have been rather limited. Today we are establishing networks. As many as possible. Horizontally as well as vertically? Nationally as well as internationally.

We try to establish co-operation with target groups, as well as research libraries, with a view to teaching them about accessibility and in order for us to learn from their situations. This will make it possible for us to support and inspire them with our unique profile and goal.

Better Results

So what is it all worth? Apart from the visionary considerations of complete technological equality, we, at DBB, have committed ourselves during the next four years to improving our results as follows:

- All new audio production must be digital
- 20 % increase in audio production
- 40% more copies of publications.
- Converting 32.000 master tapes from analogue to digital
- Experiments with speech synthesizers
- Achieving accessibility of two new products in cooperation with commercial information vendors
- Special emphasis on:
- Braille users
- Business and PC users
- Persons who have become deaf and blind
- Children
- Refugees and immigrants
- New interactive library system
- Advisory centres for the public and research libraries regarding accessibility issues
- New salary structures
- PC workstations for all employees

Conclusion

In this day and age, there are many interesting challenges in working with the library for the blind.

The opportunities present large demands on management as well as staff. We clearly need the ability and will to change at all levels of our organisations. We need access to new knowledge, to integrate and profit from new learning. We need to act fast or we will lose the chance of seizing the right psychological moment. Perhaps the most difficult demand is that of the speed at which an organisation should function. Alas, there is no other way.

The time is at hand to transform strategies and implement new tasks while we are still able to influence the situation.

Some management specialists speak of rediscovering an organisation's values in a new context and marketing this revived set of values. At DBB, we follow that line, and are able to get across our ideas, advice and messages to the world that surrounds us. In this way we can get our message across to the rest of the world.